HERBAL BOUNTY!
THE GENTLE ART OF HERB CULTURE

P9-DMW-075

HERBAL BOUNTY!

THE GENTLE ART OF HERB CULTURE

Steven Foster

Illustrated by D.D. Dowden

Foreword by Dr. Richard Evans Schultes
Director, Botanical Museum,
Harvard University

Preface by Dr. Shiu Ying Hu
Arnold Arboretum, Harvard University

Gibbs M. Smith, Inc.
Peregrine Smith Books
Salt Lake City

Second Printing, 1986

Copyright © 1984 by Gibbs M. Smith, Inc.

Published by Gibbs M. Smith, Inc.
Peregrine Smith Books
P.O. Box 667
Layton, UT 84041

All rights reserved for all countries, including the
right of translation. No part of this book may be
used or reproduced in any manner without written
permission from the publisher.

Library of Congress Cataloging in Publication Data
Foster, Steven, 1957p
    Herbal bounty!

    Bibliography: p.
    Includes index.
    1. Herb gardening.   2. Herbs.   I. Title.
SB351. H5F627 1984   635.7   83-20350

Book design by J. Scott Knudsen
Illustrations, including cover, by D.D. Dowden. Photographs by Steven Foster.
Manufactured in the United States of America

For Jude . . .

and the memory of
Ozark hikes with
Richard Davis

CONTENTS

PREFACE

Shiu Ying Hu
Botanist, Arnold Arboretum
Harvard University

As a professional botanist who has spent forty-five years studying the medicinal plants of China (primarily in two ancient languages, Chinese and Latin) I found Steven Foster's book on herb cultivation a most welcome reference.

This work has been prepared for the layman by a self-made and practical botanist. The author reminds me of two eminent American botanists who enticed me to Harvard: They were Merritt L. Fernald, author of the eighth edition of *Gray's Manual of Botany*, and Elmer D. Merrill, who was honored as the American Linnaeus during his lifetime. I used to think it remarkable that these two professors (both from the state of Maine) could be self-taught botanists yet outstanding in their field because, at the beginning of the twentieth century, botany was relatively young in America. I was surprised indeed to meet a third person from Maine, Steven Foster, who achieved the same distinction near the close of the century.

I met Steven Foster at the Sabbathday Lake Shaker Community. At the time, Professor Walter Judd, University of Florida at Gainesville, was working on his *Monograph of Lyonia, Ericaceae*.[1] We shared adjacent research benches on the third floor of the Harvard University Herbaria and the excitement of our findings. One Monday, after a refreshing weekend in the Shaker Community in Maine, he said, "You must visit the Shakers at Sabbathday Lake. It is a beautiful and restful place, a simple and friendly society, and it has a very good herb garden." I did. There, a farm boy was assigned to take me to the field and building devoted to the drying and distribution of herbs. Our conversation reminded me of something that Confucius said two thousand years ago, "In any company of three persons, there must be one who can be my teacher." In the company of half a dozen persons who chose a lifestyle of simple living and honest dealing, I found in Steven Foster a teacher who could share a profound knowledge of economic botany (the study of useful plants), particularly in the cultivation and uses of herbs.

Steven Foster's botanical knowledge is not limited to herbs. He knows the native flora of Maine intimately and has an extensive association with botanists and herbalists throughout the United States. He first showed me where to find wild American ginseng in New England. When I knew him better, I said, "Your botanical knowledge is as broad and sound as that of some of my friends who hold a college degree. Have you ever thought of registering in a university and working towards a degree?" In answer, he showed me his library and said, "I have taken the money which I should have used for a college education and invested it

in these books. To me, practical work and extensive reading constitute a more economical way for obtaining botanical knowledge." Indeed, his library has an extensive collection of old herbals as well as modern textbooks, manuals, floras, and current botanical and horticultural publications. He has not only read them all, he knows exactly where and how to locate needed information in them. An excellent photographer, he has recorded his field observations in numerous slides and pictures. Readers of his book will soon find that this work crystallizes the author's philosophy of education and his practical approach to pursuing botanical knowledge.

In the first part of the book, after explaining the reasons for preparing the book, the author shares his knowledge of Latin botanical names, his ideas about designing herb gardens, and his experiences in the propagation, harvesting, and drying of various herbs. Part two characterizes, and identifies individual herbs, their folklores, phytochemistry, and usages. This portion contains eighty common herbs useful in American homes and recommended for the herb-trade market, arranged alphabetically by their common

names. Sixty of the entries represent one species. The remaining twenty entries contain two or more species, making a total of 124 plant species or hybrids covered by the work.

The material is illustrated with forty-five line-drawings prepared by an amateur botanical illustrator, eight color-plates covering twenty species and/or hybrids of the more familiar herbs, and forty black and white photographs. A glossary is provided for users unfamiliar with some of the descriptive terms. Those desiring more information about herbs may peruse the bibliography. A classified resources list is given for those who want to buy seeds or plants. Each section and entry contain useful information for users, growers, and dealers alike.

---

1. Published in Journal of Arnold Arboretum 62:(1981):63-128-209, 315-436.

FOREWORD

Richard Evans Schultes
Paul C. Mangelsdorf Professor
of Natural Sciences and
Director, Botanical Museum,
Harvard University

The recent upsurge of interest in the culinary use of herbs and spices has led to an interest on the part of the general public in the plants themselves. Thousands of gardeners are interested in growing many of the source plants and herb gardens are common, especially in cities where space for many of the ornamental horticulturals is limited.

The last two or three decades have seen many books on the source plants, their lore, history, and role in human affairs. Most of these books have been written in a popular vein. Some have been well prepared. Others have not. And almost nothing comprehensive exists on the cultivation of herbs.

Steven Foster has produced such a book and, in doing so, has contributed significantly to our total knowledge concerning herbs and their uses. A very appealing aspect is Foster's first-hand acquaintance with herb cultivation. But, while stressing the growing of these plants, he has presented a well-rounded discussion: brief descriptions of the plants in nontechnical terms, notes on the chemistry of the species, their value in folk-medicine, occasional folklore, and other relevant points of interest to devotees of herb use.

The beautiful illustrations by D. D. Dowden add immeasurably to the artistry and utility of the book.

Here is a volume which will easily find a place in the hearts of many who yearn to grow their own herbs and reap enjoyment from a hobby which brings us one step closer to the timeless rhythms of Nature in our hurried, harried world.

Herb garden at Sab-
bathday Lake Shaker
Village

ACKNOWLEDGEMENTS

For the past several years I have pursued herb growing while collecting information on useful plants that captured my interest. During this time, I have been the fortunate recipient of much inspiration, help, and support from many people who influenced the contents of the book. Special appreciation goes to the Sabbathday Lake Shaker Community, particularly Sister Mildred Barker, Sister Francis Carr, and Brother Theodore Johnson for endless encouragement; David Serette for showing me which end of a camera to peer through; Les Eastman who taught me appreciation for plants in their native habitats; Dr. Shiu Ying Hu of Harvard University's Arnold Arboretum for continually broadening my view of life; Paul Lee for adding a laugh to every situation; Billy Joe Tatum for a constant flow of inspiration; Bill Coperthwaite for showing me how to look at every moment in a fresh way; Brysis Buchanan for her insightful observations; Genevieve Paulson for pointing me in the right direction; my grandmother Lena Foster for teaching me artistic appreciation; and my parents, Herb and Hope Foster, for allowing me to do what I felt was best. And thanks to Frank Lloyd Wright for saying, "The truth is more important than the facts."

In addition to those individuals I would also like to express deep gratitude to persons who helped at various stages of the book's preparation. Thanks begin with Paul and Charlene Lee for everything; Mark Blumenthal "sold" me the right attitude; Wesley Wong of Harvard University's Botanical Museum Library helped locate obscure and important references;

Kent and Betty Taylor gave plants, information, and hospitality; Joe and Angel Brunner provided a much-needed place to stay; Jeanmarie Morelli shared her gardening wisdom and work on Angelica; Louis and Virginia Saso welcomed me to their gardens; Lon Johnson and the folks at Trout Lake Farm put theory into practice; Barbara Huston provided a gardener's view of a writer's task; Dr. Norman R. Farnsworth gave literally a pile of information; William J. Dress of the L. H. Bailey Hortorium educated me on lavender; Dr. Brent Davis shared copious *Echinacea* notes; James Sanders III provided darkroom wizardry and Edwin Luther the darkroom. My thanks to Gene Dunaway for technical assistance; to Gibbs Smith for taking me seriously; and to Donna Farar for patience and persistence in typing the manuscript. Appreciation goes to Willie Nelson for recording "The Last Thing I Needed," a song Donna wrote. A special thanks to Ella McDonald for conducive oblations. The list could go on, but I've reached the prescribed page limit.

Lemon thyme, Trout Lake Farm

SO
YOU'RE
INTERESTED
IN
HERBS

Cat Thyme and friend

THE WONDERFUL WORLD OF HERBS

1

Any plant used for culinary, fragrant, or medicinal purposes is an herb. Botanically, an herb is any plant that does not possess a persistent woody stem and dies back to the root each year, even though woody plants having medicinal or culinary uses are herbs according to the first definition. Botanists estimate that there are between 200,000 and 800,000 members of the plant kingdom.

How many can be considered herbs by our first definition? It is impossible to say; but the following story, related by a friend returning from a trip to India, illustrates the plant kingdom's herbal potential. In India, my friend met an apprentice of an herbal healer who had recently finished his indenture. For a final test, the student's master directed him to go to the hills and gather plants *without* medicinal qualities. After several days of roaming the surrounding hills, the apprentice returned with his head hung low.

"Master," he lamented. "I was unable to fulfill the task. I found no plants without medicinal uses." The teacher threw back his head in laughter and announced, "You have passed the test."

Interest in things herbal has skyrocketed since the late sixties and early seventies. Companies which began as cottage industries barely a decade ago are now multimillion dollar businesses. Celestial Seasonings is a prime success story. Major food manufacturers, including Lipton, have followed suit and introduced successful lines of herb teas to supermarket shelves. In the health food industry, herb sales are second only to vitamins. The herb tea industry had an estimated $150-300 million dollars worth of sales in 1980 when only twelve years ago it was nonexistent.

Culinary herbs are gaining more popularity too. The spice trade approaches $900 million in annual sales. The American Spice Trade Association reports that U.S. consumption of spices continues to grow faster than the growth rate of the population. In 1982 spices were imported at a record 162,292 metric tons valued at $221 million.

A resurgence of interest in natural foods has helped to accelerate the herb renaissance while a general discontent with the cost of orthodox medicine and the not-so-wonderful side-effects of wonder drugs contributes to renewed interest in herbs and self-health care.

Between 75 percent and 95 percent by weight of the herbs sold in North America are imported—many from Third World countries. Hungary is a major camomile producer, much oregano comes from Greece and Yugoslavia, lemon grass is a product of Mexico, hibiscus flowers come from Guatemala, Indonesia is a major clove producer, and the renewed

trade with China brings an abundance of herbs and spices to the American market.

While working for the Herb Department at the Sabbathday Lake Shaker Community from the fall of 1974 to the fall of 1978, I became aware of the quality difference between commercial imported herbs and those produced in our own gardens. Most often, our herbs were superior in flavor and fragrance to those we could obtain from importers.

When consumers enter natural food stores or other herb outlets and view the intriguing display of dried roots, barks, flowers, and leaves, they are often left with an impression of a wholesome, pure, natural, or organic product. Looks can be deceiving though, for labels rarely offer information about the origins, processing methods, agricultural practices, or other treatments and handling of an herb jar's contents. Often we have no concept of quality when it comes to purchasing herbs. For many of us, herbs are a relatively new addition to daily life, and we don't know how to determine herb quality.

Quality is not simply a matter of flavor. The Third World has become a dump-

ing ground for pesticides severely restricted or totally banned in the United States. U.S. law governing the sale of pesticides allows for pesticides severely restricted or banned by the Environmental Protection Agency to be exported to other countries. Approximately 40 percent of the 1.6 billion pounds of pesticides sold in the United States are sold for exportation with 15 percent "unregistered"– never tested, licensed, or reviewed by the E. P. A. This is a perfectly legal practice under existing U.S. law.[1]

On 5 October 1981, David Weir, coauthor of *Circle of Poison*, appeared on a PBS special on pesticides, stating that between 50 percent and 70 percent of all pesticides used in the Third World are not applied to local food products, but to export crops.

Substances such as DDT, 245-T, aldrin, chlordane, endrine, BHC, dieldrin, and heptachlor are among the E.P.A.-banned or -restricted chemicals used outside the U.S., in many cases, supplied by American companies.

We do not know how many chemicals are used in producing herb crops imported to the United States. Many herbs are fumigated with phostoxin or methyl bromide to prevent unwanted insects as they enter the U.S. In addition many tea bags used in packaged herb teas contain polyvinylchloride—a known carcinogen.

Furthermore, relatively few herb crops are produced commercially in the United States. The garlic industry is controlled by an oligopoly of about nine major packers and shippers in a five-county region of central California. A number of shippers are also major growers. Just before the crop is harvested, some growers side dress their rows with a high-nitrogen fertilizer while watering heavily. The bulbs swell quickly, thus increasing weight and market value.

American ginseng growers and gatherers produced 293 metric tons of ginseng *Panax quinquefolius*, valued at $39 million, for export in 1980. This figure represents close to 97 percent of the total amount of ginseng grown and gathered in the United States. Phytar 560 and paraquat are among the herbicides used by commercial ginseng growers. Diathain, M-45, Capton 50, Malathion, and Sevin are among the pesticides used in ginseng culture.

Traditionally, only one ginseng crop can be grown on a given piece of land. Although no one knows the real reasons for this, one theory is that ginseng robs the soil of nutrients. Some theorize that it also sucks in residues of chemicals present in the soil.

About 60,000 acres of peppermint and 26,000 acres of spearmint grow in Indiana, Wisconsin, Michigan, Idaho, Washington, and Oregon; 75 percent of the nation's mint is produced in the Pacific Northwest. Most of these farms produce distilled mint oil for the essential oil trade while only a handful market dried mint leaf for herb tea. About 70 percent of the dried mint leaf consumed in this country is imported.

Ingesting one to four ounces of a 5 percent solution of paraquat can result in death. This substance is used as an herbicide in commercial mint fields in Oregon, as is diuron, methomyl, Sinbar, and other substances. Soil sterilants, used in mint fields, include Telon II, Telon C-17, Terrocide 15-D, vapam, and vorlex. Methomyl, malathion, Dyfonate, metaldehyde, Kelthane, Omite, and Comite are insecticides used in mint fields.

Are you beginning to sense problems with the quality of commercial herbs? The possible presence of biocide and fertilizer residues in imported or domestic herbs is only one problem. Storage and shelf-life considerations, the quality of cut and sifted versus whole herbs, adulterations, mislabeling, and deceptive labeling are also problems.

Safety considerations thus point out a direction for herb users: grow your own. If your experience is anything like mine, you'll find your home-grown herbs far superior in flavor and fragrance to many available from commercial sources, a double reward.

Many of the plants familiar to the herb garden—parsley, sage, rosemary, and thyme—are Eurasian natives which over the centuries have found use as condiments and medicine. It is taken for granted that such plants deserve a place in herb gardens. There are, in addition, many native North American plants that are equally useful, easy to cultivate, and equally deserving of appreciation. About twenty-five of the species included in this book appear in an herb gardening book for the first time; they are indigenous to this continent and have a long history of use. The list includes wildflowers, woodland herbs, prairie plants, trees, and shrubs. In addition to indigenous American herbs and a strong complement of familiar herb garden inhabitants, I have included a couple of Eurasian novelties and an African herb which I felt herb gardeners would find interesting and enjoyable. An additional twenty plants included grow here on their own, although they were originally native to other regions. The United States has dozens of climatic ranges, making it difficult to produce any horticultural book with national appeal. A Maine gardener invariably experiences different conditions than those of the Southern California gardens. But if any one category of plants lends itself to a greater variety of climates, soil types, rainfall figures, and sun exposure, it is herbs. Many herb species including bearberry, bee balms, cat thyme, echinaceas, sweet goldenrod, horehound, lady's mantle, lavenders, wormwoods, sages, oreganos, and santolinas are exceedingly drought resistent. I have had equal success growing many of the herb species listed in this book in the harsh cold of Maine, the cool coastal mists of the central California coast, and in the sandy, acid soil of an arid south-facing slope at my present Ozark home in north central Arkansas. In August of 1983 we had fourteen days in a row with temperatures over 100° F. with no rain for over a month. While most of my neighbors' vegetable gardens shriveled away, my herb garden stood lush. Most of the herbs in this book will do as well in New England as they will in arid Utah or the wet world of the coastal Pacific Northwest. Herbs are incredibly adaptable. As a general rule, an herb garden will require much less attention than a vegetable garden.

The potential for herb use in cooking is infinite. Many people don't use herbs simply because they don't know where to begin. If you shy away from herbs because you think they are reserved for French chefs, put away your fears and start stroking herbs to become familiar with their fragrance. Nibble a leaf. Imagine the dishes you prepare which may be enhanced by that herb. Experiment and enjoy!

Most books on herb gardening ignore medicinal aspects even though the history of plant use is preserved in pharmaceutical history right up into the twentieth century. It is only in the past fifty to eighty years that American culture has lost touch with the local flora as a source of medicine. Perhaps industrialization of western culture and the attendant corruption of traditional folk wisdom have caused this loss. The promotion and acceptance of synthetic medicines in treating disease, beginning with the accelerated development of modern chemistry and its resultant application to pharmacology, have also contributed to the decline of herbal medicine. Certainly, it is reassuring to have the expertise of the doctor and the pharmacist when you are dealing with potent—and potentially lethal—medicines. Still, expertise in the medicinal use of herbs is hardly beyond the grasp of most people, though herbal medicines must be approached with intelligence, respect, and caution.

An estimated 50 percent of prescription drugs are derived from natural sources. About 25 percent come from higher (flowering) plants.

Worldwide, more people are treated with herbs than with Western orthodox medicine. Many age-old cures have a rational scientific basis. Where scientific research vindicate folk uses, I have tried to supply the information. I used terms such as *diaphoretic, stimulant, carminative,* etc., to describe a plant's traditional or modern use. These terms are not necessarily specific. For example, *tonic* points to a general effect on a particular organ or body system. A diaphoretic, for example, brings on sweating. Many herbs will produce diaphoresis as does a bowl of hot chicken soup.

The medicinal uses for herbs included in this book are intended as reference information, not medical advice. Some of these plants can produce toxic reactions or may adversely affect individuals suffering from certain conditions. Please take reasonable precautions in harvesting, preparing, using, or administering all plant medicines. Remember, any substance, synthetic or natural, may produce undesirable effects. Medical reports exist of people dying from an overdose of water! I strongly recommend seeking the advice of a qualified medical practitioner and following his or her guidance rather than relying on self-diagnosis which, all too often, is improper, inadequate, or incorrect. Qualified medical diagnosis is essential. The author and publisher hereby disclaim any and all legal responsibility resulting from the use of the traditional and scientific medical information reported in this book.

The descriptions of plants I've included are my interpretation of technical botanical descriptions and my own observations. I've tried to keep terms simple trying to give the reader a visual picture of the plant. D. D. Dowden's sensitive illustrations capture the visual spirit of the plants and, in some small way, the descriptions enhance her work. Propagation and cultivation information to a large extent is based upon my experience and that of herb gardeners in various parts of the country who have shared their experiences. Projections for potential yields per acre are provided for those who contemplate growing and drying herbs for sale. The figures are in large part based on the work of USDA researchers D. M. Crooks and A. F. Sievers, 1941; W. W. Stockberger, 1935; and my own experience.

Information on chemical constituents has been provided for general interest and comparison. It is no coincidence when a person smells sweet goldenrod for the first time and thinks of tarragon. Both plants contain estragole—the substance in their respective essential oils responsible for their flavor and fragrance.

In essence, I have attempted to write the book I needed when I began herb gardening, plus provide new, useful information to the experienced herbarist. But nature's school is one in which we are all—and always will be—students.

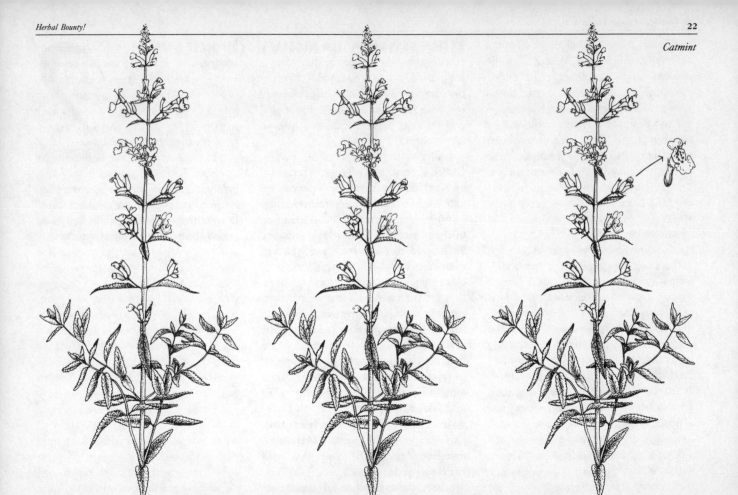

THE COMMON LANGUAGE OF BOTANY

That botany is a useful study is plain; because it is in vain that we know betony is good for headaches, or self-heal for wounds unless we can distinguish betony and self-heal from one another." John Hill, *The Family Herbal*, 1812

Names are reference points, symbols—vehicles for communicating and distinguishing one thing from another. The nature of a person, place, or plant does not change because of its name as Juliet reminds us: "What's in a name? That which we call a rose by any other name would smell as sweet. . . ."

Although the plant doesn't care what you call it, people do. Confusion inevitably arises if simultaneously more than one name is applied to a person, place, or plant. Similarly, if the same name is given to several plants or persons over a period of time, ambiguity may persist.

With a name like Steven Foster, I lived with quips about "my" songs, taking such comments with a smile and my standard response, "I haven't written any songs for a hundred years." What am I to say if someone asks if I'm the real Steven Foster? Yes, I'm real. But so was the other one.

As I sit here writing, I am brewing tea in a pot made by my sister-in-law's sister-in-law, that is to say, my brother's wife's brother's wife. Obviously it is much easier to say that the teapot's maker is Ann Gordon. Before Linnaeus introduced the Latin binomial system into general use by life scientists, scientific plant names were long and cumbersome phrases. Overlapping and confusion threatened the sanity of scientific minds. In the early

1600s when the gardener to Charles I, John Tradescant, introduced spiderworts (*Tradescantia species*) to England from North America, they were known as *Phalangum Ephenerum Virginianum Johannis Tradescanti.* The need for concise, well-defined, and unambiguous names soon becomes evident. Despite any inherent deficiencies such names are indispensable.

At workshops when I mention the need to use Latin binomials instead of relying on common plant names, about half the audience yawns, slumps down, and tunes out. Many people think Latin binomials are archaic, difficult to pronounce, hard to remember, and, as it was once put to me, a reflection of the patriarchal structure of our society. Most people, though, can pronounce and remember sassafras, coleus, rhododendron, geranium, asparagus, and petunia. These are all generic plant names as well as common plant names.

In today's herb market, *ginseng* has been applied to numerous plants and products. In product-labeling, ginseng has referred to several species of *Panax (Panax ginseng, P. quinquefolius, P. pseudo-ginseng);* Siberian ginseng *(Eleutherococcus senticosis),*

a shrubby member of the ginseng family native to parts of China and Russia; canigre or desert dock, *Rumex hymenosepalous,* a member of the buckwheat family native to the American Southwest; and even vitamin C. Several of these represent obvious marketing hoaxes. In most cases, I believe applying the name *ginseng* to plants or substances other than species of *Panax* is a marketing strategy designed to deceive consumers into buying a product on the reputation of a name.

In another example, sage generally refers to *Salvia officinalis,* an herb familiar to the fragrant garden and spice shelves; but it might also refer to certain species of the genus *Artemisia* (sagebrush) or to any number of the more than 700 species in the mint family's genus *Salvia.*

Aralia spinosa, the largest North American member of the ginseng family, and *Zantholxylum clava-herculis,* a member of the rue family, both share the common names Hercules's club, prickly ash, toothache tree, and tear blanket.

Dried French lavender sold in herb shops is not the same French lavender sold by herb nurseries. The French

lavender of the herb shop is usually English lavender *Lavandula angustifolia,* grown in France and sold on the American market under the name French lavender. "French" in this case denotes country of origin rather than the plant itself. The French lavender available from most herb plant sellers is *Lavandula dentata,* a plant not known for the quality of its dried flowers. *Lavandula stoechas,* sold mainly as Spanish lavender, is also sometimes sold as French lavender. The potential for confusion is obvious. Common names do not clearly distinguish different plants.

You don't have to be a botanist to appreciate and use Latin binomials. Not only do they clarify and distinguish one plant from another, they may also give us some insights as to the appearance, habits, uses, and history of a plant. The Latin binomial *Panax quinquefolius* clearly distinguishes American ginseng as a distinct entity. The generic term *Panax* is derived from the Greek *pan* meaning all and *akos* meaning cure, signifying cure-all or panacea. The name *quinquefolius* means five leaves. American ginseng's binomial thus tells us something of the plant's uses and leaf structure.

Some plants may have a hundred or more common names in several languages. On the other hand, only one Latin binomial can validly apply to a plant. These names are precise and internationally recognized.

The naming of plants is governed by the rules and regulations of the International Code of Botanical Nomenclature. Every few years botanists the world over convene at an International Botanical Congress where certain rules or articles for applying names to plants are established or revised. The results are published as the *International Code of Botanical Nomenclature*, a standard botanists voluntarily follow to make plant names universal and unambiguous.

Every living organism has certain definite characteristics. Some features differ greatly, such as those between a rattlesnake and an eagle. Other items like peppermint and spearmint, have very similar features. These characteristics are used to classify organisms into taxonomic groups. Taxonomy, as Arthur Cronquist defines it, is "a study aimed at producing a system of classification of organisms which best reflects the totality of their similarities and differences."[1]

Botanists have estimated there are between 200,000 and 800,000 species in the plant kingdom. To conveniently study such a great number of organisms, the kingdom is divided into smaller groups based on natural relationships. Major taxonomic groups of the plant kingdom include divisions, classes, orders, families, genera, species, and several groups below the rank of species. The family, genus, species, and subgroups of species serve as the most useful reference points for herb gardeners.

The family can be likened to a broad group of motorized vehicles known as automobiles. There are several genera in the family automobile including Chevrolets, Fords, Cadillacs, and Toyotas. In the genus Toyota, indigenous to Japan and naturalized throughout North America, is the species *corolla*. Thus for a specific organism in our hypothetical automobile family we have the binomial *Toyota corolla*.

The plant family is composed of one or more genera (genus) that resemble one another in general appearance and structural characteristics. Family names end in *aceae* with only eight exceptions, but either of the two names—regular or irregular—is used. These eight genera include several of the most important families of interest to the herb grower: the *Labiatae*—mint family (*Lamiaceae*,) *Umbelliferae*—carrot family (*Apiaceae*,) *Leguminosae*—pea family (*Fabaceae*,) *Compositae*—aster family (*Asteraceae*,) and the *Cruciferae*—mustard family (*Brassicaceae*.) For tradition's sake and the convenience of cross-referencing with other herb books, I will use the old family names not ending in *aceae*.

The mint family is perhaps the most important plant family to herbalists with about 180 genera and over 3,500 species. In fact, while the family's members represent only 1-1.5 percent of the world's flowering plants, over one-fourth of those plants commonly called herbs belong to this family. Members include sage, rosemary, thyme, pennyroyal, peppermint, savory, and dozens of others.

The first word of the Latin binomial is the generic term (genus), the second word is the specific epithet. The genus name is a noun, always capitalized, and may stand alone. The species name is an adjective, possessive, is not capitalized, and may not be used alone.

Binomials may be followed by the name or abbreviation of the name(s) of one or more persons. In *Panax quinquefolius* L., the "L" stands for Carl Linnaeus who "authored" the name for American ginseng. In 1793, Linnaeus regularized the Latin binomial system through the publication of his *Species Planatarum* (the species of plants), which included the descriptions and names for 5,900 plants. He named many of the herbs included in this book. Under the botanical code the author of a Latin binomial is the first person who validly publishes a plant name and description.

Sometimes you will find two or more names or authorities written after a Latin binomial with the first name in parentheses. This double citation means the plant has gone through a change in taxonomic position or classification. The first name in parentheses is the person who originally named the plant, the second the person who reclassified it. Authority citations have a number of other variations which we need not explore here. Suffice it to say that the authority cita-

tion is an abbreviated bibliographical reference, a useful tool for those who name plants. The citation, however, is not considered an essential part of the botanical name.

The appearance of a multiplication sign in the binomial means the plant is a hybrid produced by sexual crossing. *Mentha × piperita,* peppermint, is considered a cross between *Mentha spicata,* spearmint, and *Mentha aquatica,* watermint.

Several ranks of classification are recognized below the species level including subspecies, varieties, and forms. If one of these ranks is used, the term or an abbreviation for that term (variety, e.g. var.) must be included in the name of the plant.

One botanical name illustrating a double citation, subspecific rank, and hybrid is that for orris root, *Iris × germanica* var. *florentina* (L.) Dykes. Orris root is a hybrid of two species, (*Iris germanica* and *Iris florentina*) that was first named *Iris florentina* by Linnaeus, then reclassified by William R. Dykes, receiving its present name.

The cultivars, cultivated plants distinguished by certain characteristics

which are retained by asexual and sexual reproduction, are the most important subspecies rank of classification relevant to cultivated plants. Cultivar names begin with capital letters and are preceded by the abbreviation cv., or are placed in single quotation marks. Those of you who are still prejudiced against Latin plant names will be happy to know that since 1 January 1959 the International Code of Nomenclature for Cultivated Plants allows cultivar names only from modern languages. Latin names may not be used. However, many Latin cultivar names were published prior to 1959 and are still used.

Sometimes Latin names are changed. These changes tend to be annoying and reduce the efficiency of the nomenclature system. The Botanical Codes try to keep such changes to a minimum, but nevertheless it is sometimes necessary to change the rank or classification of a plant based on solid new information. This means a change in name as well. The nomenclature system is by no means perfect, but it is the best and most generally adopted system we have for relating to plant names.

There are no set rules for pronouncing binomials. Latin binomials may be pronounced differently by people from various regions or countries. In various parts of the United States, I've heard the generic name for Mayapple, *Podophyllum*, pronounced three distinct ways by professional botanists. People tend to pronounce binomials as they pronounce words in their own language. It is only important that you are understood by the person with whom you are talking.

In this book, the Latin binomials and author citations follow those given in *Hortus Third*, cited below. To help make the binomial more familiar to the reader, I have included a pronunciation for the genus and main species described in each entry. Rolling the names over on your tongue a few times is just another taste treat!

References for further reading:

Bailey, Liberty Hyde. *How Plants Get Their Names*. New York: Dover Books, 1963.

_____, and Ethel Zoe Bailey. *Hortus Third*. New York: Macmillan, 1976

Foster, Steven. "Ginseng—Are You Confused?" *Well-Being*, 46 (Oct. 1979):43-50.

_____. "Latin Binomials: Learning to Live with the System," *Well-Being*, 48 (Dec. 1979):41-42.

Jeffery, Charles. *Biological Nomenclature*. New York: Crane, Russack and Co., 1977.

Tippo, Oswald, and William Louis Stern. *Humanistic Botany*. New York: W.W. Norton and Co., Inc., 1977.

Hops climbing a trellis at the Farm and Garden Project, University of California, Santa Cruz.

DESIGNING AN HERB GARDEN

3

Cultivating herbs means more than planting seeds, watering, fertilizing, and weeding. Cultivating is nurturing, refining, and encouraging. As the cultivator you must establish a relationship with another living being—the plant. An herb garden will repay you equally for the energy you contributed to its growth.

The Shakers started the first medicinal herb gardens in North America; by the mid-1800s they had over 200 acres of herbs under cultivation. These herbs were sold in dried form and used for manufacturing high-quality herbal extracts sold the world over. One of the gentle glowing leaders of the Shaker movement, Elder Frederick Evans, said in 1867, "A tree has its wants and wishes, and a person should study them as a teacher watches a child to see what he can do. If you love the plant and take heed of what it likes, you will be well paid by it.[1]" I think this is the key to a successful and vibrant garden—the mystery of the green thumb.

Chinese philosophy assumes that the universe is in a constant process of change—rhythms of life and death, growth and antithesis, waxing and waning, yin and yang. The cycles are never static. The garden is in constant metamorphosis with the rhythms of the seasons and everchanging forces of weather and soil life. Garden design must conform to natural forces and not become stagnant under a gardener's management.

Romans practiced topiary gardening, clipping and trimming plants into the shapes of birds, animals, or geometric forms. Sculpted boxwoods, myrtles, and bays mimicked a myriad of shapes, often reflecting architectural style. In Francis Bacon's 1625 essay *Of Gardens*, he disapproves of "images cut out of juniper and other garden stuff," saying, "Topiary work is for children." In Bacon's day, though, cutting yews and rosemary into green gargoyles was common in the gardens of the rich. W. Robinson writes in his *English Flower Garden*, "What right have we to deform things so lovely in form? No cramming of Chinese feet into impossible shoes is half so foolish as the wilful and brutal distortion of the beautiful forms of trees."[2]

I believe foliage and flower should not be clipped and tamed to satisfy the whims of a person's time and tastes. If you want a six-foot hedge, plant a shrub that grows to six feet rather than chopping off a shrub that naturally grows twice that height. To me the ultimate achievement of the gardener is to be shaped by the forces within the garden, rather than to shape the garden by force.

A garden is a place for growth. A quiet mind can become one with nature's cycles. Respecting other life forms by cooperating with their natural needs fosters the growth of both the plants and the gardener. Life's greatest treasures are often silent and unseen; the gentle gardener will find more in the garden than useful and beautiful plants for healthful and aesthetic consumption.

Most artistic endeavors are based upon control of the medium. The gardener, on the other hand, is more like the brush of a painter, the words of a writer, or the instrument of the musician. The gardener is dependent upon the variables of sun, climate, weather, season, insects, soil life, planetary and lunar influences, and the unseen architects of the natural world. The gardener is steward rather than creator in the truest sense, though designing a garden necessitates recognizing all influences affecting plant life and creating a harmonious balance of growth factors for individual plants and the garden as a whole.

When designing an herb garden you must have a starting point. Walk around your potential garden site and observe what surrounds it. Existing architectural lines, pathways, driveways, trees, fences, native plants, building materials, present use, projected use, even the view from the neighbor's yard should be taken into consideration.

Before working out a design on paper, go to the garden spot, become quiet, and imagine yourself expanding into the soil, nearby plants, a tree, and the surrounding area in general. Imagine that you are your favorite herb plant. What does it feel like to be on that spot? Keep a piece of paper and pencil handy to write down any impressions you may have. Visualize how you would like the garden to appear. I know this may sound airy-fairy, but you may be amazed at the ideas that pop into your head.

Before diving into a grandiose plan, consider how much time you have for gardening. Is the garden going to be a weekend hobby or a passionate career? Start small and expand as feasible. Other considerations include how and when the sun hits the site, soil type and conditions, water availability, and the herbs best suited to your climate. If you have several sites to choose from you may wish to create a variety of habitats most favorable for your desired herbs.

Once you've chosen a site, test the soil using any of the kits available to gardeners. County extension offices offer basic soil analysis at minimal costs. Tell the agent that you want recommendations for organic amendments, otherwise you'll receive a list of chemical amenders.

Herbs produce the most potent essential oils, responsible for most of the flavors and fragrances, when they receive at least six to eight hours of sunlight each day. In the mint family, oil glands are usually located on the underside of leaves. When the plant comes into bloom the oil glands can be observed with a low-power hand lens.

Most herbs do best in sun except for those indigenous to the deciduous forests, plus angelica, sweet cicely, woodruff, Corsican mint, and *Salvia divinorum*. As a general rule, herbs prefer a slightly alkaline situation. If you have an acid soil the pH can be balanced with the addition of lime or wood ashes. Good drainage is essential. Poorly drained soils can be improved by deep cultivation or by adding sand or compost. Herbs require less water than most vegetables. Many herbs originate in the dry, gravelly soils of the Mediterranean region; therefore, watering will be required only in times of drought. Some herbs, such as mints, angelica, lovage, and basil grow best in a fairly moist soil. Most soils will accommodate herbs. These are general guidelines, but each herb's specific requirements are listed in the plant-by-plant entries which follow.

Now put your design on paper. Graph paper is wonderful for designing. Another good idea is to take an eight-by-ten black-and-white photograph of your house, yard, or plot, then on a piece of tracing paper placed over the photo, sketch in general outline the garden's appearance, discovering how it contrasts and blends with architectural lines.

A garden design is a personal thing. Indeed, there are as many ways to garden as there are gardeners. The garden should reflect the lifestyle and inspiration of the gardener rather than reproduce a classical design—unless, of course, the garden is designed for preservation or restoration purposes.

To a great extent herb gardens have become stylized and stagnant over the past fifty years. They echo gardens of old with little new creative input. The same ol' plants are often depicted in the same ol' settings. However, elements of historical garden design cannot be discounted as major influences in creating new herb gardens. They are a source of ideas. If you have the opportunity, visit historical display gardens at museums. The herb gardens at Mount Vernon and the Williamsburg Restoration in Virginia, Old Sturbridge in Sturbridge, Massachusetts, the William Penn Museum in Harrisburg, Pennsylvania, the National Herb Garden in Washington, D. C., and Strybing Arboretum in San Francisco and numerous other museums and botanical gardens can be a source of inspiration for your herb garden design.[3]

When considering designs, it is fun to borrow ideas from several traditional horticultural themes such as the intricacies of the formal English knot garden, the peace of the medieval Hortus Inclusus, or the reverence for stone and flowing lines in a Japanese garden. Concepts from these traditions can be blended with contemporary practices such as double-dug beds from biodynamic/French intensive methods, the permaculture principles of centering agricultural design around perennial plantings, the biodynamic ideas on companion planting, and the inclusion of native plants in landscaping.

The following designs are presented to generate new ideas, rather than to be copied. They blend elements from traditional and contemporary horticultural themes. They are meant to complement one another. The designs should be considered collectively and separately. Use the ideas to help conceptualize the best herb garden design for you and the plants under your care.

Design 1. A backyard is a retreat for quiet and relaxation—a place to enjoy family and friends. Paul Lee, friend of herbs, has turned his backyard into a place to enjoy those friends.

As a student of Paul Tillich's at Harvard, Paul Lee became fascinated with *thymós*—an old Greek word for courage and vitality–"the courage to be." Discovering that the names for thyme and the thymus gland were both derived from *thymós*, he set out to learn as much as he could about both. Paul opened a restaurant in Santa Cruz, California called The Wild Thyme featuring sweetbreads or *ris de veau* (calves' thymus glands) as the house specialty. He also put herb beds in his back yard and started collecting varieties of thyme. Today, in a peaceful residential neighborhood in Santa Cruz, Paul's entire back yard is a checkerboard of herb beds, perpetuating Paul's love of thyme and the biodynamic/French intensive techniques of Alan Chadwick.

While a professor at U.C. Santa Cruz, Paul met Alan Chadwick and invited him to start a garden on the U.C. campus. A Shakespearean actor and horticultural genius, the British-born Chadwick was once a student of George Bernard Shaw and Rudolf Steiner. He had served as gardener to the state of South Africa and was a musician and artist. At the U.C. campus he turned a hillside covered with rock and poison oak into a brilliant paradise abounding with lush vegetables, flowers, fruits, and herbs. Over the next decade Chadwick gardens graced a number of California sites inspiring all who experience their magic. Since Chadwick's death in 1980, his teachings are carried on through his apprentices. Those apprentice programs are listed in the resource section of this book.

Chadwick's methods combine techniques from biodynamic agriculture, begun in 1924 with a series of eight lectures delivered by the Austrian philosopher and spiritual scientist Rudolf Steiner, plus French intensive horticulture, begun in the 1890s outside Paris.

Steiner's lectures on agriculture responded to farmers' questions about the formative forces of nature, the "etheric" nature of plants, and the decline of crop quality and productivity on a given piece of land. Steiner taught that the farm itself is an organism. Soil is a living entity rather than just a chemical mix. Soil health, the basis of a healthy farm organism, is achieved by using compost treated with preparations from fermented plant and animal materials, intended to support microbial soil life and enhance plants' utilization of light. The effects of soil depleting and improving crops are kept in balance through crop rotation. Companion plantings make use of the subtle interrelationships between plants. The life of the soil, atmospheric influences, and lunar influence are considered along with the effect of human spiritual nature on the farm organism. Over the past sixty years, the biodynamic approach has proven successful in practice by farmers and gardeners the world over. Like the Chinese

Design 1

concept of the universe, the biodynamic farm organism never remains static.

In French intensive gardens, vegetables were grown on eighteen-inch deep beds, heavily fertilized with horse manure. Plants were grown close together so that their mature leaves would touch, creating a green mulch that reduced weed growth and helped to retain soil moisture. During winter months, bell-glass jars were placed over seedlings to help them get an early start.

One of the basic tenets of biodynamic/French intensive gardening is the preparation of a raised bed. The beds are usually three to six feet across and as long as desired. The soil is double-dug to a depth of two feet, allowing roots to breathe and encouraging the microbial life of the soil.

This technique is an old gardening practice. In 1821 William Cobbett writes of double-digging, or trenching as he calls it, in his *American Gardener:*

"As to the experience of this preparatory operation, a man that knows how to use a spade, will trench four rods [sixty-six feet of two-foot-wide beds] in a day . . . . Supposing the garden to con- tain an acre, and the labourer to earn a dollar a day, the cost of this operation will, of course, be forty dollars. . . .Poor ground deeply moved is preferable, in many cases, to rich ground with shallow tillage; as when the ground has been deep- ly moved once, it feels the benefit for ever after. A garden is made to last for ages. . . . It is well known to all who have had experience on the subject, that of two plants of almost any kind that stand for the space of three months in top soil of the same quality, one being on deeply moved ground, and the other on ground moved no deeper than usual, the former will exceed the later one half in bulk. And, as to trees of all description from the pear down to the currant bush, the difference is so great, that there is no room for comparison."[4]

You may find it best to start with 100- or 200-square-foot beds, which can be dug in a day or two, rather than spend- ing forty days trenching an acre, but you'll find the toil necessary for initial preparation worth the effort in higher yields and healthier crops. The beds should be three to six feet wide so you can comfortably reach the center of the bed without step- ping on it. In wide beds, I place a stone or two at strategic points on which to step or lean so as to prevent soil compaction. The soil should be moderately moist before digging. It is too dry if you can- not squeeze it into a ball in the palm of your hand and too wet if it clings to your shovel. If the soil is dry, water it for two hours a couple of days before digging. Add a one-to-four-inch layer of compost on the top of the bed before digging as well as any other desired soil amendments – lime, wood ashes, rock phosphate, or well- seasoned manure.

To double dig a bed, start at either end and with a garden spade dig a trench about one foot deep and one foot wide, across the breadth of the bed. Pile this soil at the end of the bed, or put it directly into a wheelbarrow. You'll need it to fill the last trench. Once the first trench is dug, take a spading fork and loosen the soil at the bottom of the trench to a depth of one foot. If the soil is hard, pry the bottom with a fork and break large clods into smaller pieces as you come to them. Repeat the procedure down the entire length of the bed, piling the soil dug from each trench into the previously dug trench, and forking about a foot deeper. Once you reach the end, the soil from the first trench is transferred to the last trench. It can be transported by wheelbarrow or shovel. During the digging process, stand on a piece of plywood placed across the bed so as to minimize soil compaction. For more detailed information on double digging and biodynamic/French intensive gardening, see John Jeavon's *How to Grow More Vegetables* listed in the bibliography.

The double-dug bed is the skeletal structure of the herb garden designs to follow. Paul Lee's backyard herb garden consists of about forty beds, many of which are three feet by three feet and separated by eighteen-inch sections of grass. His collection includes over 150 herb varieties.

Using your own design inspired by the Lee's garden you can plant perennials in some of the beds, reserving others for annual herb crops. In intensive annual beds, plantings can be close together creating a "green" mulch. Design 1 is simple and elastic. It can be stretched along existing walkways and borders, or placed in the middle of a lawn. The shapes

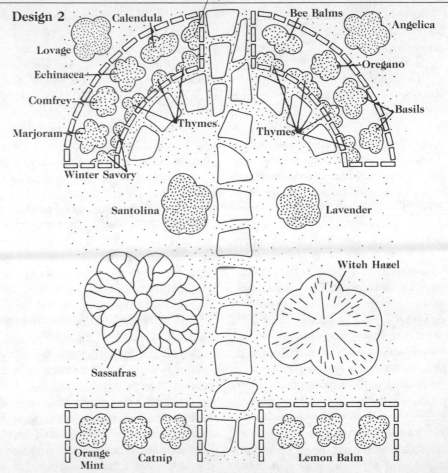

Design 2

Calendula

Lovage

Echinacea

Comfrey

Marjoram

Winter Savory

Thymes

Thymes

Bee Balms

Angelica

Oregano

Basils

Santolina

Lavender

Witch Hazel

Sassafras

Orange Mint

Catnip

Lemon Balm

can be round, oval, square, or rectangular. You can put in one bed or thirty beds – it depends on the size of your lot and inclination.

Design 2. The herb garden is often considered independent from the vegetable garden or the overall landscaping scheme. Herbs, however, can serve as primary elements in landscape design. They can be used as borders, as ground covers, and for shade. The warm orange-yellow blossoms of calendula can brighten a border, lavenders planted against a foundation offer a fragrant contrast to a dark-colored house, camomile and creeping thymes can be used as ground covers in a sunny situation, woodruff and corsican mint are useful ground covers for shaded areas. Sweet gum, sassafras, and slippery elm trees provide good summer shade. Witch hazel gives shade and brilliant fall foliage culminating with a display of delicate blossoms after the leaves have dropped. Double-digging methods can be used in preparing a spot for one tree or, over a period of time, preparing the soil for the entire garden.

It takes about five minutes to prepare and double dig each square foot of sur-face area. The 288 square feet of surface area in this design would take a total of twenty-four hours to dig by hand.

In this design, Roman camomile, either the petalless variety or the flowerless cultivar 'Treanague,' is used as a ground cover along with creeping thyme or the gray-colored creeping woolly thyme. I once had a six-foot by twenty-foot bed of creeping woolly thyme which was started from ten seedlings. Over a period of three years, they spread to fill in the entire 120-square-foot area. Maintenance was minimal. Occasionally we watered it. The plant stands less than one-half inch tall so it never needed mowing. We walked on it, sat on it, lay on it, even drove tractors over it with little sign of wear or injury. The soft fuzzy gray-green foliage satisfied the senses of smell, vision, and touch. Roman camomile doesn't mind some traffic either, as long as it's random. Stepping stones can be worked into the design to save wear on heavily traveled paths.

Start out with a four-foot-by-four-foot plot the first year, then increase the size of the ground cover each year for a three-year period until the entire area is planted. By the fourth year the herbal ground cover will be ready for full use and enjoyment. It's a great summer project for bored high school or college students. If they start working on it their freshman year, it will be completed by graduation time – the growth and expansion of the garden symbolizing the progress of the student. Ecology Action sells a booklet entitled *Self-fertilizing Herbal Lawn* listed in the resource section offering excellent information on establishing herbal ground covers.[5]

The raised bed at the rear of the lot can be planted with a mix of annuals and perennials for kitchen use. Tall angelica and lovage can flank either side of the walkways at the bed's ends. Plantings of thymes, prostrate rosemary, or winter savory can spill over the sides of the stones bordering the bed. Calendula and echinacea can be added for color. Just off the walkway in the middle of the herbal groundcover are miniature island beds of lavenders or grey santolina. Their foliage produces a striking and harmonious contrast with the ground cover.

The foundation plantings can be in groups – three or more plants of the same species. In this design, the beds against the house are planted with lemon balm or catnip, both of which will do well in the partial shade of the sassafras tree and witch hazel planted near the entryway. Orange mint can be planted under a dripping faucet for use in fresh iced mint tea.

Design 3. The Japanese feel that nature is mysterious and incomprehensible. Early inhabitants of Japan viewed their beautiful landscape as the home of numerous nature spirits called *kami*. *Kami* inhabit mountains, rivers, trees, stones, or any natural objects unusual in shape or form. Stones are thought to be hollow and as the *kami* dwelling inside grows, so does the stone. The *kami* have personalities that can be soothed and persuaded into cooperating with the garden.

This garden design is for those who live in a spot where gardening might be perceived as impossible—among large rocks. It is inspired by the reverence for stone in the Japanese garden and an appreciation for the weathered limestone bluffs of the Ozarks. Here the twisted forms of the native Ashe's Juniper, *Juniperus Ashei*, bow from rocky crags reminding me of conifers in a Han dynasty jade carving. This must be the home of *kami*.

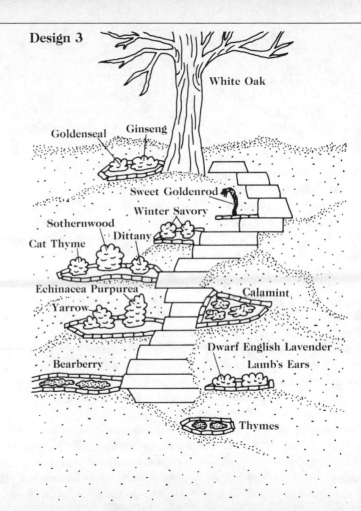

Design 3

White Oak

Goldenseal Ginseng

Sweet Goldenrod

Winter Savory

Sothernwood

Dittany

Cat Thyme

Echinacea Purpurea

Calamint

Yarrow

Dwarf English Lavender

Lamb's Ears

Bearberry

Thymes

The design is dictated by the lay of the land. Paths are quietly laid between immovable rocks. Next to the path, spaces between rocks are dammed with small stones to hold soil. Balance and harmony are achieved by striking a casual order in the seemingly random disorder of the eroding bluff.

In a hundred-yard radius, nature provides all of the material for the garden: soil, stones for paths and bed walls, even some plants for the garden. Growing of its own accord near the garden entrance, sweet goldenrod *Solidago odora* is absorbed into the design. Calamint *Satureja arkansana,* a local mint, is transferred from its nearby habitat to a garden bed. If this were California, native yerba buena (*Satureja Douglasii*) or mugwort (*Artemisia Douglasiana*) might become part of the garden. The garden gently eases into the natural surroundings.

In a 150-square-foot area, we create nine individual beds—all at different levels and ranging in size from one to six square feet. Half the garden gets full sun, the other half is under the shade of a white oak—the bark of which is a powerful herbal astringent. This makes a unique combination of herb species in a limited space. Wild ginger, goldenseal, and the shade-loving *Echinacea purpurea* grow under the oak's shadow. Thymes and germander are used as evergreens. At the south end of the garden, thymes drape themselves over stones. Native calamint decorates one bed with sprays of delicate foliage and lavender blooms. Can *kami* possibly take refuge in the tortured shrubbery and cement-entombed earth of the average suburban yard? Perhaps *kami* delight in sensitive human integration rather than the usual destructive dominance.[6]

Design 4. A place of solitude created within an enclosed garden space dates to Roman times. The Hortus Inclusus of medieval times was a garden within a garden enclosed by hedges or fencing. Planted entirely in turf, it made a quiet space for contemplation and meditation. Such a space, placed in the center or rear of a modern herb garden, provides quiet escape from garden toil and household tasks. An enveloping buffer of hops or passion flowers can filter out environmental noise and create a pleasing shaded habitat just right for relaxing. Lattice sides make a good home for climbing herbs and provide shade and valuable screening. Sides can be rustic wood posts latticed with thin half-inch diameter branches of willow, sassafras, oak, or any pliable native wood. If hops or passion flowers are trained up the sides of the structure, they will die back in autumn. Using short flexible wood sticks as lath, you can create a pleasing design for winter scenery. The top can be covered, left open for a view of the sky, or protected by an overhanging tree branch. Simplicity of design, materials, and execution make the modern Hortus Inclusus quick and easy to build, serene, and private.

A bench can be arranged among a floor of yerba buena, Corsican mint, woodruff or other shade-loving ground covers. The seat can be a slab of oak supported by a stone foundation, flat rocks laid in appropriate positions to provide a reasonably comfortable seat, a simple wooden bench, or metal garden furniture. The enclosed space can be closet-sized or as large as desired.

In Design 4, the Hortus Inclusus is the garden's focal point. The enclosed area can face the garden, providing a place to reflect upon the garden's design, or it may be placed back-to, enhancing the feeling of seclusion. All paths—those of foot and the flowing visual lines—lead to the space of quietude.

Herbal borders leading to the peaceful space can be in waves of soft textures and subtle coloration. Low-growing *Artemisias* producing a silver-gray foliage can blend with spring-time sprays of spiderwort and calamint blooms. Rose or golden yarrows spark the colors of late spring and early summer. A background of tansy or St. John's wort provide late summer yellow hues.

Over thirty-six million Americans have home gardens. A rapidly growing number of Americans—two million to date—are involved in community garden programs. One herb garden designed as the focal point of a community garden site with a Hortus Inclusus in the center can provide herbs for fifty gardeners or more and a relaxing retreat for resting between work spurts. Design 4 is inspired by an herb garden designed by David Lansford and volunteers for a community garden site in Santa Cruz, California, a vacant lot that recently fell victim to development.

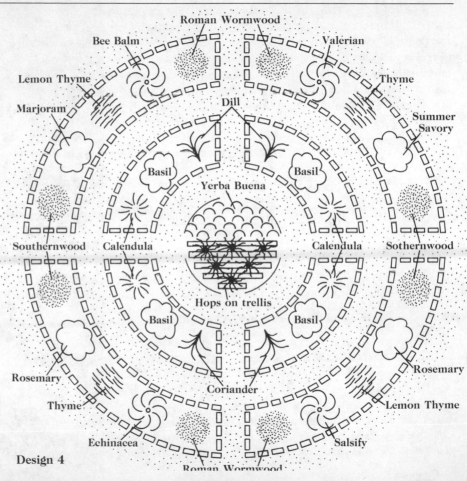

Design 4

Rooted cuttings.

PROPAGATING HERBS

4

I n his 1790 *Metamorphosis of Plants,* Goethe observes that plant growth is a rhythm of contractions and expansions; and in its growth progression, the metamorphosis of one plant organ to the next is simply a modification of the previous organ. Thus, flower parts are modified rhythms of leaf growth. According to Goethe's theory, the formative forces of a plant are most highly concentrated in the seed. With the germination of the seed comes the first unfolding expansion in the leaves. At this point, the form concentrated in the seed spatially expands in the leaves. In the flower's calyx, the forces again contract, this time around a central axis. The corolla (a flower's petals) produces the second expansion. The stamens and pistils are produced by the next contraction, the fruit by the third and last expansion, and in the seed, the final concentration of the forces of plant life are concealed in dormancy until life's rhythms are again activated by suitable environmental conditions.[1]

As an herb grower, you are the catalyst to set an herb seed's latent life forces in motion, perpetuating a species for use and enjoyment. Herb gardeners should consider themselves herb propagators. By mastering the simple techniques of propagating annuals, biennials, and perennials, you will find that the potential for expanding garden design, size of plantings, ability to save money on plant purchases, and opportunities for increasing stock for sale or trade, are limited only by the amount of time you can devote to generating new plants.

"Propagating herbs is simple. Anyone

At Taylor's Herb Garden, seed-grown herbs are sown directly into pots.

can do it," says Kent Taylor. And Kent should know. He and his wife Betty operate North America's largest herb nursery, Taylor's Herb Gardens, in Vista, California. Chances are, if you buy herb plants at a commercial greenhouse, natural food store, or from many small herb plant sellers, the original stock came from the Taylors.

The Taylor nursery is nestled on a peaceful twenty-five-acre spread only minutes away from the suburban sprawl bordering San Diego. Herbs thrive in Vista's Mediterranean-like climate through most of the year. Most of Taylor's seedlings are grown outdoors to produce a heartier stock more likely to endure shipping and display.

A two-acre shade house dominates a visitor's view of the nursery. Here shade-loving herbs such as yerba buena, gota kola, corsican mint, woodruff, and chervil are matured. Ivy, *Hedera helix,* is also grown in the shade house as a supplemental cash crop. This well-known evergreen perennial is not well-known as a medicinal plant; but in both the European and Chinese traditions, a decoction or poultice of the leaves was used to treat skin eruptions and itching.

Each year the Taylors sell over one million herb plants. In one day as many as 50,000 plants of one species may be shipped to a broker. Rows of tens of thousands of potted herb seedlings fill an acre and a half near the nursery's en-

trance. Some of these plants are being started from seed, though most are ready for sale. In this section of the nursery, annual and biennial herbs are started from seed. Hundreds of dill, marjoram, summer savory, caraway, coriander, anise, and fennel plants are at various stages of growth, from tiny emerging leaves, to eight-inch-high seedlings ready for sale.

At Taylor's Herb Gardens, seed-grown herbs are sown directly into the pots a consumer will purchase, but you can sow seed for annual and biennial herbs directly in your herb garden as soon as danger of frost has passed. To get a jump on the growing season, start them in flats indoors about eight weeks before the last spring frost. As a general rule of thumb, it is best to start most annual and biennial herbs from seeds.

When you sow seeds outdoors, prepare the seed bed well. Level the soil with a rake, removing any rocks larger than an inch in diameter. Make shallow furrows with a rake or the edge of a hoe as a guide to planting. Seeds should be covered by two to four times their diameter with soil. Tiny seeds, like German camomile, can be mixed with fine sand to help insure even distribution. Fine seed can also be sown on the surface of a well-prepared seed bed then tamped down to bring the seed in contact with moisture-holding soil particles. At the Taylor nursery, fine seeds start in flats under shade to prevent the seeds from drying out. After you plant the seeds, keep the soil moist but not soggy. The germinating seeds should never be allowed to completely dry out.

Young seedlings can be thinned or transplanted after the first two true leaves appear. What look like first leaves are not actually leaves but the food-storing tissue of the seeds, known as cotyledons. The true leaves, which have the general appearance of the plant's mature leaves, emerge after the cotyledons. Seed-sown plants at the Taylor nursery take about six to eight weeks to reach a saleable size. Most herb seeds germinate in seven to fourteen days, though parsley takes patience. It may need six weeks or more to germinate.

Seeds can be started indoors in almost any type of container. If commercial nursery flats are unavailable, take an empty gallon milk jug and cut it down with

Row of tens of thousands of potted herb seedlings fill an acre- and-a-half near the Taylor's Herb Garden entrance.

scissors or a knife to make a two-inch-deep tray. Cut slits in the bottom for drainage. My favorite seeding medium is a mixture of one part sterile potting soil, one part fine sand, and one part peat moss. Commercially prepared seed-starting mixes are also available.

Fill the containers with soil mix to about half an inch of the top. Firm the soil down with your hand, then with a pencil, ruler, or finger, mark out rows at two-inch spacings. Sow seed evenly in rows and cover with soil. Make sure the seeds are not planted too close together as crowded seedlings tend to be weak, leggy, and difficult to transplant.

Spray with a mister to keep the soil moist or place the container in a larger pan with an inch or two of water so moisture can soak up into the mix through capillary action. Remove from the pan as soon as the soil surface becomes visibly moist. Repeat as necessary. Avoid letting the seeds dry out, but keep the mix from becoming too moist.

The flat can be placed in a window and maintained at a temperature between 65° and 75° F. Seedlings may also be placed under a grow light. Sill-grown seedlings will have to be turned every couple of days as they will bend toward the light.

Poor circulation and excess moisture in a warm situation may cause damping off. Damping off is a fungus disease that appears as a greenish mold on the soil's surface. The primary culprits are the fungi *Pythium ultimum* and *Rhizoctonia solani*. Damping off may cause rotting before germination, stem rot near the surface of the medium, or girdling of the stem which stunts growth and eventually kills

To make a cutting cut the desired stem two to five inches long, leaving two leaf nodes or joints.

the plant. It can be controlled by proper environmental conditions for seedling development or by starting out with sterilized soil and containers.

Once seedlings have developed two true leaves they can be transplanted into larger containers or planted in their garden location if danger of frost has passed. Before planting in the garden, seedlings must be "hardened off" or acclimated to the outdoors by placing them in a shaded area outside and gradually exposing them to full sun over a week's time. Bring plants indoors if there is a danger of frost. Young seedlings should be transplanted on an overcast day or in the late afternoon and watered well.

Seeds of some perennials, particularly woodland plants, go through a period of dormancy. This may be the result of impermeable seed coats. The seed coats can be softened to allow for faster water uptake and aeration using one of several presowing treatments. In some species, dormancy may also result from immature embryos that need to grow and develop before germinating, or the food storage tissue and the embryo must undergo physiological changes before germinating.

Seeds of such species need to be stratified to break the dormancy and hasten the germination process. Stratification is a long-term treatment (two to three months) under temperatures just above freezing. Successful stratification has three basic requirements: a source of moisture for the seed; low, near-freezing temperatures (35° to 45° F.), and aeration—seeds need to breathe too. Seeds can be stratified in moist sand, peat moss, sphagnum moss, vermiculite, or weathered sawdust. Usually I'll place seeds in a jar of moist sand in the refrigerator for the winter months. I punch holes in the top of the jar for aeration as for a captured butterfly. The stratification medium must be kept moist but not wet. After about three months, plant the seeds in a well-prepared seed bed. Ginseng, goldenseal, sweet gum, spice bush, and witch hazel are among the species whose seed will need to be stratified.

One section of the Taylor nursery is devoted to preparing and maturing seedlings from cuttings or slips. Nearly all of the perennials at Taylor's Herb Gardens are regenerated by this method. Dozens of flats of herb cuttings line tables in

Dozens of flats of herbs cuttings line tables in checkered patterns as they develop roots and mature into seedlings.

checkered patterns as they develop roots and mature into seedlings. Kent feels propagating herbs from cuttings is one of the easiest and most economical ways of increasing his stock.

Test cutting to see if it has grown roots simply by tugging gently on the stem.

"We can produce ready-for-sale plants faster from cuttings than by seed. They take four to six weeks to develop roots. Then we pot them and they are ready to sell," Kent explains. "To make a cutting, take pruning shears, scissors, or a knife and cut the desired stem two to five inches long, leaving two leaf nodes or joints. Select cuttings from the vigorous growth of the spring and summer months. Fall cuttings take longer to root. New tip growth is most desirable. With woody stemmed herbs such as rosemary and lavender we chose the tender wood.

"After making the cutting, carefully remove the leaves from the lower inch of the stem and stick this section into your rooting medium. Our rooting medium is clean coarse sand or sponge rock. It should be kept moist until the cuttings develop roots. After several weeks you can test a cutting to see if it has grown roots simply by tugging gently on the stem. If it firmly resists, it is ready for transplanting."

A half-acre planting of fully matured herbs serves as a specimen garden for visitors and as propagating stock for herbs started from cuttings. Here beds of English camomile and thymes reach their full potential, lavender blooms entice honey bees, and stately rosemary shrubs grow to splendor. Experimental crops not listed in Taylor's catalog grow in this garden as well. Some of these herbs are propagated in the spring or fall by root divisions; others are increased by layering.

Many perennial herbs such as catnip, thymes, the mints, wormwood, bee balm, and tarragon can be propagated by root divisions. Simply dig the plant in the spring or fall and cut the root into several pieces with a shovel, or pull the roots apart with your hands. Plant in the desired location and water well. The only expenditure with this technique is time.

Layering can be used successfully with lavenders, thymes, rosemary, and other perennials. This method produces new plants while they are still attached to the parent plant. Select a healthy flexible stem that is growing close to the soil or can be easily bent toward the ground. Dig a small hole with a trowel, place a portion of the stem into the hole, and cover it, leaving three to eight inches of the stem's terminal end above ground. If necessary, pin it down with a tent peg

or a hooked stick. It is helpful to remove the leaves and scrape the underside of the stem to be placed in contact with the soil. Within a few weeks this stem will develop roots and can be clipped from the parent plant for transplanting. The process can be hastened with frequent watering. This is a good way to increase stock in the small garden.

For Kent and Betty Taylor, propagating herbs is a livelihood. For you the herb gardener, it is a way to increase the enjoyment of the garden and the size of your stock at little or no cost after you master the skills required for the best propagating techniques for individual plants. It may seem like magic to unleash the concentrated life forces of a seed or coax a stem into producing roots, but you needn't be a wizard to perform the magic. Just follow the simple instructions given in this book for each species and gain confidence in your ability to create the best herb garden for your needs.

Peppermint field, Trout Lake Farm

Tools for the Harvest

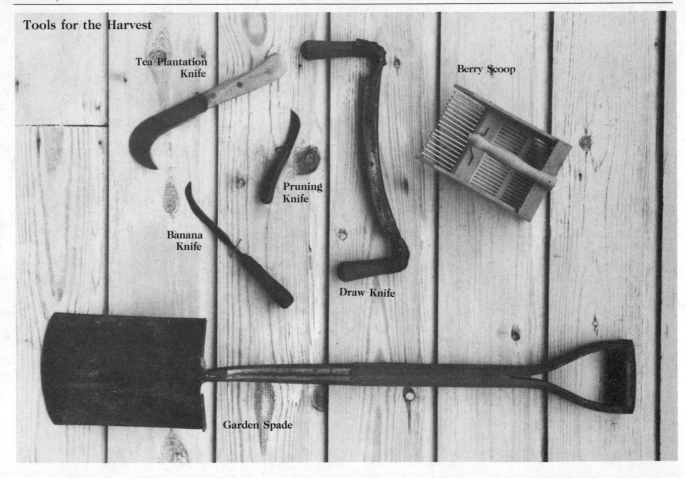

Tea Plantation Knife

Pruning Knife

Berry Scoop

Banana Knife

Draw Knife

Garden Spade

HARVESTING AND DRYING

5

The Algonquin tribes of the Northeastern United States and many other peoples with a close tie to nature regard plants as real beings, alive and vital as humans are. In many Indian cultures, medicinal herbs are gathered with respect and with attention toward maintaining the good will of the plants. When plant lives are to be sacrificed for human benefit, their gifts of food, fragrance, and healing should be respected. Herbs often receive grateful thought and prayers before they are harvested. Usually an offering is made, frequently of tobacco (Algonquin practice) or cornmeal (Hopi practice). If too many plants are pulled or injured, an herb gatherer will replant roots and even offer a prayer for the plant's reincarnation, if the species is rare. If the colony of plants is small, care is taken not to eliminate the population or show disregard for family relationships. Goethe called the relationship of one plant to another the real science of botany, though little information (beyond observations of plant ecologists) exists on this subject. The gatherer's motivations are gratitude, hope for the continuation of the species, and respect for dependence on nature. Ingratitude and wastefulness are considered sins against the forces that created the universe.

Herbs can be considered allies of humans. Dozens of plants counteract human ills. If you are growing herbs for health purposes you are seeking the goodwill of a plant. Harvesting herbs requires sensitivity. Although it is difficult to measure the quality of herbs harvested with care compared to plants that are mined, I believe the attitude and methods of the harvester have a substantial effect on an herb's quality.

I'm not really advocating that you don headdress and beads and recite incantations, dancing circles around your basil bed. What I am advocating is due respect for another life form. If the very existence of the ecology movement has taught us one thing, it is that Western industrialized society has lost respect for the earth and her myriad life forms. A fear of nuclear desecration shadows the world like a vulture. The attitude that produced this ultimate monstrosity of industrialized society continues to breed thoughts encouraging disregard and disrespect for all life on the planet. I feel it's time civilized men and women start relating to nature with a greater degree of civility. What better place to start than in an herb garden?

Before harvesting herbs, weeding, trimming, mowing, or injuring a plant in any way, let it know what your intentions are. If you're concerned about other people's opinion of your sanity, look around to make sure no one is watching you.

Speak to the plant in a clear voice of appreciation and gratitude. The gentle genius George Washington Carver said, "How do I talk to a little flower? Through it I talk to the Infinite. And what is the Infinite? It is that silent small force . . . . When you look into the heart of a rose there you experience it."[1]

Given this respectful and appreciative attitude of the herb gatherer, here are some specific practical points. If you plan to use fresh herbs from the garden, pick sparingly from the plant throughout the growing season. Pinch off flower buds as they develop to encourage a more vigorous and bushier leaf growth. To insure a plentiful supply, water frequently and side-dress with compost. For many culinary purposes, fresh herbs are superior to dried herbs. It's like the difference between the flavor of a store-bought tomato and one freshly plucked ripe from a backyard vine.

Herbs harvested for leaf material should be cut just as the plant comes into bloom. At this point, the essential oil content of most herbs peaks. This timing is best illustrated by the chemical changes in the essential oil of peppermint at various stages of growth. Premium quality peppermint oil contains a high percentage of menthol. In the tissue of young peppermint plants pulegone (the chief chemical constituent of pennyroyal oil) is the predominant aromatic chemical along with menthofuran. Low quality peppermint oils contain relatively high amounts of menthofuran. This substance produces a bitter flavor in mint. Before flowering, menthone is the chief constituent of peppermint oil. It possesses a harsher flavor than menthol. As the plant blooms, menthol becomes the oil's primary constituent, producing a clean sharp peppermint flavor. When flowering ceases, menthol is replaced by methyl acetate, giving the herb a somewhat bitter, fruity flavor. Such studies indicate the importance of the timing in harvesting peppermint. Because peppermint is such an important economic plant, many studies have been made on its chemical constituents. Unfortunately, clear information of this nature is not available for most herbs. Therefore, the experience of herb gatherers is your best information on the harvest.

The best time to harvest is in the morning just after the dew has dried off the leaves. Later in the day as the sun becomes more intense, chemical changes may occur in the essential oil, lessening its quality. Herbs should be harvested on a clear day—avoid overcast or rainy days as drops of moisture on newly harvested herbs can cause undesirable rust spots or browning.

Catnip, though, is an exception to this rule. At the Sabbathday Lake Shaker Community we had a patch of 130 lush catnip plants, a real favorite with honey bees. On sunny days the catnip bed hummed like an electrical transformer as the bees feverishly worked the blossoms. After a few stings on sunny days, we resorted to harvesting catnip on overcast days when the bees were more subdued.

Many leaf herbs will give several cuttings during the growing season. In one Maine summer, I got as many as seven cuttings off a quarter acre of comfrey. Alfalfa may produce three cuttings and commercial mint fields are often harvested twice during the growing season. Annuals such as summer savory and basil will produce a second crop if you leave the lower three to six inches of the stem during the

A blueberry rake works well for harvesting camomile blossoms.

first harvest. The remaining stem will soon sprout new shoots, and in a few weeks another harvest can be expected.

Herb flowers such as camomile and calendula should be harvested just as the plant comes into bloom. Hand picking such crops can be a slow and tedious task. I have found that a blueberry rake works well for harvesting camomile and calen-

dula blossoms, as well as seeds of some members of the carrot family. The combing action of the blueberry rake allowed me to harvest four 300-foot rows of camomile in about ten minutes. If we had picked the same camomile by hand it would have taken several hours.

For best performance in herb harvesting, blueberry rakes need a slight modification. On a blueberry rake the base of the teeth is blunt edged, causing the rake to pull up the entire plant rather than simply cut off the flower heads. A thin strip of metal can be soldered at the base of the teeth to serve as a cutting edge. A length of piano wire strung across the base of the teeth can serve the same purpose. Drill holes in both sides of the rake near the base of the teeth. Stretch the piano wire across the teeth and fasten it in the holes with appropriately sized screws or nuts and bolts. This modification disassembles easily, allowing the rake to be converted to its original intended use.

An herb harvester needs the proper implements for the job. A good sharp knife is indispensable. A nurseryman's pruning knife is also a good herb harvesting tool. The pruning knife has a curved blade useful for slicing off one bunch of herbs that can immediately be tied and hung to dry. A tea pruning knife is another wonderful tool for harvesting herbs. Designed for pruning tea bushes, it has a hooked point and is great for cropping a comfrey patch. My favorite herb harvesting tool is a banana knife. Banana knife blades are four to six inches long and slightly curved at the end. A new banana knife is difficult to find; but on an average, one out of every four junk stores with a tool display will have one or two banana knives. A good pair of pruning shears works well for harvesting woody-stemmed herbs. A sturdy, well-sharpened garden spade is indispensible for harvesting root crops. For those who wish to harvest tree barks, a draw knife is the tool you need. See the resource section for these and other tools.

Roots are dug either in the spring before leaf growth commences, or in the fall after the leaves have died back. Spring-dug roots generally contain more moisture than fall-dug roots and therefore take longer to dry. Roots need to be washed before drying. Calamus, and other plants with small lateral rootlets, are washed with greater ease if the rootlets are cut off. Angelica has a tendency to entangle upon itself, forming pockets where dirt collects. Care should be taken to wash as much dirt as possible from these areas, but a stiff brush will easily whisk away what remains after drying.

Larger roots such as those of comfrey will need to be split lengthwise to expose a greater portion of the root to the air so they can dry without molding.

Biennial roots are best harvested in the fall of the first year's growth or in the following spring. As the plant flowers in the second year, the strength of the root is exhausted. At this time the roots may become woody, pithy, and hollow.

Barks of trees and shrubs are time-consuming but fun to harvest. If you must strip the bark from the main trunk because lower branches are too high to reach, take care to insure that the tree survives. Never girdle the tree. Cut only from one side. The north side is the best place to gather bark as it tends to be more constricted and dense there. The growth does not have the added catalyst of direct sunlight as it does on the south and west sides. Anyone who makes maple syrup hangs buckets on the south and west side of trees where the sap flow is greatest.

Many barks can be gathered in the winter. The outer barks of many trees including slippery elm, sassafras and wild cherry are discarded. Only the inner bark is used.

Herb seeds should be gathered as they begin to ripen. Some seeds such as anise tend to ripen on the plant over a period of time so that immature and completely ripe seeds are found on the same seed head. If the seed is fully grown but not ripe, harvest the unripe seed along with the mature seed and cure it in your drying space.

Commercial anise growers harvest the seed while it is still green, tie the tops in bundles, and then stack in conical piles until the seed has ripened. Early harvesting insures that seeds do not shatter from the plants. The tips of anise, as they begin to turn a gray-green color, should be harvested. If left to the weather, seeds may turn an undesirable black color, lessening the quality.

Every herb gardener should let a small patch of each annual herb mature, then collect the ripe seed for planting the following spring. A few calendula or basil plants left to go to seed will produce more than enough seed for the next year. Some plants can be left to self-sow in the garden, and the resulting seedlings can be transplanted the following spring. If given the chance, coriander, dill, German camomile, and angelica will replant themselves.

You can grow the finest, lushest, most potent herbs; but if you dry them poorly, all your efforts could be for naught. Drying is simply a means of preserving herbs. By removing moisture you prevent molding, enzyme activity, or chemical changes.

Unless you have a specialized drying structure where air flow and temperature can be monitored and controlled, you will deal with new circumstances each time you dry an herb. Herb drying is an art, and book knowledge is no substitute for practical experience.

Herbs should be dried in the shade. Direct sunlight will cause leaves to turn dark brown or black. The object in herb drying should be to retain as much of the original flavor, fragrance, and color of the fresh herb as possible.

Rapid evaporation of the essential oil or changes in its chemical constituents may occur if an herb is dried at temperatures exceeding 90° F. If heat is forced too quickly over the outer cells of a leaf, those cells may harden before they can be replaced by moisture from the leaf's inner tissue, thereby sealing moisture in the leaf and causing it to mold in storage. Air temperature should be kept relatively low at first (80° to 85° F.) then increased when the plant material is almost dry. Temperature control and continuous air flow over plant material are the most important factors for efficient drying.

Herbs can be spread to dry on racks covered with muslin, newspaper, wood splint, or lath. About one pound of fresh leaf material can be dried on a square foot of drying space. Pile herbs loosely at first. Adequate air circulation is essential.

For small amounts of herbs, tying them in bunches and hanging them to dry work best. Bunches should be relatively small; a loose handful allows for good air circulation. Once I lost forty bunches of comfrey because, in attempting to save space, I had made bunches that were too large and tight. The leaves on the inside of the bunches literally composted. For your own interest you might want to record fresh weight, dried weight, and the percentage of weight lost to moisture. Experience will show you the limitations.

As soon as herbs are dry—when they feel crisp to the touch—they should be stored in air-tight containers. If left to hang after drying, some herbs will reabsorb moisture from the air. On a humid day, wormwood may reabsorb 25 percent of its dried weight. Glass containers are best. Plastic and paper bags "breathe," allowing essential oils to evaporate.

Catnip field, Trout Lake Farm

MEET YOUR FRIENDLY NEIGHBORHOOD HERBS

Angelica

Angelicas. *Angelica archangelica* L., *A. atropurpurea* L.
(an-jell′-ik-a ark-an-jell′ik-a; at-ro-pur-pur′-ee-a)
Umbelliferae—Carrot family

The genus *Angelica* is represented by about 100 species. *A. archangelica*, a European species, and *A. atropurpurea*, a North American species, are bold, stout biennials or short-lived perennials (lasting three to five years) which die after forming seed. These stately plants are useful as a focal point in an herb garden. Before producing flower stalks, the immature stems are about a foot high. After maturing, the average height is around six feet. The stalks of *A. archangelica* are large, ribbed, smooth, hollow, and often have a light purple cast. *A. atropurpurea's* stalk is usually dark purple. When backlit by the sun,

the leaves are a pleasing chartreuse color. Each leaf consists of numerous leaflets divided into two or three main groups which are again divided into smaller groups. The edges are finely toothed. The leaf stalks flatten horizontally as they clasp the main stem. The flower head is a spherical umbel, often as large as a softball, with numerous tiny greenish-white flowers. The seeds are about one-fourth inch long, flattened on one side and convex on the other with three ribs. They have thin paper-like winged sides. About twenty-five to thirty oil tubes (vittae) adhere to the seeds in each fruit. The taproots are short, thick, and fleshy, with numerous intertwining rootlets. The taste of the fresh leaves is warm and pungent, sweet at first, with a slightly bitter aftertaste. *A. atropurpurea* has a lovage-like odor while the fragrance of *A. archangelica* can be likened to musk. (Lovage is a close relative of Angelica in the carrot family.)

Angelica is propagated from seeds or by dividing offshoots from old roots, possibly a better method since angelica seed has limited viability. Angelica seed generally remains viable for about six months. It is best to plant seeds in late summer or early autumn soon after the seeds have ripened. The seed can also be refrigerated for planting the following spring. Kent Taylor has frozen angelica seed and kept it viable for two years. Be patient. Angelica may take a month or more to germinate. Occasionally self-sown seedlings appear and can be transplanted to a permanent location in the spring. Sow seed in the fall or spring one-half inch deep in well-prepared seed beds. Give the plants two feet of space in each direction.

Angelica enjoys a fairly rich, light, well-drained, but moist loam. It loves partial shade and being close to running water, yet is adaptive to most garden soils. It prefers a slightly acid soil with a pH of 5 to 7. If you dig the plant without disturbing the roots, angelica transplants with ease and in hospitable habitats will grow

eight feet high. An acre will produce eight to eleven pounds of seed and 800 to 1,300 pounds of dried root. Large roots may weigh up to three pounds. Planted as a companion with angelica, stinging nettles reportedly increase angelica's oil content by 80 percent. Angelica is subject to aphid attacks. Spray infested flower heads with a cup of water that has had six crushed cloves of garlic soaked in it.

All parts of the plant are useful. The leaves should be harvested carefully in the fall of the first year so that the main stem is not damaged. The root is harvested in the fall of the first or second year, or in the spring of the second year. Two-year-old roots are most desirable. The globe-shaped umbels are harvested as the seeds ripen and dry in shade at 80° F. Roots should be carefully cleaned before drying, and larger roots should be sliced into smaller pieces. Dried angelica is subject to insect infestations and should be stored in sealed containers. The root must be harvested soon after the seeds ripen as it will quickly rot in the ground after the plant has matured.

The young stalks of angelica can be peeled and eaten sparingly in salads or

cooked in two waters as a vegetable. Honey added to the second boiling creates a delightful sweetmeat. The Laplanders preserve the main stalks as seasoning for food. The dried leaves make a delicate tea substitute. Norwegians use the powdered root as a flour for bread baking. The Laps preserve fish by wrapping them in angelica leaves. As vindication of this bit of folklore, researchers have found angelica root oil to have antibacterial and antifungal properties.

Angelica species have diaphoretic, expectorant, nervine, carminative, stimulant, and emmenagogue qualities. In Europe, angelica is used for treating colds, coughs, bronchial troubles, urinary disorders, and indigestion.

In China, at least ten species of angelica are used, the most common being *Angelica sinensis* (Oliv.) Diels., commonly called dang-qui. It was listed in the earliest Chinese materia medica, *Shen-nung's pen-ts'ao Ching* (ca. A.D. 200). Dang-qui means "proper order." Dr. Shiu Ying Hu states, "The root stock of Chinese angelica is by far the foremost drug consumed in China. It is used more frequently and in larger amounts than the generally recognized commonest drugs in China; licorice and ginseng."[1] It is used for menstrual irregularity, dysmenorrhea, rheumatism, boils, ulcers, anemia, and other ailments. Water extracts cause the smooth uterine muscles to contract and alcohol extracts cause them to relax. It tranquilizes the cerebral nerves and serves as a cardiotonic.

Both the seeds and roots contain about 1 percent of an essential oil. The root oil consists mainly of phellandrene, alpha-pinene, and limonene. The seed oil is similar to that of the root. The oils are rich in coumarins including osthol, angelicin, umbelliferone, and bergapten. The seed oil contains imperatorin, a coumarin. Next to juniper berries, angelica is the main flavor in gin. It is also used in liqueurs such as benedictine and chartreuse.

Anise. *Pimpinella anisum L.*
(pim-pi-nel′-a an-ize′-um)
Umbelliferae—Carrot Family

Of the 140 species in the genus *Pimpinella*, only anise, *Pimpinella anisum*, is familiar to gardeners. Anise, native to the Mediterranean from Greece to Egypt, has sporad-

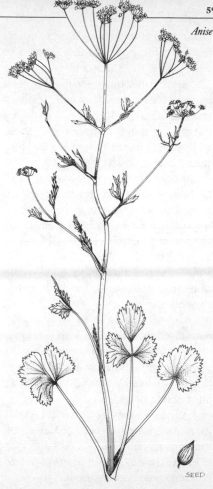

Anise

ically escaped cultivation in North America. It's an erect, though sometimes sprawling, annual which grows to twenty inches in height. The leaves are long-stemmed, rounded or three-lobed, and coarsely toothed at the base of the plant. As the plant matures, the leaves become more finely divided, producing feathery wisps toward the flower head. Delicate yellowish-white flowers are borne on large umbels. The greenish-gray fruits (generally called seeds) are pear-shaped and about one-eighth of an inch long with ten prominent ribs and short hairs. Each fruit contains about thirty vittae (tubes containing essential oil).

Propagation is by seed. Because anise does not transplant well, it should be sown directly in the garden. Seed should be planted in the early spring as anise takes 130 to 140 days to mature. It needs a temperature of 70° F. to germinate. Use fresh seed as its viability deteriorates rapidly after two years. Sow to a depth of one-fourth to one-half inch. Three-inch seedlings should be thinned to six-inch spacings. They will germinate better if sown with coriander. Seedlings develop slowly and must be kept free of weeds.

SEED

One ounce of seed should sow a row 150 feet long; five pounds will plant an acre with rows every three feet.

Anise is the most persnickety of all herbs. It likes perfect weather—relatively uniform rainfall and temperatures during the growing season. Long wet or dry spells will not help this fastidious plant. Anise wilts under excessive heat and therefore is difficult to grow in the South. A light, well-drained, moderately rich sandy loam is preferable. A beneficial fine-textured moisture-retentive soil can easily be created in a raised bed. Soil pH should be around 6.0 to 7.5. Anise needs full sun. An acre grown under good conditions may produce 400 to 600 pounds of seed.

The ripening fruits should be carefully monitored as some seeds on the same umbel ripen quicker than others. As soon as the tip of the fruits turn gray, harvest. If left to the weather, seeds may turn an undesirable black color.

Anise's culinary potential far exceeds its traditional use in breads, cookies, cakes, candies, and liqueurs. Try a half-teaspoon to one teaspoon in four quarts of potato or lentil soups. Crush one-half teaspoon

of seed with a mortar and pestle and add to salads. Use your imagination!

Anise is an aromatic stimulant, carminative, expectorant, stomachic, and galactogenic. It is one of the best herbal remedies for relieving gas in the digestive system. Used in laxative formulas, anise helps prevent cramping in the bowels. A strong tea will break up bronchial mucus and stimulate milk flow.

The oil of star anise *Illicium verum* is chemically almost identical to that of anise. They are used interchangeably in the distilling, confectionary, and perfumery industries.

The seeds contain one to four percent by weight volatile oil. The oil contains 75 to 90 percent *trans*-anethole, estragole, beta-caryophyllene, and anise ketone. Anethole is the main substance responsible for anise's so-called licorice flavor.

Anise hyssop. *Agastache foeniculum* (Pursh) O. Kuntze
(a-gas-take′-ee fee-nik′-you-lum)
Labiatae—Mint Family

I often wonder where some common plant names originated. Anise hyssop is a com-

Anise Hyssop

mon name that could confuse even a botanist. The plant does not resemble hyssop or anise, though its flavor is anise-like. The thirty or so members of this genus are collectively known as giant hyssops. They are native to Eastern Asia and North America, where they are found in the north central United States in dry thickets, plains, and barrens. The plant is robust and attractive, an erect, hardy perennial growing three to four feet high. Usually after growing about a foot it begins to branch. The stems are smooth and square. The leaves are opposite, generally oval-shaped, rounded at the base, tapering to an acute angle at the apex. They are about three inches long and two inches wide. The margins have sharp-edged teeth. Small soft gray hairs cover the lower leaf while the upper surface is hairless but rough to touch. Flowers are borne on dense terminal cylinder-shaped spikes four to six inches long. The flower head has large conspicuous bracts often casting a slightly lighter hue of purple than the flowers. The flowers are blue-purple, about five-sixteenths of an inch long, and have two pairs of stamens; the upper pair curves downward, the lower pair curves upward,

causing the pairs to cross. Anise hyssop's showy violet display begins from June to August, and lasts well into autumn.

Propagation is by seed sown in the spring or fall, cuttings, or root division. The seed germinates easily. Self-sown volunteers often pop up under established plants. Young seedlings are easily transplanted, and even the mature plant transplants with ease at any point in its growth cycle.

It thrives in a sandy, well-drained loam and grows lush in a rich soil. Full sun is preferable, but it will grow without stretching under light shade. Plants should be given eighteen-inch spacings.

Anise hyssop was used by northern Plains Indians as a beverage tea and the infusion was also used as a sweetener. The flowers were often included in Cree medicine bundles. The Chippewas used the root for coughs and respiratory problems.

Anise hyssop makes a fine tea. I feel it is a classic example of an herb tea with good economic potential. It is easy to grow, harvest, and dry; it produces well and it has a familiar and much-enjoyed flavor.

Basils. *Ocimum basilicum* L. *O. kilimandscharicum* Guerbe, *O. sanctum* L. *O. gratissimum* L.
(oss'-i-mum ba-sil'-ik-um)
kil-i-mand-shay'-ree-um; sank'-tum; gratis'-i-mum; Labiatae – Mint Family

If I had space for only one herb in my garden it would be reserved for basil, *Ocimum basilicum*, or its varieties. Basil is probably the most widely cultivated herb in American gardens. The genus *Ocimum* is represented by over 160 species of annuals and short-lived perennials native to warm temperate regions of Asia, Africa, and South and Central America.

Ocimum basilicum and its large-leafed 'Italian' and 'Lettuce Leaf' varieties are extensively cultivated in the United States. Most seeds sold as sweet basil are usually one of these varieties. *O. basilicum* is an erect, branched annual and grows three feet high. The leaves are bright green, smooth, oval, and acutely pointed, with entire or slightly toothed margins. Leaves of *O. basilicum* are about 1½ to 2 inches long, though the leaves of the lettuce leaf variety may reach four inches in length. Flowers are arranged on racemes. They

Basil

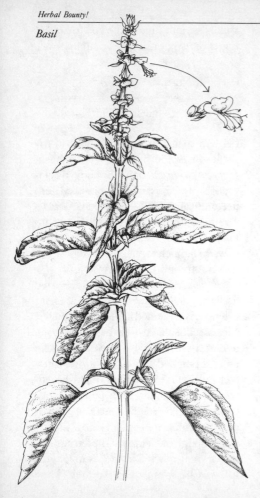

are one-fourth to one-half inch long, in whorls (verticillasters) of six flowers, with two opposite groups of three flowers. The whorls may be compact or spaced some distance apart. Two tiny leaf-like bracts are arranged opposite one another below each whorl. The cup-like calyx has a broad, rounded upper lip, its margin curving upward. The lower lip has four sharp pointed lobes, two on the sides and two at the lower edge. The flowers are white to purple in color, with broad four-lobed upper lips and a narrow four-lobed lower lip. The black seeds are about one-sixteenth of an inch in diameter and produce mucilage when soaked in water.

Bush basil *O. basilicum* 'Minimum' (*O. minimum* L.) is a dwarf variety with tiny leaves, usually eight to twelve inches tall. The flowers may be in short terminal spikes with three or four whorls, or on the stems among the leaves. One form grows in a round mass or ball-shape, another has purple leaves and flowers.

Ocimum basilicum 'Purpurascens,' purple basil, has deep purple stems and leaves sometimes mottled with green. The flowers are lilac toward the centers, becoming a paler white-lavender on the flower's edges. The cultivar 'Dark Opal,' developed in the 1950s at the University of Connecticut, is consistently purple with no mottling.

Ocimum basilicum 'Citriodora,' lemon basil, has a pleasing citrus scent. It grows to be about a foot tall and has small leaves about five-eighths inch wide and 1½ inches long. This tender annual hails from Southeast Asia and Australia.

O. kilimandscharicum, camphor basil, is a tender perennial native to tropical Africa, growing more than three feet high. The leaves have a strong camphor odor and are about one inch wide and three inches long. This is a good perennial for southern climates but will not survive a freeze. Unlike sweet basil, the leaves of this species have tiny hairs, giving it a grayish cast. It is best propagated from cuttings. The racemes may be up to one foot long.

O. sanctum, holy basil, is a native of Malaysia and India. It grows from one foot to two feet tall and has many branches. In India it is called *tulasi* and is venerated by the Hindus. *Tulasi* is used as an amulet to protect the body in life and death and is a "giver of children." An immortal plant of the gods, it is worshipped in hymns and embodies perfection itself—the mystery of the creator is in the mystery of *tulasi*. According to Helen H. Darrah, author of *The Cultivated Basils*, in the United States most seed sown as *O. sanctum* or "spice basil" is probably a hybrid of *O. canum* and *O. basilicum var.* True *O. sanctum* is seldom seen in American gardens.

O. gratissimum L., East Indian or tree basil may grow six feet tall in regions with no frost, and the hairy leaves may be as long as six inches with a width of 3½ inches, though the plant seldom attains such size under cultivation in North America. Smaller forms grow from two to three feet tall. It has a strong clove scent.

Basil is started from seed sown indoors in late March or early April, or directly in the garden as soon as the danger of frost has passed and the soil has warmed up. Seed germinates in five to fourteen days, blooming begins eight to ten weeks after planting, and full bloom takes twelve to fourteen weeks. Seeds may rot in a cold damp soil, as happened to my basil planting in the spring of '78. We had over twenty-five days of rain in the month of June. The soil surface became crusty on the few sunny days we had, and the seed was sealed in the ground, rotting before it could germinate. Seed may also slip up to the soil's surface after a rain because of the slippery coat produced by the mucilage in the seed. Sow to a depth of one-fourth to one-half inch. The seed will remain viable for over a decade if refrigerated. About six pounds of seed will plant an acre.

O. basilicum and its varieties like a fairly rich, moist garden soil and full sun. If the soil is too rich, the plants will produce lush leaf growth with poor oil content. The soil should be well-aerated—a double-dug bed is perfect for basil culture. The soil pH should fall between 5 and 8. Cultivate the plants when young, being careful not to damage the fast-growing root system. After the first crop is cut, the soil around the roots should not be disturbed. Pull weeds by hand. Give basil seedlings eighteen- to twenty-four-inch spacings. Water basil at the base of the plant as cold water may produce spotting on the leaves—especially if it's watered in the morning and exposed to intense sunlight. The basils are tender annuals, usually succumbing to the first frost. An acre of basil may produce one to two tons of dried leaf.

Leaf harvesting may begin just before the plants bloom. At this time, the lower leaves begin to turn yellow. Cut three to six inches above the ground to insure a good second growth. For fresh harvest pinch off the flower buds as they develop, causing the plants to branch. Take leaves as needed. From the field to the drying area, basil must be handled with care. Bruising the leaves releases the essential oil and causes the leaves to turn black. Basil has a fairly succulent stem and takes longer to dry than other herbs.

Basil is perhaps the most useful cooking herb with diverse culinary potential. It is excellent with tomato dishes, carrots, green beans, lentils, zucchini, chicken, red meats, and fish. Chop fresh leaves for soups and salads. Use the following recipe for a delicious pesto:

1 cup fresh basil leaves
1 cup fresh parsley leaves
½ cup olive oil
⅓ cup water
3 cloves fresh garlic
1 handful of chopped almonds

Mix ingredients in blender starting out with the olive oil and about one-fourth of the basil and parsley. Slowly add the remaining ingredients. Serve cold on pasta or any of the foods mentioned above.

Make basil vinegar for salads by placing one plant's leaves in a pint of your favorite wine, rice, or cider vinegar.

Basil is high in vitamin A, vitamin C, calcium, and iron, and contains about 14 percent protein and over 60 percent carbohydrates.

In his *Family Herbal,* John Hill states, "Basil is little used, [medicinally], but it deserves to be much more. A tea made of the green plant is good against all obstructions. No simple is more effectual for gently promoting the menses, and for removing the complaints which naturally attend their stoppage."[2] In old herbal literature, crushed leaves are recommended for the stings of bees and scorpions. Basil has been used for mild nervous disorders and rheumatic pains. A snuff of the dried leaves is used for nervous tension headaches. In Central America, *O. basilicum* is put into the ears to cure deafness. The Chinese use basil to relieve stomach spasms and kidney

ailments, and to promote blood circulation before and after childbirth. Mexican Americans use basil for menstrual and labor pains. For earache, the powdered leaves are steeped in olive oil.

Camphor basil, *O. kilimandscharicum,* is used in Nigeria for colds and children's stomach aches. The fresh leaves are chewed or the roots are boiled in water.

The leaves of *O. gratissimum* are used in India for chutneys and as a cooling agent in gonorrhea. Rheumatism and paralysis are treated with fumigations and baths made from the herb. A soothing decoction is made from the mucilaginous seeds.

The sacred *tulasi* (Sanskrit) or *tulsi* (Hindu) *O. sanctum* is an ingredient in rheumatic prescriptions, is an expectorant, and its root is boiled for fevers. Tulasi has been used to alleviate vomiting, expel intestinal worms, and remove cold and evil spirits. In the Philippines, a tea of the roots was given to women in childbirth, and the flowers are rubbed on the head as a perfume.

O. basilicum has stomachic, tonic, carminative, galactogenic, emmenogogic, and gastric antispasmodic qualities.

The essential oil of basil contains

delta-linalool and estragole as the main components, with varying amounts of methyl cinnamate, eugenol, borneol, ocimene, geraniol, anethole, safrole, camphor, and other components. Concentrations of these chemicals vary greatly depending upon the species, variety, time of harvest, soil, and weather conditions. Basils having a strong clove scent contain high amounts of eugenol – clove bud oil contains up to 90 percent eugenol. Basil oil reportedly has worm expelling qualities. The oil is used commercially for fragrance in perfumes, soaps, toothpastes, mouthwashes, and in flavoring liqueurs such as chartreuse.

Bearberry, uva-ursi. *Arctostaphylos uva-ursi (L.)* K. Spreng.
(ark-toe-staf'-il-os oo-va-er'see)
Ericaceae – Heath Family

Bearberry, a prostrate evergreen shrub of northern climates, is creeping its way into herb gardens. There are about fifty species in this genus, most native to western North America. However, *A. uva-ursi,* a perennial four to six inches tall hails from northern Europe, Asia, and

North America. Its stems are generally short, trailing, and woody. The leathery, bright, glossy leaves are oval, entire, one-fourth to one inch long, and the undersides are a lighter color than the upper surface. They turn a dull reddish-purple during winter cold. The urn-shaped, waxy, white-rose blossoms are borne in clusters on terminal racemes, blooming from May to June. The shiny bright-red fruits have tough skins and contain five stone-like seeds.

Bearberry is propagated from cuttings or layerings made in the early spring, summer, or fall. Cuttings take about twice as long to root as most herbs.

For dense vigorous growth, bearberry needs a very acid soil with a pH of 5 or less. It is happy in a poor gravelly soil with full sun or light shade. Plants are slow to start and must be kept free of weeds until well established. Bearberry transplants with difficulty. Disturb the roots as little as possible and give new plantings plenty of moisture to encourage root growth. This plant loves a coastal breeze and is good to grow on steep slopes interspersed with rocks. It makes a good ground cover, controlling erosion in the

Bearberry

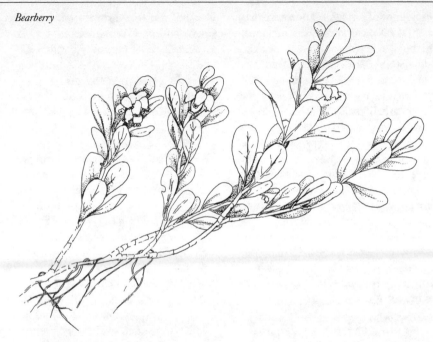

cool regions of the Northwest, mountain areas, and Northeastern United States. It will stand a freeze of -50° F.

Kinnikinnick, as the leaves were known to Indians, was smoked alone or mixed with tobacco. Apparently the smoke was swallowed and retained for a few seconds for an intoxicating or stupefying effect as is the custom among marijuana smokers. Medicinally, the dried leaves are used as a tea or tincture for their diuretic, strong astringent, tonic, and urinary antiseptic qualities. Bearberry has proven useful in chronic cystitis, nephritis, bronchitis, gonorrhea, kidney and gall bladder stones, and urethritis. Make tea by soaking the leaves in cold water for twenty-four hours or by adding one ounce of the dried herb to a quart of boiling water, then infuse in a covered container for about fifteen minutes. One to two fluid-ounce doses are taken three to four times daily. This is an effective urinary disinfectant only if the urine is alkaline. Sodium bicarbonate should be taken first if the urine is acidic.

The leaves contain mostly arbutin. In the body it hydrolizes to form hydroquinone which gives it antiseptic qualities. Methylarbutin, tannins, and allantoin are also found in the leaves.

In large and frequent doses, hydroquinone can irritate the mucus lining of the stomach and cause vomiting, ringing in the ears, diarrhea, delirium, and convulsions. In cystitis, when the urine decomposes in the bladder, the urine may turn a dark green color after drinking bearberry tea.

In Scandinavia, bearberry leaves have been used to tan high-quality leathers.

Bee balms, horsemint, bergamot, Oswego tea. *Monarda didyma* L., *M. fistulosa* L., *M. Russeliana* Nutt., *M. punctata* L.
(mow-nar'-da did'-i-ma); fis-too-low'-sa; rus-el-ee'-ay-na punk-tay'-ta)
Labiatae – Mint Family

The genus *Monarda* has twelve species native to North America, occurring primarily in the eastern continent, from Ontario to Mexico. Most are perennial though some species are biennial or annual.

Monarda didyma L. is the best known of garden-grown bee balms. It grows to four feet tall and has smooth, toothed, oval-shaped opposite leaves with acutely pointed tips about three inches long. The leaf stems (petioles) are about one-fourth inch long. The leaf-like bracts blend the colors of the leaves and flowers. Flowers are borne on a single head-like whorl (verticillaster). The calyx is star-shaped; individual sepals are sharply pointed. The curved-lipped corollas are about 1¼ inches long. Vividly scarlet, they bloom from July into September. Plants spread from root runners creating colonies in open woods. It ranges from New England, south to Georgia and west to Tennessee. Numerous cultivars exist including scarlet, pink, salmon, deep red, purple, and white-flowered varieties. I've heard of a plant breeder who produced a cultivar with almost black flowers.

M. fistulosa L. ranges from western New England to Georgia west through the southern coastal states, to east Texas, and north to Minnesota. It is a hardy perennial to four feet with bright lavender flowers about 1¼ inches long. One form has white flowers.

M. Russeliana Nutt. grows to two feet tall and blooms earlier than other species of *Monarda* from April to mid-June. It grows in open rocky woods from Kentucky to Iowa, south to Arkansas and northeast Texas. Its leaves are shiny above, dull green beneath, and have widely spaced teeth. Bracts are pale purple. Mid-ribs of the leaves occasionally have purple coloration. The flowers display a creamy white throat speckled with purple. The first flowers come from the center of the head and, as they develop, blooming corollas progress from the center to the head's outer edge, crowning each plant with a wreath of blossoms.

M. punctata L. is annual, biennial, or perennial and grows in sandy soil. Its branching stems grow to three feet high. The four-inch-long leaves are oblong or lance-shaped ending in a sharp point. The bracts are light yellow to purple. Purple spots dot the yellow corollas. The whorled flower clusters are stacked in tiers of two or more whorls. *M. punctata* and its varieties grow on the eastern coastal plains, west to Minnesota and south to northern Mexico.

Monarda grows easily from seed or may be propagated by root divisions made in spring or fall. Three-or four-year-old plantings should be divided, as they tend to die out in the clump's center and become scraggly.

Monardas can be grown in a variety of habitats. *M. didyma* likes a fairly rich, moist, slightly acid soil under full sun or partial shade. It should be protected with shade in the hot South. A fairly light, dry, limey soil, and full sun are preferable for *M. fistulosa*. *M. Russeliana* favors partial shade and dry, sandy, acidic soils. Essentially a lime-loving plant, *M. punctata* likes an alkaline, dry, sandy soil and full sun. All of the *Monardas* make good border plantings – some under shade, others in full sun. At least one species should be grown in every herb garden.

Bee balms make a pleasant beverage tea, especially *M. didyma*. Also called Oswego tea, it was drunk by Indians and early settlers. Harvest the leaves before blooming for a mild minty tea. After blooming, the leaves are more pungent and bitter. I add individual blossoms as a colorful and spicy treat in salads.

M. punctata is an aromatic stimulant, diaphoretic, and carminative. It is useful for settling an upset stomach and treating colds accompanied by diarrhea. Hard-to-find horsemint oil is useful as a liniment for neuralgia and muscular rheumatism.

Monardas are sometimes called bergamot. Bergamot oil, readily available on the natural food market, comes not from a *Monarda*, but from the rind of a citrus fruit closely related to oranges. The two should not be confused.

Teton Dakota boiled the leaves and flowers together as a tea to relieve abdominal pains. The Tewa Indians used the leaves to flavor meat and rubbed the dried or powdered leaves on the head to cure headaches. The Winnebagos applied a preparation of the boiled leaves to pimples and other skin eruptions.

Oil of *M. fistulosa* and *M. punctata* contain limonene, carvacrol, and cymene. *M. punctata* is a rich source of thymol, a major ingredient in Listerine and other antiseptic preparations. Thymol is strongly fungicidal and anthelmintic. *M. punctata* has been commercially cultivated as a source for thymol, though today thymol is produced in the laboratory.

Borage. *Borago officinalis* L.
(bor-ray'-go of-iss-i-nay'lis)
Boraginaceae – Borage Family

The genus *Borago* is represented by three species native to the Mediterranean region. *Borago officinalis* is the familiar species of the herb garden. This coarse annual usually grows to 1½ to 2 feet tall, though in a rich soil it may exceed five feet in height. The leaves are thick, covered with stiff rough hairs, alternate, oval-shaped, and pointed at the ends. They grow from three to six inches long. The stems are succulent, hollow, and hairy like the leaves. The terminal flowers are star-shaped, bright blue, and distinguished

Borage

by prominent black anthers forming a cone-like structure in the center of each blossom. The flower clusters nod downward. Each flower produces four brownish-black nutlets.

Borage grows well in an average garden soil and will tolerate poor dry soils. Soil pH should fall between 5 and 8. Full sun or partial shade are suitable. It grows readily from seed and self-sows profusely. Plant on a back border or central focal point. Borage sprawls and should be given two-foot spacings. The seeds produce broad large cotyledons similar in appearance to those of cucumbers. Borage develops a tap root making it difficult to transplant. Plants take about eight weeks to mature. They will continue blooming until the first frost when they wither to a black mass. One ounce of seeds will plant about a 500-foot row. We had three 250-foot rows of borage at the Sabbathday Lake Shaker Community gardens from which we harvested the flowering tops for drying and packaging. The three rows produced about fifty pounds of dried material—more than enough to supply our limited demand for the dried herb.

This planting was literally humming with bees. Standing close to borage on a sunny day is like listening to the steady buzz of high-tension electric wires. And there is high tension for the gardener who tries to pick a drooping flower before checking to see if a bee is busy collecting nectar!

Harvest borage as it begins to flower. It can be harvested two or three times during the growing season, or you can make a couple of successive plantings. Drying must be done with care. If you are drying small amounts, carefully remove the leaves from the succulent stems, and if time allows, peel the stems for a noon salad. Fast drying under moderate heat is preferable. Borage tends to turn brown or black without good air circulation. If you spread it to dry on an open frame drying rack, make sure the leaves are not overlapping, potentially hampering air flow.

The fresh leaves and flowers of borage possess a delicate cucumber-like flavor. Young leaves are good chopped in salads. The leaves may also be boiled as a pot herb. The flowers are a colorful and tasty addition to salads. Gently grasp the flower stem directly behind the sepals, then pinch

Two-acre herb garden at Sabbathday Lake Shaker Community. Borage in foreground.

Calamint. *Satureja arkansana* (Nutt.) Briq.

(sat-you-ree´-a ar-kan-say´-na)

Labiatae – Mint Family

In the seldom-admired rocky glade where few plants bloom in splendor, a native American member of the mint family resides, flaunting a soft spray of lavender blooms in the transitory summer-weathered days of late spring. This plant begs for a place in herb gardens. Botanists have been confused by its plethora of names and ranks including *Satureja glabra* (Nutt.) Fern., *Satureja glabella* (Michx.) Briq var. *angustifolia* (Torr.) Svenson, *Clinopodium glabrum* Ktze., *Calamintha Nuttallii* Benth., *Calamintha glabella var. Nuttallii* Gary, *Micromeria Nuttallii* Torr., *Micromeria glabella var. angustifolia* Torr., *Hedeoma glabra* Nutt. (where it all started), and the name we're going to use, *Satureja arkansana*. Botanists do agree, however, on several points about this plant. Its leaves are glabrous or smooth, they are narrow (angustifolia), and it was first described by naturalist Thomas Nuttall (1786-1859) who encountered this pennyroyal-like plant, "upon the banks of the St. Lawrence

and pull the anthers, and the entire corolla will slip from its pedestal.

Medicinal uses are somewhat limited. Borage is diuretic, demulcent, emollient, and diaphoretic. It is used in kidney ailments, pulmonary troubles, and for fevers. A poltice of the fresh leaves with the hairs scraped off is used for inflammatory swellings. A handful of fresh leaves steeped in a quart of water with a sprig or two of spearmint added makes a cooling, soothing summer beverage. Borage contains mucilages, calcium, and potassium nitrate.

Calamint

and the upper lakes" and on calcareous rocks at Niagara Falls.[3]

Calamint, a perennial native to the eastern United States and south central Canada, occurs from Minnesota to Ontario, western New York, south to Arkansas and Texas and grows in limestone glades, and on banks of streams, moist ledges of limestone bluffs, and escarpments. The plant stands only six to twelve inches tall. The leaves are smooth, with upright branching flower stems. They are one-half inch long or less, oblong, linear, entire (no teeth), and peppered with oil glands. The gaping almost inquisitive-looking, two-lipped flowers occur in clusters starting halfway up the stems. Flowers are a bluish-lavender color about one-eighth to one-fourth inch long. Like European pennyroyal *Mentha pulegium*, calamint sends out root-runners after blooming.

Thickly growing calamint brushes the calves of bare legs like seeding grasses. Stroke the leaves and the surrounding air explodes with a sweet pennyroyal-like fragrance.

Propagate by dividing the runners in spring or late summer after it has finished blooming. Calamint likes a limey, gravelly soil with good drainage. It prefers full sun but will tolerate some shade. A group planting of calamint makes a soft-textured mid-summer border.

The individual blossoms make a colorful and spicy addition to salads. A tea of the flowering herb has a pennyroyal flavor. It is diaphoretic and soothes an upset stomach.

I hope this obscure little plant finds popularity among herb gardeners.

Calamus, sweet flag. *Acorus calamus L.* (ayk´-or-us kal´-a-mus) Araceae—Arum Family

Most people glancing at boggy areas harboring calamus might pass it by as a grass, sedge, or cattail. Trudging through the bog, though, you will notice a sweet musky fragrance and will soon discover this arum with grasslike leaves. Calamus is a perennial inhabitant of marshy places in Europe, Asia, and North America. The smooth slender leaves, 1 ½ to 6 feet high arise from horizontal rhizomes creeping in all directions just below the soil's surface. The sword-shaped leaves are a light green color and have a prominent mid-

Calamus

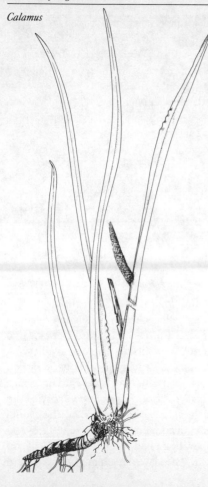

rib. The minute flowers are borne on a fingerlike green spadix, protruding one-third to one-half way up the leaf stalk at a 45° angle. The tiny yellowish-green flowers are arranged on the spadix in diamond patterns. Calamus inhabits the edges of slow-moving creeks, ponds, and marshes. Because its roots spread, it grows in thick mats. The branching rhizomes are about as big around as a finger. The undersides of the rhizomes are anchored by numerous stringy rootlets. The fresh rhizome has a spongy texture. A seldom-seen cultivar 'Variegatus' has yellow-striped leaves.

Despite its propensity to grow in water in wild habitats, it may be grown in a fairly rich, moist garden loam with a pH from 5 to 7.5. Calamus enjoys full sun, but will do well under partial shade. Plants are easily propagated by root divisions. Plant crowns with an inch or two of attached rhizome.

Commercial plantings of calamus have been made on upland soils which produce crops of corn or potatoes, yielding 2,000 pounds of dried root per acre.

Harvesting is easy with a sharp garden spade. Roots should be dried between 85° and 90° F. The root shrinks considerably when dried, losing 70 to 75 percent of its fresh weight. I've often dried it in the sun on the dashboard of a car. Before drying, cut off the rootlets on the underside of the rhizome or remove them by rubbing when dry.

Calamus has many uses. The root has long been esteemed as an aromatic bitter to tone and settle the stomach and relieve indigestion, gas, and heartburn. Small bits of dried or candied calamus root are chewed for these purposes. The root is considered a stimulant, carminative, tonic, bitter, and aromatic.

Tribes of the Great Plains used a decoction of the root for fever and chewed the root for coughs, colds, and toothache. Teton Dakota warriors chewed the root and applied the resulting paste to their foreheads and temples to help them be fearless in the face of enemies.

During the Depression, calamus was chewed as a tobacco substitute, and some people claim chewing the root will deter the desire to smoke. At least it's a good oral fixation!

In American Indian, European, and East Indian traditions, the root is considered useful for clearing the throat of phlegm. In India, calamus root is used as an insecticide, worm expellant, and for diarrhea, dysentery, and bronchial trouble. Aphrodisiac properties are also attributed to the root.

Hoffer and Osmond in *The Hallucinogens* report numerous uses of flag root, rat root, or sweet calomel by the Crees of Northern Alberta. One Indian informant stated that calamus dispelled fatigue on long walks and made him feel as though he were walking one foot off the ground. Hoffer and Osmond also report that large doses of calamus root in controlled experiments created an experience like that of LSD.[4] Several tribes ascribed mystic powers to the plant, and Pawnee mystery ceremonies included songs about calamus. Whether the plant was used hallucinogenically by North American Indians and whether, in fact, the plant is hallucinogenic remains a mystery to modern science. However, after chewing calamus root for several years, I've found that one or two inches of the dried root ingested over an hour's time does leave me feeling vigorous. Nibbling on the root during long drives helps to keep me awake.

The chief chemical constituent of the oil, asarone, resembles mescaline in structure though it has an opposite effect. Calamus oil also contains beta-asarone, eugenol, azulene, pinene, cineole, camphor, and other components. In rats and cats the oil and extracts of calamus have exhibited hypotensive, anticonvulsant, and central nervous system-depressant activities.

Experiments with rats have shown the Jammu variety from India to be carcinogenic. Because of this potential carcinogenicity, in 1968 the FDA forbade the use of calamus root, oil, and extracts in human foods. However, this blanket action covering all calamus products must be questioned as only the Indian variety was used in the testings. American, European, and East Indian calamus oils vary considerably in composition.

Calendula, pot marigold. *Calendula officinalis L.*
Kal-end′-you-la off-iss-i-nay′-lis
Compositae – Aster Family

The common pot marigold has captured the appreciation of poet, gardener, and

Calendula

healer alike. Calendula is native to south central Europe and north Africa. The genus has about fifteen species. A venerable annual for borders or garden nucleus, the buoyant light-yellow-to-orange blossoms bring color and vitality to the lush shades of summer and the fading hues of autumn. With coarse surfaces and many branches, it reaches a height of two feet. The leaves are oblong, without teeth or with small inconspicuous teeth. Leaves are three to six inches long and their stalks gently clasp the stem. The flower heads, 1½ to 3 inches across, consist of several rows of ray florets and a central cluster of tubular flowers. Calendula blooms continually from the appearance of the first blossoms about six weeks after planting to the first light snows of late autumn. In Maine, my calendula beds continued blooming into November. The seeds (achenes) are curved and taper to a point at one end. The blossoms close at night and on overcast days, but open with the sun. One cultivar, 'Chrysantha,' produces double blossoms that are a rich buttercup yellow. Kieft Seeds, a Dutch firm, lists thirty-four calendula cultivars in its catalog (see resource section). Herbalists consider single-flowered varieties to be medicinal.

Calendula should not be confused with other marigolds—members of the genus *Tagetes*. This genus of familiar marigolds is represented by about thirty species and numerous cultivars. They are indigenous mainly to south and central America, though several species are found as far north as Arizona and New Mexico.

Sow seeds as soon as the ground can be worked in the spring. If allowed to go to seed, calendula self-sows freely, and the resulting seedlings can be transplanted the following spring. Thin to one-foot spacings.

They grow well in moderately rich, well-drained soil with a pH range of 5 to 8 and tolerate full sun or partial shade. In Southern states, plantings do better under partial shade.

At the Sabbathday Lake Shaker Gardens we planted four 300-foot rows of calendula from four ounces of seed. We harvested the flower crop three times. A week after each cutting, the rows were again covered with blossoms. About twenty pounds of dried flower heads were gathered from this planting.

The plant's most useful part is the ray florets or petals, though the entire flower is usually harvested as a matter of economy. Try spending an afternoon plucking the individual flower petals from the central disk and you'll soon realize why commercial growers choose to harvest the whole flower head. Gathering individual flowers is great for the home gardener, but unfeasible for the farmer.

Petals stripped from the disks dry much faster than the whole flower head, but I find it easiest to dry the entire flower, then remove the dried petals by hand as needed.

Calendula is referred to as "poor man's saffron" since the flavoring and coloring potential are similar to that of true saffron. Calendula adds a subtle saline flavor and a delicate yellow hue to food. It can be used for coloring rice and other grains. Calendula lends itself well to soups and chowders. In medieval Europe, calendula blossoms were used as a base for soups and broths and could be found literally by the barrel in market places. Use the fresh flower petals in salads.

A tea of calendula promotes sweating and is useful in treating ulcers, both internally and externally. Calendula was at one time a popular home remedy for jaundice. Today it is used as an embrocation on sprains, bruises, cuts, and burns.

A wash of calendula helps promote reconstruction of tissue, and reduces swelling and discharges. It lessens scarring from burns and helps abcesses and abrasions.

The first edition of the *United States Homeopathic Pharmacopoeia* (1878) lists two methods for preparing calendula. One method expresses the juice of fresh calendula gathered in summer, then adds alcohol equal to the volume of the expressed juice. In the second method, the plant is soaked in five parts alcohol for two weeks.[5]

A ninety-year-old friend who had been using a homemade calendula tincture for all of his family's cuts, abrasions, burns, and scalds for close to seventy years, made a tincture by soaking the whole fresh plant in vodka for two weeks. He diluted the tincture with nine parts water with each use.

The flowers contain a resin, a bitter compound, a saponin, and an essential oil with carotene, calenduline, and lycopine.

Camomile. *Matricaria recutita* L. and *Chamaemelum nobile* (L.) All.
(mat-ri-kay'-ree-a rek-you-tie'-ta; kam-ee-mel-um no'-bil-ee)
Compositae–Aster Family

Camomile is one of those ambiguous common names applied to a variety of closely related species. We will concern ourselves with two species: Hungarian or German camomile, *Matricaria recutita (Matricaria chamomilla)*, and Roman or English camomile, *Chamaemelum nobile (Anthemis nobilis)*.

German camomile is an annual native of Europe and western Asia, growing from one to two feet high. It has a pale green, smooth, shiny stem with striations. The finely divided linear leaf segments are borne on numerous branches. The many terminal flower heads are in a comb-like formation and are about one-half to five-eighths of an inch in diameter. The disk flowers are yellow surrounded by ten to twenty white ray flowers. The receptacle is smooth, conical, elongated, and hollow inside. The fruit is a slightly curved, pale gray, smooth achene.

English or Roman camomile, a perennial native to Europe, is a low-growing herb with a creeping rhizome reaching a foot in height. The stems are branching, slightly hairy, and usually prostrate or drooping, though sometimes erect. The downy, alternate, green-gray leaves are flattened and feathery in appearance. The flower heads are about an inch across and sparse compared with German camomile–a solitary head sits atop each

German Camomile

flower stalk. The disk flowers are yellow; the ray flowers are white though sometimes absent. The receptacle is conical and solid. One showy double-flowered variety has large white blossoms. Nearly all the yellow disk flowers become white ray flowers. A petalless flower form is available from some herb plant sellers. 'Treanague,' a cultivar named after the estate from which it originated, is flowerless.

German camomile is grown from seeds sown directly in their garden location. The plants will self-sow freely. Watch out. They can become weeds! The seed bed should be well prepared as these seeds are very tiny. They can be scattered on the soil's surface, then gently tamped down with the flat side of a hoe. Sow as early in the spring as possible, as seedlings tend to become leggy and flower quickly under hot summer sun. Young seedlings, about one to two inches tall, are easily transplanted. Older seedlings do not survive transplanting well. If planted around 1 June in the North, expect flowering late July or early August. Blooms develop continuously. Here in the southern Ozarks, self-sown plants complete their life cycles by mid-June.

Full sun and a moist sandy loam suit German camomile. Soil pH should fall between 6 and 8.5. English camomile likes full sun and a slightly acid-to-neutral garden soil with good drainage. It does not tolerate hot, dry weather.

English camomile can be started from seeds, cuttings, or by root division. Seedlings should have a six-to-twelve-inch spacing. When cultivating with a hoe, cover exposed or loose roots with soil.

At the Sabbathday Lake Shaker Village we planted double rows of German camomile ten inches apart and harvested the flowers with a blueberry rake. Once flowering commences, harvesting is possible every ten days to two weeks. An acre may produce 300 to 500 pounds of dried flowers.

A rich soil will produce a lush leaf growth but few flowers of English camomile. An acre may yield 400 to 600 pounds of the dried flowers. England produces most of the flowers.

Most seeds purchased as camomile, and dried camomile for tea, can be expected to be *Matricaria recutita*, grown commercially in Hungary, Egypt, Argen-

Petalless English Camomile

tina, Belgium, Russia, Bulgaria, and Germany. To determine whether dried camomile flowers are German or English, carefully slice open the receptacle of the flower head. The receptacle of the German is hollow; the English is solid. Tea-bagged camomile often contains seeds. Tear open a package, plant the contents, and see what happens.

Camomile is perhaps the best known of herbal teas besides peppermint. English camomile tea has tonic, stomachic, diaphoretic, soporific, and antispasmodic qualities. German camomile is tonic, sedative, carminative, emmenagogue and diaphoretic. It is used in treating colic, diarrhea, insomnia, indigestion, toothache, swollen gums, skin problems, gout, sciatica, and a host of other ailments. Both camomiles have been used to treat cancers.

As a good rinse for blonde hair, steep the dried flower heads in hot water, cool the infusion, then strain. Extracts of the two species are used in cosmetics such as hair dyes, shampoos, sunburn lotions, bath lotions, and other products. The oil is used as a fragrance in soap, detergent, perfumes, and lotions.

The oil of German camomile contains chamazulene, farnesene, alpha-bisabolol and other components. High-quality oil should be of a deep blue color. The oil has bacteriacidal and fungicidal properties. The component chamazulene is anodyne, antispasmodic, anti-inflammatory, and anti-allergenic. The plant also contains flavonoids, coumarins, a polysaccharide, choline, and amino acids.

Individuals allergic to ragweed pollen may, theoretically, suffer life-threatening symptoms by drinking camomile tea. However, only one report exists in the periodic scientific literature confirming an anaphylactic reaction produced by drinking camomile tea. Its long history of safe use would suggest that the great majority of people will have no adverse reactions from an occasional cup of tea. In large doses, Roman camomile may be emetic.

Caraway. *Carum carvi L.*
(kay′-rum kar′-vy)
Umbelliferae—Carrot Family

Caraway is a biennial herb native to Europe and Western Asia, widely naturalized in North America. Of thirty species of Eurasian origin, only *Carum carvi* is grown in American gardens. Caraway grows to a height of 2 ½ feet. The leaves are finely divided, resembling those of carrots. White, sometimes pink, flowers are borne on terminal or lateral compound umbels. The roots are thick and carrotlike. The seeds (fruits) are crescent shaped and

Caraway

about three-sixteenths of an inch long. Each half of the fruit (mericap) contains one seed and six oil tubes (vittae). It flowers from May to August.

Caraway is easily grown from seed sown in early spring or autumn. Seed sown in September will flower and produce seed the following summer. In the first year, an annual cover crop such as dill or coriander can be planted along with caraway. Caraway will grow rapidly after cover crops are harvested. Side dress with compost or seasoned manure in the fall or following spring to help speed growth. Sometimes caraway matures in the third summer of growth. Thin seedlings to stand at six-inch spacings. Four to eight pounds of seed will sow an acre.

Caraway likes full sun and will grow well in a dry heavy clay soil containing a fair amount of humus. Soil pH can range from 6 to 7.5. Cultivate plants when young to remove competing grasses. An acre may produce about half a ton of seed.

Harvest as soon as the fruits begin to ripen to minimize shattering, which causes caraway to self-sow and possibly become weedy. Seeds may ripen from June to August of the second year. Place harvested plants on a ground cloth to avoid seed loss.

The roots, leaves, and seeds are all useful. The roots with a flavor suggesting a mix of parsnips and carrots, can be boiled as a vegetable. Use young shoots and leaves cooked with other vegetables or chopped in salads. The seeds, of course, are the familiar little flavor morsels scattered through a loaf of ryebread. They are good in sauerkraut, cheeses, applesauce, soups, salad dressings, and apple pie. Caraway seeds contain small amounts of protein and B vitamins.

The seeds are diuretic, carminative, astringent, anthelmintic, and galactogenic. In India, a bath of the seeds is used to relieve swellings of the womb, as a poultice for hemorrhoids, and as an eyewash. Combined with laxative herbs, caraway seeds will help prevent griping. Rheumatic pains are lessened with an external wash made with the seeds. The seeds are chewed to relieve toothache, and a tea is used for pleurisy.

The main constituents of the oil are carvone and limonene. The oil is antibacterial, antispasmodic, and antihistaminic.

Catnip. *Nepeta cataria L.*
(nep-ee′-ta ka-tare′-ee-a)
Labiatae – Mint Family

Nepeta cataria is the best known of the more than 250 species in its genus. Native to the dry temperate regions of the Mediterranean, inland Europe, Asia, and Africa, catnip is a hardy perennial growing to four feet in height. The fuzzy grayish leaves are somewhat oval in shape, acute at the tip, heart-shaped at the base, and toothed, and range from one to three inches in length. The flowers occur in tight terminal spikes. Individual flowers are about three-eighths of an inch long, and are white with light purple spots. Flowering begins by the end of May in the South, lasting through late summer in northern climates. This Eurasian native has become naturalized worldwide. A lemon-scented cultivar, 'Citriodora,' is available from some plant sources.

Another commonly encountered species in American herb gardens is *Nepeta mussinii* K. Spreng ex. Henckel. This low-growing sprawling perennial reaches to one foot in height. The gray-green leaves look similar to *N. cataria* but are only an

Catnip

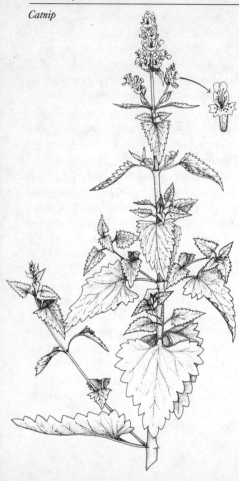

inch long. The flowers are borne on a loose raceme, are about three-eighths of an inch long, and are rich blue. This species has a peculiar pungent citrus-like fragrance and is the showier of the two species. It is often sold under the name catmint, and cats do enjoy it.

Catnip is easily propagated from seeds or root divisions. Seeds can be sown directly in the garden in spring or fall. Root divisions can also be done at either time. Young seedlings should be spaced eighteen to twenty-four inches apart. Established plants will self-sow. Commercial plantings can be expected to produce between 1,500-2,000 pounds per acre.

"If you sow it cats won't know it, if you set it cats will get it" is a bit of folk wisdom the herb gardener will find true more often than not. Plants sown from seeds seem to be left undisturbed by cats until harvested or transplanted. Bruised leaves release essential oils and attract cats. Once after harvesting catnip, I visited a nearby farm to look at some machinery. I hadn't changed my clothes or washed, and to the discerning nose I smelled like a catnip plant in human disguise—or so the twenty-three cats on this farm thought.

I hadn't been out of the car for more than two minutes before more than a dozen cats surrounded me. When two of them clawed my pant legs, I decided on a quick retreat.

Catnip thrives in a variety of habitats. I've seen it growing well in the poorest dry garden soils and in rich, deep-shaded woods. It enjoys full sun but will tolerate partial shade. It will thrive in almost any garden soil and become weedy if given the opportunity. Soil pH can range between 5 and 7.5. The plants will become more fragrant when grown in a sandy soil in full sun than in a heavy loam under shade. Frequent shallow cultivation encourages vigorous growth.

The flowering tops are the most desirable part of the plant. Catnip is by weight 60 to 80 percent stem material. Dried catnip available on the herb market is often of inferior quality, being mainly stem chards.

Though mainly thought of as a feline euphoric, catnip has a rich tradition of folk use. Catnip tea is used for headaches, stomachache, and colic and sleeplessness in children. The fresh leaves are chewed for headache. It's an old home remedy for colds, nervous tension, fevers and nightmare. It is diaphoretic and anti-spasmodic. Sister Mildred Barker of the Sabbathday Lake Shakers told me cat-nip tea was the sole medication given her as a young child at the Alfred, Maine, Shaker Community. A seventy year-old friend, native to Aroostock County, Maine, related that his grandmother would give him a tea of boneset, *Eupatorium per-foliatum*, turtle head, *Chelone glabra*, and catnip to remedy the symptoms of cold and flu. Herbalists use it to allay diarrhea and chronic bronchitis. Catnip has also been used for anemia, as well as menstrual and uterine disorders.

The essential oil contains carvacrol, beta-caryophyllene, nepetol, thymol, and nepetalactone.

Cat Thyme. *Teucrium marum* L.
(to´-kree-um may´-rum)
Labiatae—Mint Family

If you think cats like catnip, you should see how they react to cat thyme. A cat's curiosity is tantalized by the tingling essential oil as they fuss, nibble, and caress this herb. The inquisitive herb gardener will be amazed at the explosive bite in the nose this herb's fragrance inflicts.

The genus *Teucrium* is represented by over 300 species, mainly originating from the Mediterranean region. *T. marum* comes from islands of the western Mediterranean and one island off the northwest Yugoslavian coast. It is a small perennial shrub reaching twelve to eigh-teen inches high, with slender stems and linear-lanceolate to oval-shaped leaves three-eighths of an inch long. The leaves are entire (without teeth), though they occasionally develop small teeth. The margins of the leaves curve downward. Soft white fuzz covers the leaf's upper surface, while a gray pubescens is on the underside. The flowers, tightly packed on a cylinder-shaped head, are five-sixteenths to seven-sixteenths of an inch long and of a soft rose-red to purplish color.

This tender annual prefers a chalky sandy loam with good drainage. It needs full sun and is best propagated from cut-tings. It forms a dense low mass of pleasing color. Where temperatures dip below 20°F. during winter months, bring this herb indoors. Where the temperature goes below freezing, mulch it well. If need be, protect it from cats. At Taylor's Herb Gardens, cat thymes are caged in chicken wire.

Cat thyme's odor is strongly cam-phoraceous and its taste pungent and bit-ter. As a medicinal herb it is known as *herba mari veri*, herb mastich, and Syrian herb mastich. Tonic, stimulant, diaphoretic, diuretic, emmenagogue, and expectorant properties have been at-tributed to it. It is used in chronic bron-chitis, leukorrhea, amenorrhea, gout, and stomach ailments. A snuff made from the powdered herb has been used for nasal polyps. It was once an ingredient of *pulvis asari compositus*—compound powder of asarabacca. The compound consisted of one powdered ounce each of the dried leaves of asarabacca, sweet marjoram, Syrian herb mastich, and lavender flowers. The 1789 *Edinburgh Dispensatory* listed this herbal snuff as a remedy for "cases of obstinate headache, and of ophthalmias resisting other modes of cure."[6] Its im-mediate effect was to induce frequent sneezing.

Cat thyme contains an essential oil, a saponin, tannins, and choline.

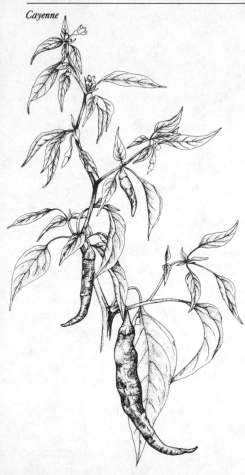

Cayenne

Cayenne. *Capsicum annuum* L. and *C. frutescens* L.
(kap'-si-kum an-you'-um; fru-tes'-enz)
Solanaceae—Nightshade Family

There are about twenty species and dozens of varieties in the genus *Capsicum*, indigenous to tropical America. In their native habitat, they are perennial and woody, growing to seven feet tall, though in American gardens they are grown as annuals reaching a height of three feet. Two species, *C. annuum* and *C. frutescens*, are cultivated in this country. *C. annuum* and its varieties include chili peppers, paprika, pimento peppers, and even the common green bell pepper. *C. frutescens* includes the tabasco peppers grown commercially in the Gulf States and New Mexico. These much-branched, smooth, shiny herbs have alternate leaves, oval to lance-shaped, one to five inches in length. *C. annuum* flowers are solitary, arising from leaf axils. *C. frutescens* may have flowers in pairs or several from each axil. The flowers on both species are white and star-shaped. Blooming begins in July to August; fruits mature by October. The familiar pods range from inch-long pea-sized fruits to banana-shaped fruits over a foot long. Their colors range from deep blues, cream yellow, green, orange, and scarlet.

Peppers are grown from seed sown indoors in flats six to eight weeks before spring's last frost. In Southern states, cayenne can be sown directly in the garden after danger of frost has passed. Young seedlings are tender and easily destroyed by frost, though mature plants may survive an autumn frost or two. Give seedlings eight-to twelve-inch spacings.

A rich, sandy loam is good for pepper culture. Peppers like full sun but will tolerate some shade. A light soil will usually produce a healthier crop than heavy clay soils. Peppers tolerate a pH range from 4.5 to 8. Irrigation may be necessary for young seedlings until the root system is well-established.

Just before a fall frost, harvest the ripened fruits and string them up to dry. Be careful not to break the stem at the top of the fruit, causing it to spoil before dry. The whole plant can be pulled and hung to dry. Peppers may take several weeks to dry, losing about 75 percent of their fresh weight.

The vitamin C content nearly doubles

as the pods turn red. Cayenne is high in vitamin A, B vitamins, calcium, phosphorus, and iron, and contains up to 15 percent protein.

Cayenne is a must for Mexican food. It will enhance the flavor of tomato dishes, egg salad, eggplant, and beans. In American herbology, the use of cayenne as a stimulant was promoted by Samuel Thomson in the late 1700s and early 1800s (see lobelia). He used it as a follow-up to lobelia to "retain the internal vital heat of the system and cause free perspiration."[7] Cayenne has been used as a gargle for sore throats. Rheumatism and arthritis have been treated with a poultice or liniment made from powdered cayenne. A teaspoon of cayenne suspended in a tablespoon of olive oil has been given to relieve nausea at the first signs of seasickness. Small amounts in food increase saliva and help digestion. Taken internally, cayenne produces great warmth in the stomach and to a lesser extent in the extremities. It opens capillaries and increases blood flow. In Oriental medicine, cayenne is considered a yin herb, bringing heat to the surface capillaries where it dissipates, and thus ultimately having a cooling effect.

Like other herbs, cayenne in excess can cause problems. It irritates the skin and mucosa. External application can cause dermatitis with blistering. Gastroenteritis and kidney lesions can result from excessive internal use.

Capsicum fruits contain a pungent alkaloid–capsaicin–and capsanthin–a cartenoid pigment. Capsaicin produces a strong alkaline reaction likened to lye, producing intense pain, dizziness and high pulse. It is not water-soluble and cannot wash off. The effect is termed "Hunan Hand." If peppers are soaked in vinegar for several hours capsaicin is neutralized.

Chervil. *Anthriscus cerefolium (L.)* Hoffm. (an-thriz′-kus sir-e-foh′-lee-um) Umbelliferae–Carrot Family

Chervil is a hardy annual, little known, yet worthy of a place in every garden of edibles for its delicate flavor in salads. It is a native of southeastern Europe growing to a height of two feet. The small, finely divided, parsley-like leaves are on erect branching stems. The fruit is linear, about one-fourth inch long with a one-eighth-inch long beak. It produces umbels

Chervil

of minute white flowers. One variety has crisped leaves. Chervil has a decidedly mild anise- or tarragon-like flavor. In the northeastern United States it has escaped from cultivation and grows wild.

Chervil is easily grown from seed sown at intervals from spring to fall. Plants take six to eight weeks to develop. It does best in the cool of spring and autumn, disliking summer heat. Seedlings should be thinned to stand six inches apart.

Chervil likes a well-drained moderately rich garden soil in partial shade. A pH range between 7 and 8 is optimum. It can be planted among taller vegetables or herbs which will shade it during the hot, dry summer weather.

Fresh chervil is best for cooking. It loses its delicate tarragon flavor upon drying. Its subtle flavor has to be tasted to be appreciated. Use more chervil than you would of other herbs, as its mild flavor is easily lost. Add it to cooked foods after the dish is done to preserve flavor. Add fresh to soups and sauces. Chervil is good in egg dishes, with baked potatoes in sour cream, or mixed (two tablespoons of fresh, 1 teaspoon dried) with a package of cream cheese or a stick of butter. It has great potential and, when combined with other herbs, glorifies their flavor.

Chervil increases perspiration, is diuretic, a blood cleanser, expectorant, and has been used to reduce high blood pressure. In the European tradition, the fresh juice has found use in treating fevers, gout, jaundice, and chronic skin problems.

The essential oil contains estragole (as does tarragon and basil), plus anethole. The leaves contain a fixed oil, high concentrations of potassium and calcium and apiin—a glycoside.

Chicory. *Cichorium intybus* L. *& C. endiva* L.
(si-koe'-ree-um in'-ti-bus; en-dive'-a)
Compositae—Aster Family

One person's weed is another person's herb. More often maligned than enjoyed in America, chicory is a culinary herb deserving greater appreciation. Chicory is thought to be native to Europe and Asia and is extensively naturalized in North America. Two species, *C. intybus* and *C. endiva*, are grown in gardens. *C. intybus*, common chicory, is a perennial growing from two to six feet high. It has a deep spiraling tap root, and its lower leaves

resemble dandelion leaves, though they are usually larger. The upper leaves are alternate, clasping the stem, becoming progressively smaller toward the top of the plant. They may be with or without teeth. The pleasing sky-blue, rarely pink, ligulate flowers hug the stems in clusters of two or three flower heads, or one head may sit alone on a short branch. They are about an inch and a half in diameter. *C. endiva* is an annual or biennial growing to three feet high, and its leaves are ruffled and more robust. My seed catalogs list nineteen chicory cultivars including red-leaf varieties, heading chicories, large root chicories, and salad varieties.

Both endive and common chicory are grown from seed sown in the late spring or mid-summer for autumn salad greens. Seedlings can be thinned to six-to-ten-inch spacings. A rich deep-dug soil and full sun provide a good home for chicory. *C. intybus* can be sown in the spring followed by a successive planting of *C. endiva* in midsummer. Azure blue flowers, edible foliage and root, and medicinal qualities make chicory an alluring plant for the herb garden.

Witloof (a Flemish word for "white leaf"), or blanched leaves, forced from winter-stored roots or roots banked with earth in spring or fall, is chicory's best known leaf product. For winter-grown witloof, the tops are cut just above the ground, then stored in sand, light soil, or sawdust in a warm cellar. Before storage the lower end of the root is trimmed, making eight inch long sections, and placed upright in the growing medium. By covering the crowns with about eight inches of soil, the roots form a "head" three to six inches long of etiolated (blanched) leaves, tender and mild in flavor. Crowns can also be forced by placing the roots in a warm, moist, dark spot or covering them in the field with flower pots.

Young unmanipulated shoots and roots may also be eaten as vegetables. The bitter taste of fresh green leaves can be reduced by cooking in several waters. Before boiling, slice the roots in thin pieces and soak them in water overnight to remove bitter principles.

The greens are high in vitamin A, calcium, and potassium. They also contain appreciable amounts of phosphorus, choline, iron, vitamin C, and B vitamins. The roots contain over 50 percent inulin, choline, tannins, and a host of other compounds.

The root is a well-known coffee adulterant. But I prefer to consider chicory an enhancer of coffee flavor, enricher of color, and acidity balancer. Adulterants are added to disguise. Coffees containing chicory should flaunt the improvement.

Gathering chicory roots is a task of excavation. The deep tap roots, often two feet long and two inches in diameter, are difficult to entirely unearth. My shovel pries broken roots of twelve-inch lengths from the Ozark's rock-ridden soil. A double-dug bed makes root harvest easy. Wash and slice the roots into one-fourth inch diameter pieces an inch or two long. Roast pieces in an oven at 250°-300° F. for one hour or until crisp. Be careful not to scorch the roots. Grind in a blender and brew a chicory root tea or add one portion of roasted root to two portions of coffee.

Chicory has stomachic, tonic, cholagogic, diuretic, and slightly sedative qualities. An infusion of the root stimulates bile secretion and tones an upset stomach. If taken in excess, chicory may cause

Chives

fullness of blood in the head and reduce the visual power of the retina.

Chives. *Allium schoenoprasum* L.
(al′-i-um skee-no-pray′-sum)
Liliaceae – Lily Family

The genus *Allium* is represented by over 400 species and is one of the most important food-producing genera in the plant kingdom. Onions, leeks, garlic, elephant garlic, and chives are all species of *Allium*. *A. schoenoprasum* is a hardy perennial of Eurasian origin that has become naturalized in North America. Chives grow from eight to twenty inches tall though they rarely reach over a foot in gardens. The leaves are hollow, round, reed-like spears. The globular flower heads are a mass of mauve pink flowers encased in paper-like bracts, borne on scapes. Flowers appear from June to August. The tightly crowded bulblets grow in clumps and have the appearance of flattened miniature onions. *A. schoenoprasum* var. *Sibericum* differs primarily in that the leaves are more robust and are shorter than the scapes. Chives are very popular in American gardens.

Seed germinates easily. Sow indoors six weeks before the last frost or directly in the garden as soon as the soil warms up. Chives may also be propagated by dividing the clumps at any time of year, except, of course, when the ground is frozen.

A fairly rich, moist soil, high in humus, is best. Chives will tolerate full sun or partial shade with a pH range between 6 and 8. Keep free of weeds – once grasses become established in a clump of chives they are difficult to eradicate. The clumps should be divided every four or five years.

The delicate piquancy that chives impart to food makes it an herb of varied use. No garden or galley should be without this little cousin of onions. Chives are primarily used fresh. They usually retain moisture after drying and, therefore, are difficult to store. Chives will produce a second, more tender crop, if cut back to about two inches. I usually thin the clumps, taking only what I need at the moment.

Chives are essential to vichyssoise and are good in asparagus, potato, and cauliflower soups. Mix the chopped leaves in cream cheese, cottage cheese, or butter. Chives are great in deviled eggs, omelettes, and scrambled eggs. And what

Colt's Foot

better place for them than in a salad!

High concentrations of vitamin A and vitamin C are found in the leaves along with measurable amounts of iron, calcium, magnesium, phosphorus, potassium, thiamin, and niacin.

Chives can be called a healthful rather than medicinal herb. They are useful in toning the stomach, reducing high blood pressure, and strengthening the kidneys.

Colt's foot. *Tussilago farfara L.*
(tus-si-lay′-go far′-far-a)
Compositae—Aster Family

The blooming of colt's foot sparks the beginning of spring and the season of the garden. It is a hardy perennial native to Europe and widely naturalized in the northeastern United States. Occasionally it has escaped from cultivation in the western United States. It should not be confused with the indigenous western colt's foot, *Petasites spp.*, though they may be used interchangeably for medicinal purposes. One species of *Petasites* indigenous to Japan is used in a manner similar to *Tussilago*.

The emerging spring blooms of colt's foot race crocuses to christen the welcome

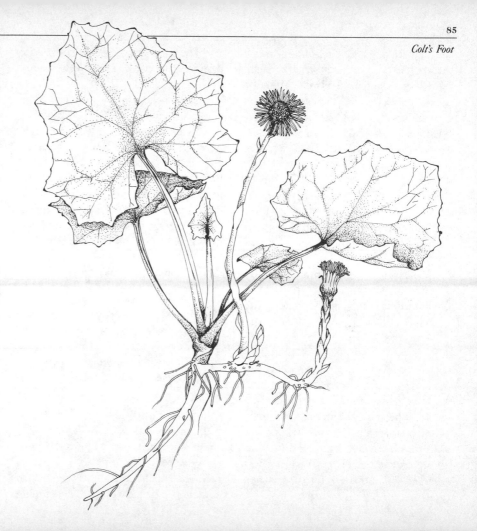

season with color. Colt's foot flowers appear before the leaves, often coming out in late February to mid-March. The light yellow dandelion-like flower heads appear on erect leafless stems or scapes. Each stem is covered with scale-like bracts of a brownish-pink color. The large (three-to-eight inches diameter) angular, heart-shaped leaves unfold as the last flower begins to wilt. They are coarsely toothed, of a dull green color above, and covered with a downy cotton beneath. The plant spreads by means of underground runners or stolons.

Colt's foot is easily propagated by dividing the stolons in the spring or fall. Give it plenty of room to spread in the garden.

It likes a heavy clay soil with a fair amount of moisture and a neutral to slightly acid pH. It will do well in sun or shade and is a good plant for borders.

The leaves, flowers, and roots are useful. The slightly bitter leaves can be eaten as a green in the early spring; but once the emergence of so many delicious spring greens begins, colt's foot is best reserved as a pot herb for times when there is nothing else to eat.

The flowers can be gathered and dried in spring. They have a mild sweet fragrance even when dried.

Colt's foot is a medicinal plant known since ancient times. The leaves and flowers are demulcent, emollient, and expectorant. The leaves have long served as a remedy for pulmonary ailments like bronchitis, and sore throats. A decoction or infusion of one ounce of the leaves to one pint of water is medicinally effective. In Germany and Scandinavia, the dried roots have been smoked to relieve coughs.

The leaves are rich in mucin and contain some inulin, tannins, a bitter glycoside, sitosterol, and other principles.

Comfrey. Russian Comfrey. *Symphytum officinale* L. *S.* × *uplandicum* Nym. *(S. peregrinum)*
(sim-'fit-um off-iss-i-nail-'ee; up-lan-'di-kum); Boraginaceae – Borage Family

There are about twenty-five species in this genus, mostly native to Europe and western Asia. *S.* × *uplandicum* and *S. officinale* are commonly grown in North America. *S. officinale* grows to a height of three feet. The erect stems often branch at the top. The eight-to-twelve-inch-long leaves are entire, oval or lance-shaped. The leaves become progressively smaller toward the top of the plant. Both the leaves and stems are covered with rough bristly hairs. From the axils of the small upper leaves emerge curving clusters of rose, purple, mauve, or sometimes white bell-shaped flowers about one-half inch long. In some regions flowering begins as early as April and lasts through September. The deep tap root has a fleshy cream-colored interior. 'Variegatum' is a cultivar with white-margined leaves. Russian comfrey *S.* × *uplandicum*, a native of Caucasus, may reach six feet in height. The leaves are rounded or heart-shaped at the base and the flowers change from pink to purple and are about three-fourths inch long.

Comfrey can be started from seed but is best propagated by dividing the roots in spring or fall. A little piece of root will produce a plant. At Taylor's Herb Gardens, inch-long roots are used. Generally I dig a mature plant and split the root into ten equal pieces with a sharp shovel. Once planted in a spot, comfrey will be there forever. The tap root may stretch six feet into the soil. If you leave a small bit of root after transplanting, another plant will soon emerge. As a consequence, plant comfrey in a permanent location and space at three feet.

Comfrey will grow in almost any soil. A well-drained moderately rich, moist loam will produce lush growth. A slightly acid to neutral pH is best. Full sun or partial shade are acceptable.

Harvest of the leaves begins as the flowers bud up. In Maine, I made my first leaf harvest on June 1 when most gardeners start planting peas and seasonal vegetables. That summer we harvested the comfrey patch seven times. Each cutting from the quarter-acre plot yielded sixty to eighty pounds of dried leaves. Leaves must be spread in thin layers to dry to insure even air circulation. Roots can be harvested in the spring or fall.

The young leaves can be boiled as a spring-time pot herb. They contain calcium, phosphorus, potassium, vitamin A, vitamin B_{12}, and up to 22 percent protein.

Medicinally, comfrey leaves and especially the root have been used as expectorants, emollients, astringents, demulcents, and hemostatics. Knit-bone is one common name. A poultice of the

Comfrey

leaves or root is placed over a sprain or broken limb to aid the "knitting" of the tissue. The root has been used to allay diarrhea, pharyngitis, tonsillitis, bronchitis, pneumonia, and whooping cough. Over the past decade, comfrey has become a very popular remedy.

The root contains allantoin – a cell proliferant. The root and, to a lesser extent, the leaves contain alkaloids in the pyrrolizidine group – symphytine and echimidine. Recently (1978), this alkaloid group has been found to be hepatoxic, causing massive liver tissue destruction and cancer. Continuous internal use of comfrey may, therefore, cause damage. On the other hand, comfrey has a long history of safe use.

A 1979 press release entitled: "Comfrey as Medicine" issued by England's National Institute of Medical Herbalists opens with the following paragraph:

"The strange saga of comfrey indicates the folly and illogicality of the approach which runs as follows. If a trace of a chemical can be isolated from a large quantity of a plant and be fed or injected into laboratory animals, the lethal results may be extrapolated to man who is then told not to take any of the original plant because it contains poison. The plant may have been eaten or made into a tea for centuries during which no single instance of ill-effect has followed its use. Today there is no single man, woman, or child in any country who has been recorded as suffering toxic effects from taking comfrey leaf or root as medicine. *Comfrey has a clean sheet and has no case to answer.* The *onus probandi* lies upon those who denigrate a safe herbal remedy by making assumptions in the absence of any evidence to justify what has tended to become an emotive rather than a scientific issue."[8]

As the old saying goes, "Everything in moderation."

Coriander. *Coriandrum sativum* L.
(koe-ree-an'-drum sa-tie'-vum)
Umbelliferae – Carrot Family

Coriander, cilantro, or Chinese parsley, native to southern Europe, western Asia, and naturalized in North America, is a strong-smelling herb, to say the least. It may reach four feet in height and is a hardy annual. The lower leaves are rounded, toothed, and resemble the young leaves

Coriander

of anise. As the plant matures, the leaves become more finely divided and feathery. The flowers are in graceful lacy umbels; the individual blossoms are pinkish-white. On each umbel group, the petals are enlarged on the outer flowers. Bees work coriander feverishly. It produces pink pollen, and bees fly about the garden with pink pollen sacks. The seeds (fruits) are about one-eighth inch in diameter, globular, ribbed, and light brownish when ripe. Each fruit consists of two halves (mericaps) both containing a seed. Mature plants may bend under the weight of the pleasant-smelling fruits.

Coriander is easily grown from seed sown to a depth of one-fourth to one-half inch in the spring or fall. Thin to stand at four-to-eight-inch spacings. Seeds germinate in seven to twenty days and mature, producing seed, in about three months. Depending upon the spacing of rows, ten to twenty pounds of seeds will sow an acre. Plants self-sow freely.

Coriander likes a deep, well-drained, moderately rich loam with a pH between 6 and 8. It needs full sun and plenty of moisture and will probably require an occasional watering.

Leaves for fresh or dry use should be harvested before the plants bloom. Seeds should be harvested after about two-thirds have turned from a green to brownish color. Cut in the early morning while the plants are still moist with dew to avoid seed shattering since coriander can easily become weedy. Yields vary; 500 to 2,000 pounds of seed per acre have been obtained.

Many Americans dislike the fragrance and flavor of fresh coriander leaves. It has been described as unpleasant, awful, noxious, and buglike. I have to admit, while tending the Shaker Herb Gardens, I usually found someone else to weed the coriander rows—until Dr. Shiu Ying Hu taught me to appreciate the flavor of this herb. In China it is eaten in salads and as a pot herb. Most people, unfamiliar with Chinese parsley, have to acquire a taste for it. Cilantro is often the secret ingredient that gives Mexican, Turkish, Indian, and certain Chinese dishes their distinctive flavor. Fresh cilantro can be found in markets wherever Mexican, Chinese, Vietnamese, Spanish, or Indian populations abound. Use the leaves in rice dishes, refried beans, curries, omelettes, soups, and salads. This much-ignored herb can enhance the flavor of many foods. I now describe the flavor as sweet, pleasant, and aromatic.

The leaves are a rich source of vitamin C, vitamin A, calcium, phosphorus, potassium, and iron. It contains 14-22 percent protein and small amounts of fiber, niacin, and thiamine.

In western cookery the seeds are used primarily for flavoring breads, cookies, and cakes.

The whole herb is used to quiet stomach ache and nausea. The seeds will correct cramping when mixed with laxative herbs. In Chinese medicine a decoction is given for dysentery and measles and is used as a gargle for toothaches. In India an eye wash made from the seeds has been used for chronic conjunctivitis and as a blindness preventative for smallpox victims. It is carminative, diuretic, tonic, stomachic, and aphrodisiac, and reportedly lessens the intoxicating effect of alcoholic beverages.

The essential oil contains coriandrol (55 to 75 percent), geraniol, borneol, camphor, carvone, anethole, and other chemicals. Commercially the oil is used

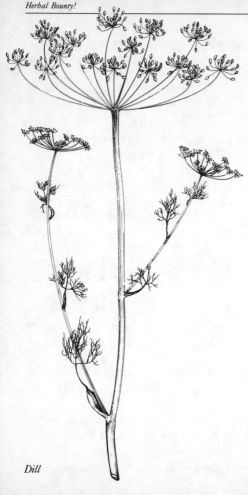

Dill

to flavor tobacco, pharmaceutical preparations, alcoholic beverages, baked goods, and condiments.

Dill. *Anethum graveolens L.*
(a-neeth'-um gra-vee'-o-lenz)
Umbelliferae – Carrot Family

An herb garden without dill is like a car without wheels. Dill's versatile culinary use and easy culture make it the perfect herb for the beginning herb gardener and a favorite of die-hard enthusiasts. *A. graveolens* is a hardy annual native to Southwest Asia and Southeast Europe. It is also naturalized in some parts of North America. It grows from two to four feet high, though 'Bouquet,' a dwarf form, is bushier and may be 1½ to 2 feet tall. The stems are smooth, ribbed, hollow, and have a bluish-green cast. The finely divided linear leaves envelop the stem with a thin sheath. The tiny yellow flowers grow on terminal umbels up to eight inches across. The flattened fruits have prominent ribs and are about one-eighth of an inch long. Dill has a carrot-like tap root.

Dill is easily grown from seed sown in early spring. Make successive plantings every three weeks from May through the first of August to insure a fresh supply of leaves for picking. Seeds germinate in ten to fourteen days and should be sown to a depth of one-fourth inch. Seedlings grow well thinned to eight to twelve inch spacings. Four to eight pounds of seed will sow an acre, depending upon the planting scheme used. I once broadcast four pounds of seed over a half acre of tilled ground. The resulting seedlings were nearly impossible to thin and weed, making harvest difficult. I recommend planting dill as a row crop with rows spaced at eighteen to thirty inches. A ready market can be found for fresh dill stalks in most urban areas, making dill a good supplemental cash crop for a family garden. A fifty-foot row will provide a child with some extra spending money for summer vacation.

Dill thrives best in a moderately rich, moist, slightly acid (5 to 7 pH) soil, under full sun. It will tolerate some shade especially in the South.

In a rich garden soil, dill self-sows in abundance. Plants produce seed about eight weeks after planting. An acre may yield 400 to 700 pounds of both seed and leaves or dill "weed."

Dill leaves are harvested just before the plant comes into bloom. Seeds can be harvested as soon as the tips begin to turn light-brown. Dill weed should be carefully spread to dry at a temperature of 90° F. When hung to dry without temperature regulation, dill often turns an undesirable brown color.

Dill leaf's delicate aromatic flavor lends a refreshing spark to otherwise bland foods such as potatoes, scrambled eggs, omelettes, carrots, sauces, and fresh cucumbers. Dill is, or course, best known for its use in flavoring pickles—and just because some find the flavor of dill pickles unpleasant doesn't mean they will turn up a nose at dill-seasoned dishes. The seeds have a pungent aromatic flavor great with cabbage dishes, potato salads, fish, stew, soup, broth, and breads.

The leaves contain magnesium, iron, calcium, potassium, phosphorus and vitamin C.

Dill leaves are little-used medicinally, though the seeds possess aromatic-stimulant and carminative properties. Drinking dill tea or chewing seeds will reportedly relieve digestive gas, soothe an upset stomach, and sweeten bad breath.

Dill weed oil contains alpha-phellandrene, limonene, and carvone. The seed oil contains the same constituents with higher concentrations of carvone. The seed also contains coumarins and a glycoside. The seed oil is antibacterial.

Dittany, stone mint. American dittany. *Cunila origanoides (L.)* Britt. (koo-nie′-la oh-rig′-an-oi-deez) Labiatae—Mint Family

Dittany is an herb from North America woods ideal for rocky, shaded crevices in the herbal landscape. It grows in dry, open, rocky woods, favoring acid soils on sandstone, chert, and granite from Florida to Texas, and north to Illinois and New York. It is a hardy, branched, erect perennial growing from one to two feet tall. The leaves are nearly sessile (without leaf stalks) oval, almost triangular in shape, with acutely pointed tips. They have small teeth, and as the specific name origanoides implies, an oregano-like fragrance. The rose-to-lavendar flowers appear in axils around the leaves or in terminal clusters from August to October.

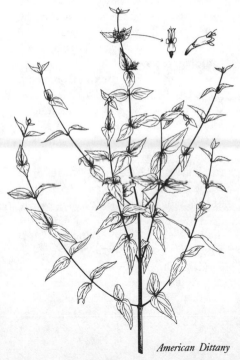

American Dittany

During the first chills of autumn frost, dittany produces frost flowers at its base—twisting, white, fluted ribbons of ice, sometimes four inches tall and two inches broad. This phenomena is caused by cell sap rising from the still-alive root into the dead tissues of the leaves and stems. The rising vapors seep through cracks in the stem, crystallizing as they contact the freezing air. Frost flowers have to be seen to be appreciated.

Dittany is easy to grow from seed. It can also be propagated from root divisions made in the spring. Plant among rocks under 50 percent shade. A sandy, dry soil with a pH around 5 and with good drainage is best.

Harvest the leaves in late summer when dittany is in bloom and hang in bunches. It dries quickly.

The dried leaves make a mild-flavored mint tea—a good wintertime beverage. The leaves can be used in cooking as an oregano substitute.

Medicinally, dittany has been used as a diaphoretic to reduce fevers, and as well for headaches and for snake bites.

Echinacea, purple coneflower.

Echinacea pallida Nutt., *E. angustifolia* D.C., *E. purpurea* (L.) Moench, *E. paradoxa* var. *paradoxa* (Norton) Britton (ek-i-nay´-see-a pal´-lid-a; an-gus-ti-foh´-li-a; pur-pur-ee´-a; par-a-docks´-a) Compositae—Aster Family

The genus *Echinacea* is represented by nine species and two varieties indigenous to North America, with distribution centered in Arkansas, Kansas, Missouri, and Oklahoma. These coarse perennial herbs occur in rocky prairies, barrens, glades, fields, along railroad tracks and roadsides, and, in the case of *E. purpurea*, in open woods. Echinaceas grow from one to four feet high with erect, simple or branched stems. Most species have rough, bristly, stiff hairs on the stems and leaves. The simple alternate leaves are oval to lance-shaped with relatively long petioles (leaf stalks) at the base of the plant. The leaves become progressively smaller and sessile (without leaf stalks) toward the flower head. The leaves are entire or have coarse teeth. The cone-shaped flower head or hemispherical receptacle with radiating ray florets ranging in color from rose, pink, purple, white, and yellow, characterize the plant. Disk flowers range from brownish-orange to reddish-brown. The ray florets are drooping (reflexed), especially in *E. pallida*. Flowering begins as early as mid-May in the South, extending into October in the northern limits of its range. The fibrous, horizontal or vertical root-stocks, pungently aromatic with a bitter flavor, are six to twenty-four inches in length. Several rosettes of leaf and flower stalks may arise from a single root.

E. pallida, *E. purpurea* and *E. angustifolia* are the most common species. *E. pallida* has long, slender, entire leaves, five to twenty times longer than broad. The purple, pink, or white ray flowers are 1½ to 3½ inches long and drooping. The plant stands sixteen to thirty-six inches tall and ranges from Michigan to Nebraska, south to Georgia, and west to Texas.

E. angustifolia is the species listed in most herb catalogs and books, though much of the root on the market tends to be *E. pallida* and *E. purpurea*. *E. angustifolia* is smaller than other *Echinacea* species, growing from six to twenty inches high. The ray flowers are as long or shorter than the width of the disk (seven-eighths to one and one-half inches long). The stiff hairs on the plant appear swollen at their bases. It grows from Minnesota to Saskatchewan, south to Oklahoma and Texas.

E. purpurea grows from two to four feet (rarely six feet) tall. Its leaves are oval with acutely pointed tips and coarse teeth. Ray flowers are rose to deep purple. This species is the most widely distributed, ranging from Georgia west to Oklahoma, north to Michigan and Ohio. The seed of this species is widely available on the horticultural trade, sometimes known as *Rudbeckia purpurea*. Several hybrids are offered including 'The King,' 'Sombrero,' and 'Bright Star.' German seedsmen offer variants known as 'Alba,' 'White Prince,' 'White Lustre,' and 'White King.' An English cultivar with heads six to seven inches across is sold under the name 'New Colewall Strain.' Ronald McGregor, author of the *Taxonomy of the Genus Echinacea*, reports that all these variants have been observed in natural wild stands.[9]

Unlike other "purple cone flowers," the paradox of *E. paradoxa* var. *paradoxa* lies in its yellow ray flowers and near-hairless smooth stems and leaves. Although rarely cultivated, it is a good candidate for the herb garden. However, it is quite rare, found only in the Missouri and Arkansas Ozarks.

Propagation is by seed or by carefully dividing branching crowns from the main rootstock in spring or fall. Echinacea seeds sprout better if stratified before germinating. This can be achieved by sowing the seeds on the surface of a sandy soil mix in an open cold frame during January. Once the weather warms in early spring the seeds readily germinate if provided moisture and sunlight. Also, they germinate easily if stratified in moist sand in a refrigerator for one month. Like many prairie plants, echinacea seeds need sunlight to germinate. Tamp the seeds into the soil mix but do not cover them. A light dusting of soil or a light straw mulch will help retain moisture.

Sown from seed, they need to grow for three or four years before sizable roots can be harvested. Plants propagated by division can be harvested two years after planting.

Most echinaceas grow in poor, rocky, slightly acidic, to alkaline (pH 6-8) well-drained soils. *E. purpurea* likes a moderately rich soil. All species are drought-resistant. Full sun is required, except for *E. purpurea* which enjoys dappled shade during hot summer months. Deep and frequent cultivation encourages healthy growth.

Harvest the roots in autumn after the plants have gone to seed. Dry in shade or under forced heat. Roots over one-half inch in diameter can be split before drying.

Echinacea was one of the most important medicinal plants of the Plains Indians. The root was used as an antidote for all types of venomous bites and stings. A piece of the root was applied to toothaches to relieve pain. The Kiowa Indians chewed the ground root slowly, swallowing the juice for sore throats and coughs. A decoction was used in steam baths so that participants could endure higher temperatures. The Sioux used the roots as a remedy for rabies. *E. pallida* was used to treat mumps, measles, rheumatism, arthritis, bad colds, smallpox, mouth sores, and many other ills. Indians used echinacea to treat more than 100 types of cancer. Kiowa women used the bristly dried flower heads as hair combs.

Dr. John King of Cincinnati, a leading botanic physician in his day, first described the medicinal uses of *E. purpurea* in the 1852 edition of his *American Eclectic Dispensatory*. In an article in an 1887 issue of the *Eclectic Medicinal Journal*, Dr. King again became the first to extol the properties of *E. angustifolia* in print. King used the herb extensively in his private practice and found it to be the only remedy to relieve his wife's "virulent cancer."[10] In the late nineteenth and early twentieth centuries, tincture of echinacea became the fastest-selling medicine derived from a native American plant, despite denunciations of the herb's usefulness in the *Journal of the American Medical Association*. By the late 1920s echinacea fell into disuse, as did plant drugs in general. Today both scientific and popular interest in echinacea are increasing rapidly, thus creating the threat of overharvesting wild populations. Cultivated supplies of the root are needed.

Echinacea preparations have been used to treat gangrene, boils, carbuncles, abcesses, mucous membrane inflammations, typhoids, burns, wounds, diphtheria, blood poisoning, mouth ulcers, and other ailments related to diseased-blood conditions. Its effects are considered antithermic, antibiotic, depurative, alterative, and antiseptic.

Two polysaccharides which stimulate the immune system have been isolated from *E. purpurea*. One, echinacin B, has strong wound-healing and infection-fighting capacities because of the formation of a hyaluronic acid polysaccharide complex that helps neutralize inflammation and swelling enhanced by the enzyme hyaluronidase. Hyaluronic acid, found in the ground substance (the material which occupies spaces between cells) of connective tissue, acts as a binding and protective agent.

Echinacea extracts increase bacteria-destroying cells (phagocytes), inhibit inflammation and accelerate wound healing. Experiments with *Echinacea* essential oil also suggest tumor-inhibiting capacity (Walker carcinosarcoma and lymphocytic leukemia). Echinacea research shows that this herb possesses resistance to herpes and influenza virus, *Staphylococci* and *Streptococci* bacteria, as well as allergies.

E. angustifolia contains an essential oil, a sesquiterpene, betaine, inulin, glucose, fructose, and other substances. *E. purpurea* contains an essential oil, tannin, inulin, vitamin C, and enzymes. Two glycozides possessing mild antibiotic activity have been isolated from echinacea species.

Preparations include a decoction of the root plus a tincture made by adding one part, by weight, of the root to two parts of a mixture of equal volumes of ethyl alcohol and distilled water. Doses of the tincture range from five to sixty drops in a little water taken four times a day.

In Europe numerous lotions and creams containing Echinacea are sold to fight swelling and inflammation and promote the healing of sores. An extract, echinacin, is used to treat chronic inflammations and prevent influenza.

Elecampane. *Inula helenium* L.
(in′-you-la he-lee′-ni-um)
Compositae—Aster Family

Elecampane is a striking plant, a good focus for an herbal design scheme. This robust perennial generally grows from four to six feet high, but I've seen specimens in double-dug beds that exceeded eight feet. The basal leaves are long and comparatively narrow, being ten to eighteen feet long and about four inches broad. The leaf stems add an additional six to twelve inches to the leaf's overall length. Above, the leaves are rough; below, they're covered with soft velvety white hairs. Moving up the stem, the leaves become successively smaller, losing their petioles (leaf stalks) at the top. Instead, the upper leaves clasp the stalks with their heart-shaped bases. Abundant long, slender ray flowers project radially from the splendid golden flower heads which are sometimes four inches in diameter. The flower heads are sparse and may sit alone or in groups of two or three on top of the stalk. The root is large and fleshy, about six inches long, one to two inches thick, with half a dozen or more lateral rootlets, six to twelve inches long and one-half to one inch across. Elecampane flowers from May to August. It's native to central Asia and naturalized in Europe and North America.

Elecampane is propagated in autumn by dividing buds or "eyes" off two-year-old roots which are being harvested for drying. Plants may also be started from seed sown indoors about seven weeks before the last frost.

Elecampane thrives on a fairly rich moist loam with an acid pH, 4.5 to 6, in full sun or partial shade. Give plants in rich soil three feet spacing; space those in average soils at eighteen inches. Deeply dug soil will help produce large roots and robust plants. An acre may produce a ton of roots.

Only the root is used, and it should be harvested in the fall of the second year. By the third year the roots often become woody and pithy. For easy drying, slice roots into half-inch-diameter pieces. They can be candied like angelica and calamus roots.

Elecampane has a rich tradition of medicinal use, especially as a home remedy for lung ailments like pneumonia, whooping cough, asthma, bronchitis, and vesical catarrh. It is considered stimulating, diaphoretic, diuretic, expectorant, tonic, emmenagogue, bechic, cholagogic, and mildly antihelminthic. Elecampane has been used for skin afflictions, upset stomach, diarrhea, intestinal parasites, and, in Chinese medicine, to treat certain cancers. Topically, elecampane has been applied to facial neuralagia and sciatica. Experiments with mice have shown the tea to be a strong sedative.

The root is prepared by decocting one-half ounce of the root in one pint of boiling water. A tincture is made by weight with two parts root and one part alcohol. One-sixth of the alcohol is added to the root and thoroughly mixed after which the remaining alcohol is added. Let it sit for ten days.

The root contains up to 44 percent inulin. The essential oil comprises up to 4 percent of the root's weight and primarily consists of the sesquiterpene lactones, alantolactone and isoalantolactone. Alantolactone is a powerful worm expellant still used in Europe. Both lactones are strongly bactericidal and fungicidal.

Fennel. *Foeniculum vulgare* Mill. (fee-nik´-you-lum vul-gay´-ree) Umbelliferae – Carrot Family

Fennel is an annual, biennial, or perennial native to Eurasia. It has become extensively naturalized in south and central California where it is often called wild anise. Fennel grows to six feet in height

Fennel

Copper or bronze fennel (var. rubrum) has bronze leaves with a metallic lustre. *F. vulgare* var.*azoricum* (Mill) Thell., like celery, has edible stalks greatly thickened at their base. It is often erroneously confused with *F. vulgare* var.*dulce* Batt. & Trab., whose leaves are not thick at the base and is primarily grown for the essential oil in its large fruits.

Fennel is easily grown from seed sown directly in the garden after danger of frost has passed. Seed usually germinates in fourteen days. Thin seedlings to stand at six-to-twelve-inch spacings. Four to seven pounds of seed will plant an acre.

Common fennel likes a light, dry, limey soil with a pH from 7 to 8.5 and full sun. Finocchio (var. azoricum) needs a rich soil with lots of moisture to produce succulent, edible stems. Once the stems become about an inch thick, they can be hilled with soil to blanch the stems and produce a milder flavor. Harvest ten days after hilling. Commercial fields have produced 600 to 1400 pounds of seed per acre.

The roots are edible and may be harvested in the fall of the first year. Leaves and stems should be harvested for fresh use before the plant flowers. Seeds are harvested in late summer as they begin to turn their characteristic grayish-green color.

The boiled, blanched stalks make a wonderful vegetable in and of themselves. The filiform leaves are a great addition to soups and salads, and especially complement fish. Fresh leaves can be chopped into a vinegar and oil salad dressing in the blender. The seeds are used in breads and cookies, and a mild anise-like tea can be brewed from the leaves or seeds.

Fennel is high in calcium, iron, potassium, vitamin A and vitamin C. It also contains some protein and phosphorus.

The seeds are used to stimulate milk flow, as an aromatic stimulant for digestive disorders, and as a carminative, especially to relieve infant colic. Fennel is also an expectorant, diuretic, and antispasmodic. In China, a poultice of the powdered seeds is used on hard-to-heal snake bites. The seeds are used in tea and in tincture form.

The fruits may contain up to 28 percent by weight a fixed oil consisting mainly of petroselinic acid, oleic acid, and linoleic

and has an erect, round, smooth, striated, jointed and branching stem. The leaves are long, linear and pointed, similar to dill leaves. The tiny yellow flowers grow on flat umbels with fifteen to forty rays. Each umbel is up to seven inches in diameter. The half-inch-long fruits are oval and greenish-gray with prominent ribs.

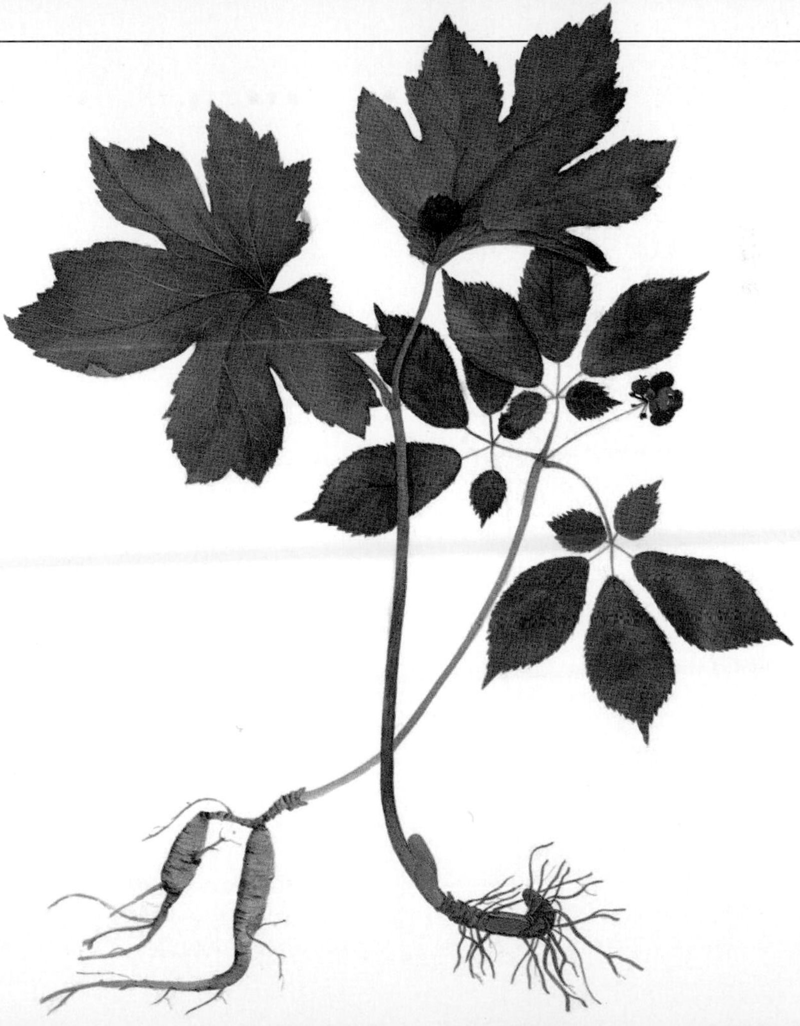

Lavandula stoechas, L. × *hybrida, L. dentata, L. multifida, L. angustifolia*
'Munstead'

Echinacea paradoxa, E. pallida (emerging), E. pallida, and E. Purpurea

Lamb's Ears, Cat Thyme, and Salvia divinorum

Spiderwort, and Passion Flower

Monarda Russeliana, M. fistulosa, M. didyma and M. punctata

acid. The essential oil, composing up to 8 percent of the weight of the fruit, contains *trans*-anethole, fenchone, estragole, limonene, camphene, and other substances. The oil reportedly checks spasms of smooth muscles in animal experiments and is antibacterial.

Foxglove. *Digitalis purpurea L.*
(dij-i-ta′-lis pur-pur-ee′-a)
Schrophulariaceae – Figwort Family

Foxglove, a biennial or short-lived perennial, is a well-known ornamental for flower and herb gardens. It is native to Europe and widely cultivated throughout the world. In the American Northwest and Northeast it has become naturalized along roadsides. When flowering, foxglove may reach six or seven feet in height. In the first year, the leaves form a dense basal rosette. In the second year the plant shoots up a thick, erect, round, downy stem. Leaves on the stem are alternate with long stalks. Leaf blades are oval to lance-shaped, with small round teeth, prominent veins, and a wrinkled appearance. They are six to twelve inches long and three to four inches wide, green and woolly on the upper side and covered with a white

or gray pelt of hairs beneath. Their flavor is extremely bitter. The showy bell-shaped flowers appear on one-sided spikes. They are usually 1½ to 3 inches long, have flared lips, and are purple, cerise, and sometimes white. The lower inside surface is whitish, covered with purple dots. Numerous cultivars are available.

Foxglove is grown from its tiny seeds, sown indoors in flats in February or March. Transplant outdoors after the last spring frost. Plants will self-sow.

An acid or slightly alkaline soil (pH 5 to 8) is acceptable. A loose, well-drained, moist, rich soil produces lush growth. Foxglove will tolerate full sun or light shade. Seedlings need to be kept free of weeds and the soil well cultivated throughout the plant's growth cycle.

In Great Britain and on the European continent the leaves have been used as an expectorant, as a remedy in epilepsy, and as a poultice on scrofulous swellings for centuries. In 1775, William Withering, an English physician, brought foxglove's diuretic and dropsy-relieving properties to light. By the late nineteenth century, it was widely prescribed by physicians as a cardiotonic and diuretic.

Foxglove

In modern South America, an infusion of the leaves or foxglove pills are used for asthma relief, sedatives, or heart tonics. Colombians use a tea made of three or four corollas of a white-flowered variety to treat epilepsy in infants. In India, wounds and burns are treated with an ointment containing digitalis glycosides.

Digitalis glycosides are used to treat congestive heart failure, as it increases the force of heart contractions while providing rest between the contractions. It also raises low blood pressure.

Foxglove contains more than thirty glycosides. Two are precursors to digitoxin and gitoxin.

Several years ago, a newspaper reporter interviewed me for an herb article. After the interview, the reporter arranged to trade some herb plants with me on the following day. He wanted to show me some comfrey, which he had tried in salads and found extremely bitter-tasting. The next day I went to his office and there, sitting on a file cabinet, was a box of first-year foxglove plants! To the novice, comfrey and foxglove have a similar appearance. Earlier that same year (1979) an elderly couple had eaten what they

thought were comfrey leaves. It was foxglove, and both died within twenty-four hours. Foxglove should be well-marked in an herb garden or not planted at all. Its utility to herb gardeners is limited to ornamental use. The plant and its preparations are highly toxic. Poisoning is characterized by nausea, vomiting, dizziness, severe headache, irregular heartbeat and pulse, convulsions, and death.

Garlic. *Allium sativum* L.
(al´-i-um sat-eye´-vum)
Liliaceae – Lily Family

Allium sativum is perhaps the most popular and pungent herb of world cuisines. This perennial close relative of onions is thought to have originated in central Asia, though it has been in cultivation throughout the world for so long it is nearly impossible to establish its point of origin. Garlic has four or more flat, grayish-green leaves about one foot long and one-half inch wide. The flower stipe may reach three feet in height. Globular clusters of white flowers unfold from a papery beak-like envelope; bulbels — miniature seed bulbs — may develop in place of flowers. If planted in early spring, flowers emerge in mid-

Garlic spread to dry.

summer. The root is a fleshy bulb, one or two inches broad. A thin white sheathing encases five or more pointed oblong cloves. Several varieties are grown commercially. In central California 'early' garlic is planted in the fall and harvested the following May or June. The bulbs are large and flat; the delectable cloves are enclosed in white sheathing. 'Late' garlic is planted soon after the 'early' harvest and has medium-sized cloves with light pink to reddish sheathing. The whole bulb is covered with a thin white skin. 'Late' has a longer shelf life than 'early'. 'Creole' is a hardy variety with small red-skinned cloves.

Garlic can be grown from seed, nursery sets (bulbels), or by planting individual cloves. Cloves are perhaps the most convenient form to plant. The outer cloves will generally produce superior plants. Place them points up in one-inch-deep holes at six-inch spacings. Fall plantings can be made in the Deep South and on the West Coast where the ground does not freeze in winter. In other regions, garlic can be planted as soon as the ground thaws.

A moist, sandy soil, moderately rich in humus, is perfect for garlic culture. Full sun is essential, and slightly alkaline soil is best. Garlic plants take very little space and can be planted throughout the garden among other herbs and vegetables. As a companion plant, garlic will help keep away cabbage moths, Japanese beetles, and aphids. Aphids can be controlled with a garlic spray made by blending a handful of unpeeled cloves with three cups of water. Strain and spray on affected plants, being sure to cover undersides of leaves and stems. Repeat as necessary until the vermin travel to more fragrant shores.

Harvest garlic when the leaves turn brown and die down. Shake off loose dirt and cut off stringy rootlets. Let the bulbs dry for a day or two then bring them in to braid. Soak the tops in water for about an hour or until pliable. Braid the leaves tightly together, adding another bunch with each twist, and knot at the top. Hang in the kitchen and remove cloves as needed.

Garlic is a most versatile culinary herb. However, there are two schools of thought when it comes to garlic breath—emphatic fans and equally energetic disdainers. The Lovers of the Stinking Rose, a garlic fan club, have a remedy for garlic breath—socializing with other garlic lovers. The fresh cloves can be used with an endless variety of meats, vegetables, soups, sauces,

Herbalist Jeanmarie Morelli in a field of garlic

and salad dressings. A highly nutritious herb, garlic abounds in fiber, magnesium, phosphorus, potassium, protein, thiamin, niacin, riboflavin, vitamin C, and especially vitamin A.

Expectorant, diaphoretic, diuretic,

carminative, vermifuge, stomachic, anti-spasmodic, rubefacient, and intestinal anti-septic qualities have been attributed to garlic. It proves useful in fevers and colds, lung ailments, intestinal disorders, and general health maintainance. At the onset of a cold, I chew up two or three cloves of garlic and without fail have been cured. Studies have shown garlic lowers serum cholesterol and reduces high blood pressure, lessening the chance of heart disease and hardening of the arteries. And to quote a bumper sticker, "Fight mouthwash–eat garlic."

The major components of garlic oil are allicin, allypropyl disulfide, diallyl disulfide, and diallyl trisulfide. The oil has been reported to have antifungicidal, antibacterial and antitumor qualities.

Wild geranium, cranesbill. *Geranium maculatum L.*
(jer-ayn′-ee-um mak-yew-lay′-tim)
Geraniaceae – Geranium Family

A denizen of open woods and field edges from Maine to Manitoba, south to Georgia, and west to Oklahoma, this in-digenous American plant is a showy ad-dition to herb gardens. It is an erect, hardy

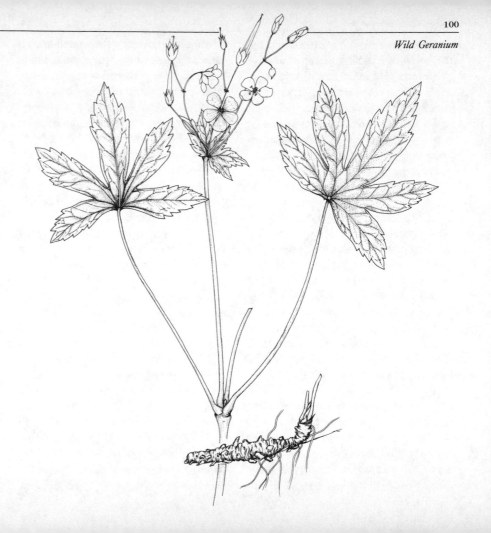

perennial standing 1 to 1½ feet tall. Long-stemmed leaves arise from the roots while short-stemmed to sessile opposite leaves grow on the main stem. They are divided into three to seven lobes with sharp teeth at the lobe's ends. The leaves are somewhat hairy and mottled with whitish-green splotches—hence the specific name *maculatum* (spotted). The attractive rose-purple flowers, 1 to 1½ inches in diameter, are borne on terminal panicles. Wild geranium blooms from April to June. One form, *G. maculatum f. albiflorum*, has white flowers. The roots are horizontal, about one-half inch in diameter, contorted, knobby, and pinkish-gray on the interior.

Wild geranium grows from seed collected in late summer and sown in fall or the following spring. Roots may also be divided in the fall. Established plants self-sow freely. Give plants six-inch spacings.

This plant is particularly attractive when grown in colonies of six or more. It needs partial shade and good drainage and will grow in a variety of soils, tolerating a pH range of 4.5 to 7.

The root gathered in autumn is the part used.

Wild geranium root was a well-known remedy among native Americans and early settlers. The Meskwakis of the upper Midwest used the root to heal sore gums, pyorrhea, toothache, and hemmorrhoids. The root boiled in milk was a popular remedy for intestinal ailments of children. Diarrhea, dysentery, leukorrhea, gonorrhea, and syphilis have all reportedly responded to treatment with the root. I have used a gargle made from the powdered root to relieve canker sores. Basically, the root is useful wherever a styptic or astringent is called for. The root contains tannins and gallic acid.

Ginseng, American ginseng, *Panax quinquefolius* L.
(pan′-acks kwin-kwe-foh′-li-us)
Araliaceae—Ginseng Family

There are about nine species in the genus *Panax*, all but two of which are native to eastern Asia. American ginseng is a perennial herb native to eastern North America, favoring north- or east-facing slopes in a well-drained humus-rich soil. It grows to a height of fifteen inches. One- or two-year-old plants—"strawberry ginseng"—produce three strawberry leaf-like leaflets. Two- to three-year-old plants often develop characteristic five-fingered, palm-shaped leaves. Older plants develop two to five prongs with five leaflets on each prong. The leaflets are oblong, coarsely toothed, and two to six inches long. The flowers are tiny and greenish-white appearing in June to July. Bright red two-seeded berries ripen in late July to October. The white fleshy tap root often develops a human-like form. The plant dies back to the ground every fall leaving a scar on the "neck" at the top of each root. The age of the root is determined by counting the scars.

Ginseng is not the easiest herb to cultivate. Propagation is by seeds which may take six to twenty months to germinate. It should be stratified before planting. Pre-stratified seeds are available from most seed sources. One- two- or three-year-old roots can be purchased for planting, but the buyer risks introducing diseased stock into his or her beds. Freshly harvested seed that has not been stratified can be planted one-half inch deep, six inches apart, in well-prepared beds in September. Seed may germinate the next spring or the following year. If seed is purchased from a large grower, it is a good idea to disinfect the seeds by soaking them in a mix of nine parts water and one part chlorine bleach for five to ten minutes. This will kill disease organisms. Stratified seed may be planted in the spring. Fifty to one hundred pounds of seed will sow an acre.

A light-textured woods loam, high in humus, is suitable for ginseng culture. Heavy clay or sandy soils will not produce healthy plants. Maintain a pH of around 5 to 6. Shade of 70 percent or more is required for ginseng and can be provided by natural tree canopies, shade screen, or a lath shed. The design of the shade structure should allow rain to reach the beds. Ginseng grown under a natural tree canopy is, of course, the least expensive. Beds can be double-dug and provided with blood meal, bone meal, and leaf mold as soil amenders. If these substances unbalance the pH, use a light application of lime or wood ashes. After plants die back in autumn, they should be mulched with a four- to six-inch layer of straw or leaves.

Plants are subject to attack by leaf blight, insects, root rot, and rodents, who consider the roots a delectable treat. Preventative control measures for the organic grower are the most effective. To avoid diseased stock, gather wild seeds when possible. Remove and destroy all affected plants in beds. Vertical metal barriers placed around the bed's perimeters can control rodent attacks. Half of a twenty-four-inch sheet of aluminum should be below the soil's surface. Commercial ginseng growers use herbicides such as Phytar 560 and Paraquat. Diathaine, M-45, Captan 50, Malathion, and Sevin are among the pesticides employed in ginseng production.

The roots are harvested in the fall of the fifth or sixth year after planting from seed. Carefully dig the roots with a garden spade, taking care to keep the whole root intact. Remove loose soil by spraying with a hose, then spread the roots on racks to dry. Stir as needed to provide adequate air circulation. Drying time varies depending upon weather conditions and size of roots. Air curing may take as long as a month. Harvest seeds after berries ripen.

The mysterious powers of ginseng are shrouded in folk fact and fiction. "The root of life" is believed to invigorate, rejuvenate, and revitalize the system. Over the past thirty years, Russian, Japanese, and, most recently, American research suggests a scientific basis for the use of ginseng as a general body tonic. Ginseng has been shown to increase work efficiency by raising capacity for mental and physical performance and allowing for better adaptation to high and low temperatures. Ginseng increases tolerance to stress. Its effect is termed adaptogenic. The life of X-ray-irradiated mice has been prolonged with ginseng. It also counteracts the toxic effects of chemicals such as choloroform and amphetamines. In Chinese medicine, ginseng is combined with other herbs to treat a wide range of illnesses. Future research may provide important new applications for ginseng in disease prevention and cures.

Saponin glycosides are responsible for ginseng's biological activity. They are called panaxosides by Russian researchers and ginsenosides by the Japanese. Eleven of these substances are found in Oriental ginseng *Panax ginseng*. American ginseng primarily contains the R_{b-1} and R_e ginsenosides.

Sweet Goldenrod, Blue Mountain Tea. *Solidago odora* Ait.
(sol-i-day′-go oh-door′-a)
Compositae—Aster Family

I've tried dozens of herb teas—some nauseating, others tasty—but my favorite is unequivocally sweet goldenrod. I feel this North American native should be grown in every herb garden, here and abroad.

More than 100 species of *Solidago* grow in North America, but only *S. odora* has a fragrance and flavor suggestive of anise or tarragon. It is an erect, sometimes sprawling perennial, three to six feet high, found in thickets, along roadsides, and in dry, open, rocky woods from New Hampshire to southern Ontario, south to Florida and west to eastern Texas. The leaves are sessile (without leaf stalks), entire (not toothed), and sharply pointed, about four inches long and half an inch wide. The leaves become successively smaller toward the top of the plant. When held up to light, the leaves are spotted with translucent dots. The stems have a purple cast. The bright yellow flower heads are arranged on one side of a stem in tight long panicles. It flowers from July to September.

Sweet goldenrod can be grown from spring- or fall-sown seed, but is most easily propagated by dividing the crowns in spring after the plants become three to four inches tall. In three or four years the crowns will spread, producing clumps six to ten inches in diameter. These older clumps can be divided into ten or more seedlings.

Sweet goldenrod will grow in a rocky or sandy soil with good drainage and a fair amount of humus in either full sun or partial shade. The soil should be slightly acid. It will generally thrive in any good garden soil and requires little moisture.

Harvest just before the plant comes into bloom as the leaves later take on a more astringent bitter flavor. Tie in bundles. Sweet goldenrod dries quickly, and the leaves can easily be removed from the stem with one stroke.

Sweet goldenrod should be grown as a commercial tea crop. It is easy to grow and produces well. Frederick Pursh (1774-1820), a well-traveled botanical explorer, reported that sweet goldenrod was exported to China at a high price as a tea substitute.[11]

Sweet goldenrod has limited medicinal applications, but has been used as a digestive stimulant, rubefacient, mild astringent, and carminative. Externally the leaves are used to relieve rheumatic pains and neuralgia. The tea is used to promote sweating in fevers, for colic, and to regulate the menses.

The oil contains delta-limonene, borneol, and estragole.

Goldenseal. *Hydrastis canadensis* L.
(hi-dras′-tis kan-a-den′-sis)
Ranunculaceae—Buttercup Family

Goldenseal is a perennial with an erect hairy stem about a foot in height with three or four yellowish scales at the base of the plant. Each plant has two leaves seemingly forking about three-fourths of the way up the stem. One branch supports a larger leaf, the other, a smaller leaf and flower stalk. The leaves' lower surfaces have prominent veins. The leaves grow up to twelve inches wide and eight inches long. They are palmate with five to nine lobes, and have sharply pointed irregular teeth. At flowering time, the leaves are partially expanded and very wrinkled. The flowers appear in late April to early May, lasting only three to seven days. The flowers are one-half inch in diameter and petalless. A round spray of forty to fifty stamens characterizes the flowers. The globular, fleshy, bright red fruits, resembling a large raspberry, ripen in July or August. They contain ten to twenty black, hard, shiny seeds. The horizontal rhizome is knotty, about one-half to three-fourths inch thick, two to three inches long, with numerous fibrous rootlets. The root is intensely yellow. The plant, which usually dies down after the fruits mature, grows in rich, moist woods favoring beech canopy from Vermont to Minnesota, south to Georgia, Alabama, and Arkansas.

Propagate by seed, division of rhizomes, or by planting the "eyes" or buds from vigorous root fibers. Seeds need to be stratified before germinating. A mixture of two parts moist sand and one part leaf mold—finer than the seeds—serves as a good medium. Place in a refrigerator for three months and plant the following spring. Most first-year seedlings only develop cotyledons. One true leaf is produced the second year; two leaves plus a flower develop in the third.

Each rhizome is studded with rootlets and undeveloped buds. Any piece of root with a bud or "eye" and a few strands of fibrous root will produce a plant. On an average, about five plants can be divided from each mature rhizome. Plant one inch deep eight inches apart. Break the roots into pieces and plant in September . Often tops will not appear until the *second* summer after planting. Being a goldenseal cultivator requires patience.

A deep, loose, friable soil is essential. Four-inch layers of leaf mold can be added to beds, along with well-composted manure, wood ashes, and rock phosphate. The soil should be balanced to a pH of 6 to 7. Soil should be well-drained but moist, and 75 percent shade is necessary, provided by training vines, a tree canopy, or lath sheds. Beds must be kept free of weeds. You can expect 1,000 to 2,500 pounds of dried root per acre after five years.

Seed-sown plants are harvested after four or five years. Plants grown from root divisions may be harvested after three or four years. Spring-dug roots shrink considerably more than those dug in the fall.

Roots should be cleaned, then dried until brittle. When dry, the fibrous rootlets are easily removed from the main rhizome by rubbing.

American Indians used goldenseal for eye ailments, skin diseases, gonorrhea, cancers, and as a dye and skin stain.

In recent years goldenseal in powdered or capsulated form has become a panacea popular for many ills. In my opinion, powdered goldenseal products should be avoided because of excessive potential adulteration.

A wash made from the roots is useful in conjunctivitis and other eye ailments. It is a useful tonic and astringent for treating inflamed mucous membranes of the vagina, uterus, mouth, throat and digestive system. Gonorrhea, jaundice, bronchitis, pharyngitis, ulcers, and many other ailments have been treated with goldenseal. Its action is antiseptic, antiperiodic, diuretic, astringent, tonic, and hemostatic.

The alkaloids hydrastine and berberine are the biologically active compounds in goldenseal. Berberine is responsible for goldenseal's yellow color and bitter taste. It has a strong antibacterial effect, increases bile secretion, is anticonvulsant and stimulates the uterus. In laboratory animals, it has acted as a sedative and lowered blood pressure. The properties of hydrastine resemble berberine.

Hops. *Humulus lupulus L.*
(who′-moo′-lus loop′-you-lus)
Cannabinaceae—Cannabis Family

Hops are native to Europe, Asia, and North America. The genus's two species are grown in gardens—*H. lupulus* which has a perennial root stock and annual shoots growing thirty feet or more in a season, and *H. japonicus*, a rapid-growing annual creating a graceful festoonery. The leaves of *H. lupulus* resemble grape leaves. They are rough, hairy, three to five lobed, coarsely toothed, about as broad as wide (three to five inches), and are in an opposite arrangement, though leaves at the end of shoots may be arranged singly. The twining stems, spiraling clockwise, are tough, flexible, and fibrous. Some plants produce racemes of male flowers from the leaf axils. Others produce female flowers and the plump, rounded, cone-like fruits called strobiles. The strobiles

Hops climbing a trellis at the Farm and Garden Project, University of California, Santa Cruz.

are about 1¼ inches long and are characterized by translucent, yellowish-green, papery bracts, each covering a seed (unless the variety is seedless). Hops flower from July to August.

Hops can be grown from seed but are generally propagated by dividing the young shoots from the main crown in spring or fall, or by cuttings rooted from older shoots and suckers in late summer. The first year, seed-grown hops usually develop slowly. Plant root cuttings in a hill—three roots per hill, spaced eighteen inches apart at the corners of an equilateral triangle. Keep well-cultivated and free from weeds.

Hops require a deeply dug, rich, moist soil with full sun. Soil pH should be between 5 and 8. By midsummer, the prickly vines may stretch from fifteen to thirty feet. Once rapid growth begins, water frequently. Cut the stems back after they are hit by a fall frost and add the refuse to your compost pile. In autumn, dress the roots with compost. Hops may require more care than some herbs, but they are worth the effort. Trained over a trellis, they create enclosed spaces in the garden—to say nothing of their food and medicinal value.

In early fall when the strobiles begin to feel firm, turn an amber color, and are covered with a yellow dust, harvest on a clear day. The strobiles will spoil rapidly if not quickly dried soon after harvest. For good keeping, the moisture must be reduced from 65 to 80 percent to about 12 percent. Place in an oven no warmer than 150° F. and leave its door ajar.

As the young shoots appear in the spring, they can be eaten as an asparagus substitute. Blanch the shoots by hilling the crowns with dirt the previous fall. This makes milder-flavored and tenderer shoots. Eat only young shoots. The older ones tend to be tough and bitter. The flavor is nutty and pleasing, though the texture is often dry and gritty. At one time, a hill of hops was part of every English vegetable garden.

Hops are stomachic, tonic, nervine, diuretic, anodyne, sedative, and soporific. A pillow stuffed with hops will help an insomniac sleep. Moisten the hops with water before going to bed so rustling strobiles don't keep you awake (assuming you're either the insomniac or sleeping in the same bed with one). An infusion of the strobiles will help relieve muscle spasms. A poultice is used externally as an anodyne on rheumatic joints and muscle pains. The bitter-tasting tea will help stimulate appetite and calm nervous tension. The tea is soothing and serves as an antispasmodic in delirium tremens.

Add one-half ounce of the herb to boiling water and give four-ounce doses of this infusion.

Ripe hops contain a yellow granular powder called lupulin. It contains the plant's active principles—an essential oil mainly composed of humulene, myrcene, beta-caryophyllene, and farnesene. Resinous bitter principles comprise up to 12 percent of the weight of the strobiles—mostly bitter acids, including lupulone and humulone. Over 100 compounds have been found in the essential oil.

Hops are best known as a flavoring for beer, but the plant has many uses. The spent hops left over from beer production make a good compost and mulch, especially for nursery trees. The ashes have been used in glass manufacturing. A pulp of the stems has been used to make paper and cardboard. Textiles such as yarns and strings are made from the stem fiber, and the stalks can be used for weaving baskets.

Horehound. *Marrubium vulgare L.*
(mar-rue′-bi-um vul-gay′-ree)
Labiatae—Mint Family

Horehound

Horehound is a hardy perennial herb native to the Mediterranean and northern Europe, and naturalized throughout the United States. It is a bitter aromatic herb standing about one foot tall with a bushy spreading habit. The whole plant is covered with a soft, woolly felt, giving the plant a whitish-gray appearance. The leaves are round or oval-shaped and arranged opposite one another on square stems. They are about an inch long, and have slight teeth and short petioles. The tiny white flowers occur in tight whorls around the leaf axils. The calyx has ten sharp pointed recurved teeth; when dried, they cling to clothing like burdock pods. It flowers from June to September.

Horehound is easy to grow from seed sown in shallow drills in fall or early spring. Resulting seedlings should be spaced eight to fifteen inches apart. Horehound may also be propagated from stem cuttings or root division. Plants grown from seed may take two years to bloom.

Horehound is one of those herbs that grows in places other plants shun. A poor, dry, sandy soil with a wide pH range (4.5 to 8) and full sun are all horehound needs. It's a good herb to plant around a border which doesn't need much attention. An acre of horehound has been reported to produce three-fourths to one ton of dried herb.

The leaves and flowering tops are harvested in peak-bloom. Horehound is easy to dry but difficult to process by hand because of its sticky calyces.

Medicinally this ill-tasting herb is a stimulant, bitter stomachic, resolvent, deobstruent, expectorant, tonic, and mild vermifuge. Its primary use is to break up phlegm, relieve coughs, soothe sore throats, and relieve bronchitis and other upper respiratory ailments. Horehound has also been useful in jaundice, chronic hepatitis, amenorrhea, and leukemia. An ointment made from freshly bruised leaves is useful for healing cuts. Large doses have a laxative effect.

Marrubiin, a bitter principle, is the main active constituent of horehound. It has been shown to possess expectorant qualities and to strongly increase the flow of liver bile. The leaves also contain tannin, mucilage, a resin, and minute amounts of aklaloids and an essential oil. The volatile oil is a vasodilator and expectorant.

A tea can be made by adding one ounce of the herb to a quart of water. Sweeten with honey before drinking.

Horseradish. *Armoracia rusticana* P. Gaertn., B. Mey. & Scherb. (ar-mor-ay'-see-o rus-ti-cay'-na) Cruciferae—Mustard Family

Horseradish is a deep-rooted, robust perennial native to southeast Europe and naturalized in North America. In bloom it may reach a height of five feet. The dock-like lower leaves have wavy-scalloped edges and may be two feet long and nine inches wide. Sometimes the leaves are divided into jagged linear segments. As the leaves progress up the flower stalk they become miniaturized and scarcely reconizable as horseradish leaves. The flowers are tiny and white, and appear in June. The root stock may be two feet long and two to four inches wide.

Propagate by root cuttings in the spring or fall. The large tap root will produce numerous lateral rootlets. Take those that are pencil thick and about two to eight inches long, cut them square at the top and slanted at the lower end. Place one foot apart six to twelve inches below

Horseradish

the soil's surface. Leaves will soon appear. Plants can be grown from any division of the root, though cuttings from the top crown are best. Horseradish may also be grown from seed, but it is not readily available.

A rampant energetic grower in a deep-dug, rich, moist soil, horseradish likes full sun or partial shade. Keep the soil loose and free of weeds. Dig compost around the roots in autumn. A pH of 6 to 8 is best.

Harvest in the fall of the second year. After that time the roots may become pithy and bitter. Plant anew every year or two, but reserve one spot in the garden for horseradish. Like comfrey, once established it will always be there unless every scrap of root is removed. The fresh roots can be stored in a cellar in moist sand or outside covered by earth that won't freeze in winter as you use them.

The young tender spring leaves can be boiled like spinach. The fresh root can be grated and used as a condiment on meats or fish. I make a horseradish spread by blending a cup of chopped root along with one-fourth cup vinegar, one-fourth cup olive oil, two teaspoons of honey, and two cloves of garlic. When you lift the lid off the blender, don't stick your nose into the cloud of fumes. The combination of sulphur compounds can literally knock you out!

The root is high in potassium and vitamin C, and contains appreciable amounts of calcium, phosphorus, iron, and vitamin B.

The root will stimulate appetite and aid digestion. It is laxative, diaphoretic, strongly diuretic, rubefacient, and antiseptic. If applied externally, it will give some people a rash with blisters. A cataplasm has been used to break up chest colds and to relieve rheumatic muscle pain. One teaspoon of the root in a glass of water with a little honey can be used as a gargle for sore throat.

The root contains an essential oil, almost identical to mustard oil, plus asparagine and sinigrin. Mustard oil has antibacterial and antifungal properties.

Hyssop. *Hysoppus officinalis L.*
(hiss′-op-us off-iss-i-nay′-lis)
Labiatae — Mint Family

Hyssop is a hardy shrub-like perennial native to the Mediterranean region. The erect stem, woody at the base, has a controlled growth making it a good plant for edging and borders. It grows from 1½ to 2 feet tall, and is either with or without hairs. The leaves are ¾ to 1½ inches long, lance-shaped, and have short petioles. The flowers occur in six-inch spikes with whorls of six to fifteen blossoms emerging from each axil. The flowers are generally a bright blue. White-, pink-, or rose-flowered cultivars also exist. Flowering is from June to October.

Hyssop is easily grown from seed sown directly in the garden, propagated from spring or fall root divisions, or from cuttings made from the vigorous summer tips. Plants should be given one to two foot spacings.

A calcareous, light, rocky soil and full sun are best. Hyssop will grow under partial shade, but becomes leggy. It will lose its pungent aroma if grown in a rich moist soil. An acre of hyssop may produce 1¼ tons or more, but the market for dried leaf is limited.

The young shoots and flowering tops can flavor tomato soups and sauces, but use sparingly.

The flowering tops or whole herb in

Hyssop

flower are harvested just as blooming begins, usually in midsummer. Tied in bunches, hyssop dries easily.

The tea is stomachic, diaphoretic, carminative, stimulating, and expectorant. Along with horehound, it is used for lung ailments including bronchitis and asthma. A gargle made from the leaves relieves sore throats. Externally, a tea, poultice, or strong bath of the leaves is used to relieve muscular rheumatism. One-fourth ounce of the herb to a pint of boiling water makes a medicinal infusion.

The essential oil contains pinocamphone, isopinocamphone, pinenes, camphene and other substances. The plant also contains up to 8 percent tannin, and a glucoside—hyssopin. Extracts of hyssop have shown antiviral effects against herpes simplex. The oil is used to make chartreuse and eau-de-cologne.

Lady's Mantle. *Alchemilla vulgaris L.*
(al-kem′-il-a vul-gay′-ris)
Rosaceae—Rose Family

Lady's mantle is a hardy perennial with elegant foliage and lacy mists of yellow blooms. It grows to 1½ feet tall and is

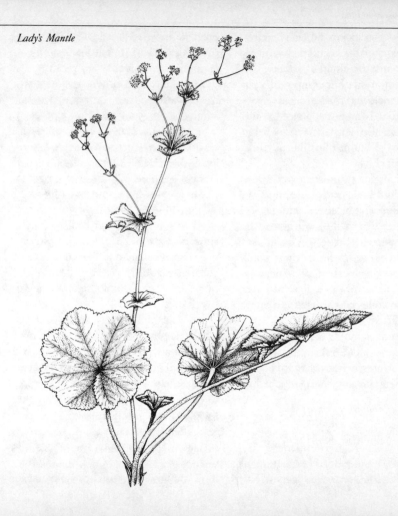

Lady's Mantle

native to Eurasia and sporadically naturalized in North America. The rounded leaves, two to eight inches in diameter, have plaited folds with seven to eleven lobes and tiny teeth. Sprays of small yellow petalless flowers bloom in June, lasting in the far north to August. Folded leaf-like stipules collar the stem. The tap root is stout and black.

Drops of dew form in the leaf folds and cups of stipules, giving lady's mantle an early morning jewel-like sparkle. This dew was thought to infuse subtle medicinal virtues from the leaf—the stuff of alchemist's potions. *Alchemilla* derives from an Arabic word *alkemelych* meaning alchemy.

Lady's mantle can be propagated from seed, but the seeds germinate slowly. Self-sown volunteers appear in the garden and can be transplanted in the spring. "Eyes" of the crown can be carefully divided, leaving some attached root for propagating new stock in the spring or fall.

Lady's mantle's taproot likes a deep-dug soil with good drainage. A poor, slightly acid soil will suffice for this plant. It grows in full sun or partial shade and is completely winter hardy. Once established, it requires little care. Plant on rocky inclines that may be hard to reach and maintain.

The root, harvested in spring or fall, and the leaves, harvested as the plant blooms in June, are used medicinally.

A decoction of the fresh root is a powerful styptic used to stop bleeding. The leaves are also astringent and styptic owing to their tannin content. They are used internally and externally to stop bleeding or profuse menstruation. One ounce of the dried leaves is added to a pint of water for medicinal purposes.

Lamb's Ear, Woolly Betony. *Stachys byzantina* C. Koch (*S. lantana* Jaqc. & *S. olympica*)
(stay'-kiss biz-an-tie'-na)
Labiatae—Mint Family

If one plant has received an appropriate common name it is lamb's ears. If you have the chance, close your eyes and rub this plant's leaves while imagining the texture of a lamb's ears. It's almost impossible to distinguish the two. *S. byzantina* is a hardy perennial native to Turkey and Western Asia, and is much enjoyed in North American gardens. Inevitably, upon first sight, a person unfamiliar with this plant will ask for its name. In a rich soil, lamb's ears may reach a height of 2½ feet. The densely woolly, grayish leaves, about four inches long and one inch wide, are oblong to spatular shaped. They grow in rosettes, forming a dense spreading mat of silvery-white foliage. In May or June, fuzzy pencil-thick stalks shoot up, bearing almost hidden mauve-rose flowers, each an inch long. About a month after flowering the plant goes to seed.

Lamb's ears can be propagated from seed, or better, by dividing the roots in spring or fall. Give plants six-inch spacings. It takes a sharp spade to cut through the thick mass of spreading rhizomes lamb's ears produces.

Lamb's ears need full sun, a moist, moderately rich soil, and good drainage for optimum growth. The soil should be slightly alkaline. This is a wonderful light-colored foliage plant for border plantings especially along pathways. It satisfies the eyes, nose, and sense of touch, and is best grown as an ornamental.

The leaves, however, can be harvested just before flowering. They have a mild aromatic taste which becomes apple-like upon drying and make a mild-flavored tea. After seeding, the leaf stalks should be cut to the height of the basal leaves.

Woundwort is another name for lamb's ears. The leaves are mildly astringent and have historically been applied to cuts to stop bleeding and used as an absorbent dressing.

Lavenders. *Lavandula angustifolia* Mill., *L. dentata* L., *L. multifida* L., *L. stoechas* L., *L.* × *hybrida* Balbiz ex Gingins (la-van′-doo-la an-gus-ti-foh′-li-us; den-tay′-ta; mul-tif′-i-da; stee′-kas; hi-bri′-da) Labiatae – Mint Family

There are about twenty species and numerous varieties of lavenders occurring mainly in the Mediterranean region, though some hail from as far east as India.

English lavender *L. angustifolia* is a two- to three-foot-tall perennial shrub with slightly hairy linear or lance-shaped leaves up to 2½ inches long. It produces one-half-inch-long blue-violet flowers arranged in whorls of six to ten blooms on loose 3½-inch-long spikes. Leaf-like bracts are in an opposite arrangement below each whorl. They are usually shorter than the three-sixteenths inch calyces. English lavender has many cultivars including the dwarf early blooming 'Munstead,' the white flowered 'Alba,' 'Hidcote,' a deep purple-flowered cultivar, and 'Rosea,' with rose-pink flowers, to name a few.

French or dentate lavender, *L. dentata*, grows to three feet in height. The leaves are grayish in color and covered with a soft fuzz. They are about 1¼ inches long, linear – oblong with well-defined rounded teeth at the margins. The tight spikes are up to 1¾ inches long and one-half inch in diameter. The one-fourth inch long purple flowers are offset by thin, purple, oblong- to oval-shaped bracts up to one-half inch in length. One variety has green rather than gray leaves.

L. multifida, fern leaf lavender, has lacy, finely divided fern-like leaves. Each segment is one-fourth to three-fourths inches long. The spikes are often in threes or solitary, up to 2½ inches long with one-half inch-long bluish corollas.

L. stoechas, Spanish lavender, is a shrub growing to four feet tall with linear to oblong, lance-shaped leaves about three-fourths inches long. The spikes are short and plump up to 1½ inches long and one-half inch in diameter. The three-eighths inch flowers are dark purple. This lavender is native to Spain and Portugal.

L. × *hybrida* Balbiz ex Gingins (*L. heterophylla*, Sweet Lavender, Taylor's Herb Garden's name) is a fast-growing perennial reaching four feet in height. The leaves are fuzzy, broad, lance-shaped to spatular-shaped, 1½ inches long, with compact groups of leaves. The compact spikes are up to three inches long. The bracts have sharply pointed tips, become enlarged toward the top of the spikes, and are sessile toward the top. Once flowering commences it continues through the growing season. This hybrid is found only in cultivation.

Lavenders can be grown from seed, cuttings, or root divisions. Cuttings taken in spring or fall are the best means of propagation. Seeds take about a month to germinate and should be planted indoors six to eight weeks before spring's final frost. Plants from cuttings or seeds grow very slowly the first year, often reaching only six to eight inches in height. They must be mulched or otherwise protected through the first winter.

Lavenders like a light, well-drained,

gravelly soil well-supplied with lime; pH should be between 6 and 8.3. *L. angustifolia* is the only species I've listed that will survive a hard, cold winter. The others hardly stand a freeze. Wet soils will inevitably winterkill the crown. A protected south-facing location is best. A heavy mulch should be provided after the ground freezes in late fall.

Harvest the buds just as the flowers are about to open. Dry in a well-ventilated space with subdued light.

Lavender is one of the most appreciated of fragrant herbs. Lavender oils are used as fragrance in pharmaceutical preparations and in cosmetic creams, lotions, soaps, perfumes, and colognes. I distinctly remember my first cup of lavender tea. It tasted more like a bar of soap than a beverage. Both *L. angustifolia* and *L. stoechas* are commercially produced for dried flowers and essential oil.

Lavender has a steady tradition of medicinal use since the time of Dioscorides, a first century A.D. Greek naturalist. It possesses tonic, stimulant, antispasmodic, carminative, sedative, stomachic, and diuretic qualities. Lavender tea, oil, or inhalants have been used for headaches, neuralgia, migraines, muscle spasms, rheumatism, and other ailments.

Lavender oil contains linalool, linalyl acetate, lavandulyl acetate, and over 100 other components. In tests with mice the oil has been found to be a central nervous system depressant.

Lemon Balm. *Melissa officinalis L.*
(mel-iss′-a off-iss-i-nay′-lis)
Labiatae – Mint Family

Every herb garden should harbor this herb with its strong but delicate lemon scent. It is an upright, tender perennial native to southern Europe and naturalized in England, France, and the eastern and western United States. Lemon balm grows to two feet high. Its stems are branching and hairy. The two- to three-inch-long leaves are oval or heart-shaped, deeply wrinkled, and have scalloped edges. The light blue to white flowers occur in whorls around the leaf axils. They are about one-half inch long and appear in May to August. One cultivar has variegated leaves.

Lemon balm is easy to grow from seed sown in the spring or early fall. Plants self-sow freely; lemon balm can become

Lemon Balm

a weed if young seedlings aren't transplanted or given to a needy herb gardener. Cuttings can be made from the vigorous summer growth or the roots can be divided, preferably in the springtime. Give seedlings one-foot spacings.

A fertile, moist, slightly acid to alkaline soil (pH 5 to 7.8) is best for lemon balm. It likes a cool habitat and thrives in moist open spots of California's redwood forest. If grown under full sun, lemon balm may wilt during hot, dry spells. Plants grown under shade tend to be larger and more succulent than those grown in direct sunlight. Light, dry soils cause the leaves to yellow. In regions where ground freezes and heaves, the crowns should be mulched during winter months. An acre may produce 800 to 1,800 pounds of dried herb.

Harvest just as the plant comes into bloom. Care should be taken not to bruise the leaves from the harvest through drying. Lemon balm dries quickly and easily but loses much of its lemon scent upon drying. When dry, store in tightly closed containers. If hung to dry in bunches, lemon balm can be rapidly processed by rubbing each bundle across a half-inch mesh screen. The leaves crumble and fall through the screen, leaving the processor with a handful of stems.

The fresh leaves make a refreshing tea, either iced or hot.

Carminative, diaphoretic, febrifuge, and mild sedative properties are attributed to lemon balm. A hot tea promotes sweating in colds accompanied by fever.

The volatile oil contains citral, citronellal, eugenol acetate and geraniol. In laboratory testing, hot water extracts have been shown to possess strong anti-viral qualities against Newcastle disease, herpes simplex, mumps, and other viruses. The oil also has antibacterial properties.

Lemon Verbena. *Aloysia triphylla* (L'Her) Britt. [*Lippia citriodora* (Ort.) HBK] (al-oiz´-i-a try-fil´-a)
Verbenaceae – Verbena Family

Lemon verbena is a deciduous shrub – losing most of its leaves in fall – native to Argentina, Chile, and Peru. In American gardens, it seldom grows to more than ten feet, but I've seen a twenty-five-foot tall specimen. It is rather scraggly. The long lance-shaped leaves (three to four inches), are entire or slightly toothed, have a strong lemon fragrance, and are arranged in whorls of three or four leaves. The flowers are small and inconspicuous, of a white to pale lavender color, and appear in July to September.

Lemon verbena is best propagated from stem cuttings. Kent Taylor of Taylor's Herb Gardens takes cuttings from pencil-sized or smaller greenwood. The cuttings have two leaf joints: one with leaves above the rooting medium, the other below. Three leaves are left on the upper joint; the outer half of each leaf is cut off. Mid- and late summer stems take best.

This fragrant shrub likes a moist, moderately rich, sandy soil with good drainage in full sun. Lemon verbena is not winter-hardy where temperatures dip below 20 ° F. In preparing for a Maine winter, I cut plants back to the ground, dig up the roots, and heel them in moist sand in a cellar. Water the roots every few weeks to keep them from drying out. Once danger of frost has passed the following spring, replant the roots. If you use this method, plants grow up to four feet high each year. They may also be grown in a large pot and brought indoors for the winter, though often the change in climate will cause the leaves to drop. Large plantings have produced three-fourths to two tons of dried herb per acre.

Lemon verbena makes a fine herb tea and can be used in potpourris, floated in iced mint tea, or just hung about the

Lemon Verbena

kitchen for its lemon fragrance. It has limited medicinal use. Sedative, febrifuge, stomachic, and antispasmodic properties have been attributed to the herb. It may be used to settle indigestion or dyspepsia.

The essential oil contains limonene, dipentene, cineole, citral, and other substances.

Licorice. *Glycyrrhiza glabra L.*
(glis-sir-ize'-a gla'-bra)
Leguminosae – Pea Family

Licorice is a fairly hardy perennial native to southern Europe west to Pakistan and northern India. It is herbaceous or slightly woody and grows to a height of three to seven feet. The leaves are divided into oval leaflets, one inch long, oppositely arranged along a mid-rib similar to acacia. Each leaf is arranged alternately on the main stalk. The small light blue or purple pea-like flowers are borne on four-to six-inch spikes arising from the leaf axils. The small pods containing two to four kidney-shaped seeds look like immature pea pods. The main root-stock is a deep penetrating taproot burrowing from three to six feet below the soil's surface. Creeping horizontal stolons branch from the main root

Licorice

traveling up to six feet just under the soil. In the second year, shoots emerge from the stolon buds.

Licorice can be grown from seed sown in spring in well-prepared seed beds, but seedlings are slow to develop. Licorice is usually propagated by dividing the root crown or by stolon cuttings. Eight- to twenty-inch stolon cuttings with a bud or "eye" can be planted vertically about an inch below the surface, spacing the plantings at eighteen inches. This is best performed in the spring. Plants will grow to a one-foot height the first year, and onions or other shallow-rooted crops can be sown with first-year licorice plantings.

Soil should be dug to a depth of two feet or more and manured well the autumn prior to planting. A moist, fairly rich, well-drained sandy loam is best. Soil pH should be slightly alkaline (7 to 8). Licorice is a plant for southern climates, dying in a hard freeze. Warm regions and mild climates insure vigorous growth.

The main root and stolons are harvested in the fall of the third or fourth years—preferably the latter. All pieces of the root must be removed from the ground, for like comfrey and horseradish, once established, licorice can become weedy. It is best to harvest plants that haven't gone to seed as the sweet sap is exhausted by the flowering process. Pinch flowers back as they develop. An acre has been reported to produce 2½ to 5 tons of root. The main root should be split as it is slow to dry.

An extract of licorice is made by crushing the fresh or stored roots, then boiling or passing steam through them and evaporating the liquid, leaving a thick paste or solid black glossy substance with a sharp fracture.

Medicinally the dried peeled root has been decocted to allay coughs, sore throat, laryngitis, and urinary and intestinal irritations. The root is expectorant, diuretic, demulcent, antitussive, anti-inflammatory, and mildly laxative. It has proven helpful in inflammatory upper respiratory disease, Addison's disease, and gastric and duodenal ulcers. Side effects may develop in ulcer treatment. Licorice may increase venous and systolic arterial pressure causing some people to experience edema, cardiac asthma, and hypertension. In some countries, licorice has been used to treat cancers. Licorice stick, the sweet earthy flavored stolons, are chewed. Licorice chew sticks blackened Napoleon's teeth.

Up to 24 percent of the root weight is glycyrrhizin, the plant's major active component. Glycyrrhizin may cause hypertension from potassium loss, sodium retention, and an increase of extracellular fluid and plasma volume. It is fifty times sweeter than sugar. Licorice also reportedly contains steroid hormones, but their relation to licorice's biological activity is yet to be determined, though extracts have been shown to be estrogenic in laboratory animals.

Licorice extracts are used to flavor tobacco, chewing gums, confections, soft drinks, liqueurs, ice cream, and baked goods. It is also an ingredient in cough medications, laxatives, and anti-smoking preparations. Licorice increases the foam in beer. It is one of the most widely consumed herbs in the world.

Lion's Ear, lion's tail. *Leonotis leonurus* (L.) R. Br.
(lee-on-ah′-tis lee-on-ur′-us)
Labiatae—Mint Family

Lion's ear is a tender branching shrub native to South Africa. Its vibrant orange whorls of velvety flowers make it one of the mint family's most striking ornamentals. It usually grows to five feet in height in the garden, though it may reach seven feet. The plant is covered by short hairs. The opposite oblong or lance-shaped leaves reach two to five inches in length and are coarsely toothed. The whorls (verticillasters) of fuzzy 2½ inch-long orange blossoms emerge from the leaf axils. Blooming may begin as early as June in southern California, lasting into autumn.

Lion's ear is best propagated by spring cuttings. They strike more readily than those made in summer or fall.

Full sun and a dry, sandy, slightly alkaline soil with good drainage suits *Leonotis* culture. This is a subtropical species and will not survive a hard freeze. Where temperatures dip below 20° F. in winter months, lion's ear will have to be brought indoors. Before an autumn frost, cut the plant back to the root, pot it, and bring it into a greenhouse. If given enough sun, lion's ear can be forced to bloom in the greenhouse during winter months. It is a fabulous border plant in temperate climates. At Taylor's Herb Gardens, a hundred-foot row of lion's ear graces the west end of the display garden.

Lion's ear has been used to promote menstruation, as a snakebite antidote, and to relieve epilepsy, cardiac asthma, and leprosy. In South Africa several species of *Leonotis* are referred to as *dagga-dagga*. Its leaves or resin are smoked alone or with tobacco for a feeble euphoric effect similar to, but weaker than, marijuana.

The plant contains a resin and essential oil.

Lobelia. *Lobelia inflata L.*
(loh-beel'-i-a in-fla'-ta)
Campanulaceae – Bellflower Family

Lobelia is an erect hairy annual growing in the wild to one foot in height, though often reaching two to three feet in cultivation. The leaves are mostly sessile, oval about two inches long and half as broad. The pale blue-white, irregular flowers, one-half by one-fourth inch long, are arranged on a spike at the end of the plant's stalk. Typical of the *Lobelia* genus, the top throat of the corolla is split its entire length. The seed capsules resemble an inflated bladder (hence the specific name *inflata*) and are filled with tiny black seeds.

Lobelia grows in fields, open woods, and along the banks of streams and ponds from Labrador to Georgia, and west to Arkansas. Flowering begins mid- to late summer, lasting until fall.

The seed is very small and must be sown on sifted or very well-prepared soil. Plant indoors in late February, sprinkling seed on the surface of the soil mix, lightly tamping it with a spatula. Place flats in trays of water to moisten soil through capillary action to prevent seeds from becoming displaced by surface watering. Seeds germinate in ten days and must have light in the red end of the spectrum to emerge. This can be supplied by sunlight or a couple of 200-watt incandescent bulbs mounted about thirty inches above the flats. When seedlings are about two months old, transplant them to larger flats at two-inch spacings or to individual pots. About one month later, plant in the field with eighteen-inch spacings. Seeds can also be carefully sown directly in the garden in spring or fall.

Lobelia will grow in a slightly acid clay loam but does best in a rich, moist loam. It will tolerate full sun or partial shade. An acre may produce 1,000 to

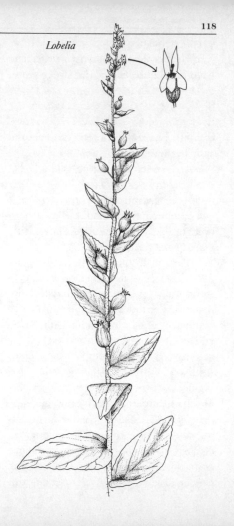

Lobelia

1,700 pounds of dried herb.

Harvest the whole herb in flower after a few seed capsules develop. Lobelia dries easily.

Over the past 200 years lobelia has sparked much controversy. Samuel Thomson (1760-1843), the guru of nineteenth-century botanic physicians, claimed to have discovered lobelia's medicinal virtues in 1793. However, in 1785, the Reverand Dr. Manasseh Cutler of Hamilton, Massachusetts, published the first mention of lobelia in "Account of Indigenous Vegetables," a paper delivered before the American Academy of Arts & Sciences. Thomson was an exceptionally popular empiric physician who popularized the use of lobelia, calling it his "No. 1" herb in a "course" of medicine which included induced vomiting, sweating, stimulating, and correcting the "morbid" action of the system.[12]

In 1809 Thomson was arrested for murder for allegedly administering a fatal dose of lobelia. In a colorful trial, he was acquitted due to lack of evidence proving willful intention to harm the deceased and lack of proof satisfactorily concluding that lobelia was, in fact, a poison. As there were no laws at the time against practicing medicine without a license, that was not an issue. The trial sparked a great deal of interest in Thomson, lobelia, and the lack of legislation defining who was eligible to practice medicine. Today, Thomsonian medicine is perpetuated in such popular books as Jethro Kloss's *Back to Eden*.

The plant's efficacy and toxicity ratio is still an open question. Its strong emetic action earned it the names "emetic herb," "gag root," and "puke weed." Simply chewing a leaf or seed capsule stimulates the vagus nerve, leaving the stomach and throat with an acrid burning sensation. You may feel nauseous without vomiting or experience violent vomiting. Action depends on the dose and the potency of the herb which deteriorates rapidly after drying; much commercially available lobelia is weak.

Lobelia has been smoked or used in powdered form or as tea to relieve asthmatic paroxysms. It is also strongly diaphoretic, expectorant, and sedative. Fevers, whooping cough, insect bites, bruises, and sprains have been treated with lobelia.

Lobelia contains over fourteen alkaloids including the pyridine alkaloid lobeline. Like nicotine, lobeline acts first as a central nervous system stimulant, then as a depressant. Overdose can cause convulsion and collapse. Lobeline is used in commercial over-the-counter anti-smoking lozenges.

Because of the conflicting nature of information available on lobelia, it must be used with caution.

Lovage. *Levisticum officinale* W.D.J. Koch (le-vis′-ti-kum off-iss-i-nail′-ee) Umbelliferae – Carrot Family

Lovage is a stout, hardy perennial native to southern Europe and naturalized in some parts of North America. It generally grows from four to six feet tall, though I've seen it stretch to over eight feet. The stems are smooth, hollow, erect, and thick. The compound divided leaves have long stalks (to twenty-four inches). The leaves are alternate on the stalk and individual leaflets are broad, flat, and wedge-shaped – much like celery leaves. Tiny yellow flowers occur on loose umbels. The elliptical curved seeds have three prominent wings on each mericap. The vertical rhizome is strongly aromatic, white, and fleshy, three to five inches long, one to three inches thick, with lateral rootlets up to eight inches long.

Lovage is easily grown from seed sown in the spring or fall. Fall-sown seed may not germinate until the following spring, but usually seed germinates within two weeks. In early spring, roots can also be divided to increase stock. Give plants eight- to twelve-inch spacings.

Lovage will do well in almost any garden soil, but thrives best in a deep, rich, moist loam with good drainage. Soil pH range is between 5.5 and 7.5. Full sun or partial shade is acceptable. Experimental plantings have shown an acre may produce about 1,000 pounds of root in the third year.

The leaves, stems, roots, and seeds are all useful. Leaves may be harvested and dried in the second or third year before plants bloom. Stems and leaves can be used fresh. The roots are best harvested in the fall of the third year. In autumn, harvest the seeds as they begin to turn light brown. Like angelica, lovage seeds are subject to aphid infestations. Its succulent leaves are best dried on screens

under low forced heat rather than being hung to dry.

The fresh leaves and peeled stems can be chopped into salads. The leaves make a rather pungent and unique-flavored celery substitute. Use half as much lovage as you would celery. I like a sprinkling of the chopped leaves on carrots, cabbage, potatoes, and in tomato dishes. The root can be candied like calamus root.

Medicinally the root is used as an aromatic stimulant, carminative, diaphoretic, emmenagogic, and diuretic. Indigestion, colic, flatulence, and menstrual problems are among the ailments treated with an infusion of lovage root.

The oil contains butyl-phthalidine, umbelliferone, bergapten, terpineol, coumarins, and acids. It is used as fragrance in soaps, lotions, and perfumes. Manufactured foods such as liqueurs, baked goods, and meats are flavored with lovage oil.

Maidenhair Fern. *Adiantum pedatum L.*
(a-di-ayn'-tum ped-ay'-tum)
Polypodiaceae—Polypody Family

Maidenhair, one of the most well-known

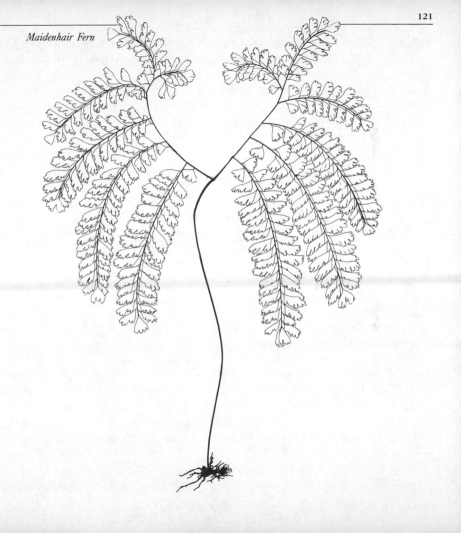

Maidenhair Fern

and appreciated ferns, is not often considered an herb, but this illusive inhabitant of dim-lit, rich, moist woods has a long history of medicinal and practical use by Europeans and American Indians. The genus *Adiantum* has over 200 species, mostly native to tropical America, though a few species grow in North America. The lacy fronds stand up to 1½ feet high and the leaves (pinnae) may be 1½ feet across. Sometimes called five-finger fern, *Adiantum's* leaves fork at the plant's summit making five or more hand-shaped divisions. The individual pinnules (leaflets) are four-sided, oblong, and wedge-shaped. Two edges of the pinnule are deeply notched. Spores develop at the tips of the notched edges which roll back to cover the spores, forming indusa. The stems are wiry and slender with a brownish-black luster. Fine bluish hairs cover the uncurling spring fronds (croziers) and the young leaflets are tinted red. Creeping rootstocks send up fronds at intervals throughout the growing season. The roots are slender, branched, and dark. Maidenhair occurs throughout the United States in moist woods. There are several varieties and forms of *A. pedatum*.

Perhaps no other fern enjoys cultivation as much as maidenhair. It is easily propagated from root division in the spring or fall. Plant in a spot where the rootstocks can spread.

Maidenhair favors deep to light shade in a moist, rich soil. It will tolerate a pH of 4.5 to 7. A slightly acid soil is best. The whole plant can be gathered for fall use. It dries quickly and easily.

Some Indian tribes used the dark polished stems of maidenhair for basket weaving. Ashes of the leaves are rubbed on the hair to make long, shiny, black strands. In Arab countries, a mix of olive oil, vinegar, and the ashes are used to grow hair on bald scalp patches caused by ringworm. Some Indians used an infusion of the leaves as a hair wash. To add body and luster to hair, boil a handful of the leaves in a pint of water for ten minutes. Cool, strain, and use as a final rinse. Northwest tribes chewed the leaves to stop internal bleeding.

Maidenhair can be considered a stimulant, demulcent, expectorant, and mild astringent. Maidenhair will activate the lungs' mucous membranes causing the expectoration of accumulated wastes.

A tea of the leaves will help soothe a sore throat, allay coughing, and break up the congestion of asthma or other pulmonary ailments. This herb is mild so the tea needs to be strong. Infuse an ounce of leaves in a pint of water. The taste is slightly aromatic and sweet with bitter overtones.

Maidenhair contains a little tannin and minute traces of an essential oil.

Marjoram. *Origanum majorana L.* (*Majorana hortensis* Moench)
(or-i-gay'-num ma-jor-ay'-na)
Labiatae – Mint Family

Marjoram is a tender, bushy perennial which must be grown as an annual in most parts of the United States. It reaches a height of two feet and is smooth or hairy. The leaves are one-fourth to one inch long, oval, entire, with short petioles on the lower leaves, and sessile upper leaves. The veins are somewhat raised. The spikelets are borne in terminal panicles on short branches. Each spikelet is one-fourth to one-half inch long. The bracts are small, rounded, and glistening with oil glands. The calyx has one lip with a deep slot down one side. One-eighth-inch long flowers are white, pale lilac or pink.

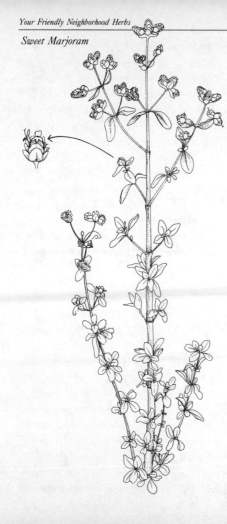

Sweet Marjoram

Marjoram, native to north Africa and southwest Asia, and naturalized in southern Europe, blooms in late summer.

Marjoram is easily propagated by seeds sown in the spring or by summer cuttings. Winter indoors in pots and replant in spring after danger of frost has passed.

A light, fairly rich, well-drained, slightly alkaline soil (pH 7 to 8) in full sun is favorable.

Harvest as soon as blooming commences. It dries easily.

Marjoram is sweeter, somewhat more piquant than oregano. It's great with tomato dishes, meats, onions, brussels sprouts, and mushrooms, and is a pleasant surprise in salads. The leaves contain up to 13 percent protein and are high in vitamins A and C.

Carminative, diaphoretic, antispasmodic, and diuretic properties have been attributed to marjoram. In laboratory experiments, extracts of marjoram have been reported to inhibit herpes simplex. The oil has been used for toothache, and marjoram was once used for cancer.

The essential oil contains terpinenes, sabinene, linalool, carvacrol, cis-sabinene hydrate, *trans*-sabinene hydrate and over forty other components. Cis-sabinene hydrate is responsible for sweet marjoram's typical fragrance.

Mayapple. *Podophyllum peltatum* L. (po-doe'-fil-lum pel-tay'-tum) Berberidaceae – Barberry Family

Under the shade of pines and oaks in damp woods from Quebec to Florida, west to east Texas and Minnesota lives the indigenous perennial mayapple or American mandrake. It grows to a foot and a half high and one foot broad. Smooth, roundish leaves with three to seven lobes unfold like umbrellas in the early spring. One leaf sits atop first-year plants; on older plants, two leaves are borne on a forked petiole. Drooping from the axil of the forked petioles, one white waxy flower, one to two inches wide with six petals, blooms in May to June. Its odor is nauseating. The fruits, the mayapples, are the shape and size of large rose hips; they are pale banana-yellow, rarely red, and about 1¼ inches long. They have a sweet, slightly acid, hint-of-strawberry flavor. The root is a slender knotty creeping rhizome about one-fourth inch thick

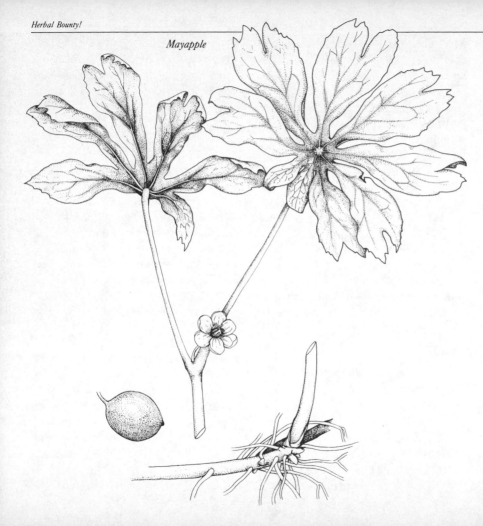

Mayapple

and several feet long.

In spring, mayapples are easily propagated by dividing any portion of the root.

A warm, shaded location, in light but moist soil, with a pH of 4 to 7 is preferable. Mayapple spreads in clumps and should be given a space where it will not crowd more delicate plants.

When ripe, the fruit is edible, but all other parts of the plant can be fatally toxic. The highest biological activity is from spring-dug roots.

When early settlers reached American shores, they found Indians using the root as a strong purgative, a liver cleanser, emetic, and worm expellant. The Penobscots of Maine used the root to treat cancers and warts. The Cherokees used drops of the fresh plant juice to treat deafness.

In the last century, mayapple was widely used as a cathartic, emetic, and vermifuge. The root was used for constipation, jaundice, hepatitis, fevers, and syphilis. Ingesting the root may cause vomiting, diarrhea, headache, bloating, stupor, and lowered blood pressure.

The root contains a resin— podophyllin consisting of lignan glycosides twenty percent of which is podophyllotoxin. Alpha-peltatin and beta-peltatin are also found in the root. Podophyllotoxin has shown promise as a remedy for certain cancers but is now considered ineffectual and too toxic for human use. It has been used to treat warts and some skin cancers. The peltatins are responsible for Mayapple's purgative effects. Podlophyllin can be fatally toxic.

Mints. *Mentha spicata* L., *M.* × *piperita* L., *M. suaveolens* J.F. Ehrh., *M. requienii* Benth.
(men′-tha spy-kay′-ta; pie-per-ee′-ta; swa-vee-oh′-lenz; rek-quee-en′-ee-eye)
Labiatae – Mint Family

There are only about twenty-five true species in the *Mentha* genus, but hybridization has created between two and three thousand variations. Most are Eurasian natives.

Spearmint *M. spicata* is a perennial growing to 2½ feet high, spreading by underground root runners. Its leaves are smooth, shiny, wrinkled, lance-shaped, sharply toothed, and about two inches long. The white, pink, or lilac flowers appear in mid-summer.

Peppermint bed, Sabbathday Lake Shaker Community.

M. × *piperita*, peppermint, a cross between *M. spicata* and *M. aquatica*, is a perennial growing to three feet tall, spreading by runners traveling across the soil's surface. The stem is usually reddish-purple and smooth. The leaves are similar to spearmint's, though often longer and less wrinkled. The pink or lilac flowers appear in mid- or late summer. *M.* × *piperita* var. *citrata*, orange or bergamot mint, has a distinctive odor like that of orange rind.

M. suaveolens, apple mint, is a perennial that grows to four feet tall with hairy, oval-shaped toothed leaves. The tight flower spikes branch and produce tiny white or pink flowers in midsummer. A smaller variegated cultivar, 'Variegata,' has a pineapple-like fragrance and is often sold under the name pineapple mint.

M. requienii, Corsican mint, is a native to Corsica and Sardinia. It is a creeping perennial herb forming a dense ground cover. The stems are thread-like and the leaves are entire, nearly round in shape, and no more than three-eighths inch long. It produces tiny, inconspicuous flowers in midsummer.

Because of mint's propensity to hybridize, buying and planting seeds is a futile effort in my opinion. You never know what will come up. Start with stem or root cuttings. At the Sabbathday Lake Shaker Community, I started a peppermint bed using ten seedlings in two-inch pots purchased from a local nursery. By the second summer of growth, the plants covered 100 square feet. In the third spring, I dug one quarter of the roots from the bed and planted them in ten 250-foot rows spaced four feet apart. After two months of growth, the plants completely covered the entire 250-by-50 foot area. It was impossible to distinguish the original rows. Any piece of root with a joint or node (about every inch) can produce a plant. Divide the root runners in spring.

Mints require a rich moist soil with good drainage; pH should be neutral to slightly alkaline. Full sun is necessary except for Corsican mint, which requires at least 50 percent shade. If planted in a small garden, mints should stand alone or have some kind of growth barrier like metal or tile placed below the soil around the beds. This will prevent the roots from taking over the garden.

The largest organic herb farm in North America, Trout Lake Farm in Trout Lake, Washington, has about fifty acres of peppermint, twenty-five of spearmint, and twenty of catnip, to name a few crops. The farm is nestled about ten miles south of Mount Adam's 12,000-foot peak. Lon Johnson, the farm's owner, plants certified mint stock from a state university experiment station. Young plants are cultivated with a special harrow until they reach a height of about four inches, when they are cultivated with tractor-mounted beet hoes and hand hoes. As the runners fill in between the rows, hand hoeing becomes particularly important. Trout Lake's fields are virtually weed free without the use of herbicides. The mints are sometimes harvested twice each season, as they reach full bloom. Harvesting is performed with a cutter bar, similar to that used for harvesting hay, then windrowed with a hay rake, and allowed to dry in the field for a day, weather permitting. The following morning, when the dew has dried from the leaves, the rows are turned with a windrow turner and allowed to dry for another day. When the leaves have dried until they easily "crack" from the stems, a combine is run through the field to separate stem and leaf material. The leaves are transferred from the combine's bin into heavy-gauge plastic bags where they are stored until cut and sifted at the farm's milling facilities. Trout Lake Farm's herbs are the highest quality available. Between 800 and 2,000 pounds of mint can be produced on an acre.

Peppermint is probably the most heavily consumed herb tea in North America. Peppermint and spearmint are often neglected as culinary herbs but can be used in tossed and potato salads, desserts, beverages, carrot dishes, or with sauteed parsnips.

Mints are high in calcium, vitamin A, vitamin C, and riboflavin, and contain phosphorus, potassium, and niacin.

Medicinally, peppermint is carminative, stomachic, stimulant, and tonic. A tea is useful for allaying insomnia, upset stomachs, nervous tension, migraines, colds, cramps, and many other minor ailments.

Peppermint oil contains menthol, menthone, menthyl acetate, and menthofuran. Spearmint oil contains primarily carvone. Extracts of peppermint have proven effective against several viruses. The United States produces more than 80 percent of the world's peppermint and spearmint oil.

Nettle. *Urtica dioica L.* and related species (er-ti′-ka die-oh′-i-ka)
Urticaceae – Nettle Family

About fifty species of nettles grow throughout the world. *Urtica dioica* is a Eurasian native widely naturalized in North America. Most people neglect this plant – until they walk through a patch while wearing short pants. Nettle is a perennial growing from two to six feet tall. The ovate sharp-pointed leaves have

Stinging Nettle

a heart-shaped base and are deeply toothed. Leaves may reach six inches in length. Both the leaves and the fibrous stems are covered with tiny, hollow, silica-tipped hairs which release an irritant when touched. Drooping from the leaf axils, racemes or panicles of inconspicuous greenish flowers emerge from June to September. The plant has a creeping persistent rootstock, forming extensive patches.

Nettles can be grown from seed, cuttings, or root divisions. Divisions are best made in autumn after the leaves have died back.

A damp, rich soil under full sun or partial shade is preferable. In their native habitat, nettles will often grow along edges of streams or in moist pastures. Reportedly when one nettle is planted among ten seedlings of such aromatic herbs as valerian, marjoram, sage, peppermint, and angelica, nettles will substantially increase the oil content of those herbs. When added to compost piles, nettles activate the decomposition process. Nettles themselves compost into a rich humus.

Harvest in May or June before nettles begin flowering. Handle fresh plants with gloves. The leaves dry quickly. Once cooked or dried, nettles lose their sting.

The sting can be neutralized by rubbing the affected area with either mashed jewel weed leaves (*Impatiens pallida* or *I. biflora*), yellow dock leaves (*Rumex crispus*), or the juice of nettles.

The spring shoots make a tasty green when cooked. The dried herb can be sprinkled in salads, soups, vegetables, and other foods for a subtle saline flavor and a rich supply of iron, magnesium, potassium, calcium, vitamin A, and protein.

The leaves have diuretic, astringent, blood building, depurative, and galactogenic properties. An infusion reportedly increases blood hemoglobin. The powdered leaves and juice will lessen bleeding from excessive menstruation, nose bleeds, and hemorrhoids. Smoke inhaled from burning leaves has been used to treat asthma and bronchitis. Nettles stimulate blood circulation and have been used as a spring tonic to clear chronic skin ailments.

The stinging hairs contain formic acid, histamine, and acetylcholine.

Oreganos. *Origanum vulgare* L., *O. heracleoticum* L., *O. onites* L., *O. dictamnus* L.
(or-i-gay'-num vul-gay'-ree, her-ak-lee-ot'-i-kum, oh-nye'-teez, dik-tam'-nus)
Labiatae—Mint Family

Oregano more properly refers to a flavor rather than one particular plant. *O. heracleoticum* is commercially cultivated and sold as oregano along with *O. vulgare* and *O. onites*. *Lippia graveolens* of the verbena family is grown in Mexico and sold as Mexican oregano. Other plants producing "oregano" include members of the genera *Coleus, Salvia, Satureja, Thymus, Monarda, Hedeoma, Calamintha,* and *Lantana*. In essence, plants containing high percentages of the phenols carvacrol and lesser amounts of thymol in their essential oils have an "oregano" flavor and aroma.

The genus *Origanum* contains about twenty species, five of which are commonly grown in herb gardens. In the mint family, this genus is characterized by tight cylindrical heads of sessile flowers called spikelets or spicules. Leaf-like bracts cover the flowers just as shingles overlap on a roof. The oreganos are dwarf shrubs or

Oregano

annual, biennial, or perennial herbs native to the Mediterranean region and central Asia.

O. vulgare L., oregano or wild marjoram, is a hairy perennial growing to 2½ feet tall, often branching at the top. The leaves are opposite, oval, entire or toothed, and up to 1½ inches long. The flower heads are in a panicle or corymb, each spikelet being up to 1⅛ inches long. The bracts are purple. Each calyx has five equal-sized teeth. The flowers are white-purple and about one-fourth inch long. Flowering begins in late July and lasts into September. The species has many variants. *O. vulgare* 'Aureum' has yellow leaves. *O. vulgare* 'Viride' has green bracts and white flowers.

O. heracleoticum L. native to southeast Europe, resembles *O. vulgare*, and in fact, was once classified as one of its varieties. It too has five equal teeth on the calyces. The bracts are usually one-eighth inch long, are densely covered with oil glands on the lower surface, and are green or purple (rare). Flowers are white, or infrequently pink.

O. onites L., pot marjoram, is a hairy perennial growing to two feet in height. The leaves are oval or rounded, one-fourth to three-fourths inch long, sessile, and sparsely toothed. The flowers are in a dense terminal corymb up to three inches across. Each spikelet is about three-fourths inch long. The bracts are pointed and about one-eighth inch long. The one-fourth inch flowers are white, sometimes purple. It is a tender plant and not cultivated as widely as other species. It is a close relative of sweet marjoram, both having calyces rounded at the top with a deep slit down one side. Pot marjoram is a Mediterranean native.

O. dictamnus L., dittany of Crete, is the genus's most distinctive looking plant. It is a tender perennial growing to a foot in height, with opposite, rounded or oval, white woolly leaves. The loose panicles of three-eighths inch long bracts have a hop-like appearance. Flowers are pink and about one-half inch long. It blooms in the summer or autumn and hails from the isle of Crete.

You can propagate oreganos from seeds, stem cuttings, or root divisions, but seeds are sometimes slow to germinate. Both dittany of Crete and pot marjoram are not hardy in cold climates and must be started anew each year. It is best to propagate oreganos asexually, as seed grown plants may not be true to flavor or completely flavorless. When buying plants, stroke the leaves and make sure the plant has some fragrance.

Oreganos like a light, well-drained, slightly alkaline soil with full sun. In a rich, moist soil, their aroma and flavor is weak.

Harvest as plants begin to bloom.

Oregano contains vitamin A, niacin, phosporus, potassium calcium, iron and traces of zinc.

I sometimes wondered why my grandmother wasn't familiar with oregano from childhood, until I discovered the post-war baby boom generation was the first group of Americans to grow up with oregano. After World War II, G.I.s who had tasted oregano-rich pizza in Italy made it popular in the United States. Oregano is good with tomato dishes, meats, omelettes, beans, and deviled eggs, and has a special affinity with basil.

Stimulant, carminative, diaphoretic, nervine, and emmenagogic properties have been attributed to oregano. It has been used in indigestion, headaches, nervous tension, insect bites, toothaches, and coughs.

The oil contains carvacrol and thymol as the primary components. These two phenols may constitute as much as 90 percent of the oil. They possess fungicidal and worm expellant properties.

Parsley. *Petroselinum crispum* (Mill.) Nyman ex A.W. Hill
(pet-ro-sel-eye′-num kris′-pum)
Umbelliferae—Carrot Family

Perhaps no other herb is as familiar in its fresh form as parsley. What plate of restaurant food is served without a sprig tucked to the side of the main course? At meal's end it is often the only thing left on the plate, even though it may well have been the most nutritious part of the meal.

Parsley is native to Europe and western Asia. It is a biennial growing to six to eight inches the first year, then reaching three feet in height when in flower. The smooth, bright green leaves are deeply divided. Tiny yellowish-green flowers are borne on loose compound umbels. There are numerous cultivated varieties. *P. crispum* var. *crispum* has curled and crisped leaves. Its cultivar, 'Perfection,' produces stiff erect stems, making a clean bunch, easy to harvest. 'Triplecurled' has tightly crisped dark green leaves, looking from a distance like broccoli heads. *P. crispum* var. *neapolitanum* Italian parsley, has flat leaves similar to celery. *P. crispum* var. *tuberosum*, turnip root parsley or Hamburg parsley, produces thick parsnip-like taproots and has tall fern-like leaves. Parsley leaves stay green during winter. When in Maine, I mulched parsley with straw and in the middle of January, excavated through snow to uncover fresh leaf bunches for salads.

The key to growing parsley from seed is patience. Seeds may take three to six weeks to germinate. Plant anytime from spring to autumn; but for an early crop, sow parsley one-fourth inch deep at the same time peas are sown. A frost or two won't deter young seedlings. Parsley can be sown indoors, but seedlings transplant with difficulty. Direct sown plantings are best. Treat parsley as an annual, planting anew each year. The second-year leaves tend to be tough and bitter. Once germinated, thin seedlings to stand at six- to eight-inch spacings. Six pounds of seed

Parsley, Sabbathday Lake Shaker Community.

be dried quickly under forced heat to retain a rich green color.

What better herb for culinary use than parsley? Add to salads, tomato dishes, baked potatoes, fish, meat, peas, egg dishes and branch out into parsley butter and parsley sauces. The list is endless. The roots of Hamburg parsley can be grated in salads or soup stocks and cooked like parsnips. Harvest roots in early spring, slice very thin, and sauté in butter with the first fresh mint leaves of the season—delicious!

Parsley contains up to 22 percent protein. It is high in vitamin A, vitamin C, fiber, calcium, iron, magnesium, potassium, and riboflavin, and contains some niacin, thiamin, and phosphorus.

The seeds and leaves have been used medicinally to treat indigestion, jaundice, menstrual problems, gall stones, coughs, asthma, and dropsy. They are diuretic, stomachic, carminative, depurative, expectorant, and emmenogogic. The leaves can be chewed as a breath freshener.

The essential oil from the seeds contains apiole, myristicin, and alpha-pinene among other substances. A fixed oil in the seed is comprised mainly of

will sow an acre.

A fertile, moist, sandy loam with 6 to 8 pH is best. Good drainage is essential, especially if you intend plants to survive a winter so you can collect seeds the following year. A friable, double-dug bed serves parsley culture well.

Harvest the leaves once they reach a height of about eight inches and at any time thereafter. Hamburg roots are dug in the fall of the first year or the following spring. They can be stored in a cellar in moist sand. Italian parsley is grown for dried leaf or "parsley flakes." Leaves must petroselinic acid. The leaf oil contains bergapten and is used in oriental perfumes and men's colognes. Parsley preparations are reported to be antimicrobial, laxative, and tonic on uterine muscles.

Passion flower, maypop. *Passiflora incarnata* L.
(pass-i-flor´-a in-kar-nay´-ta)
Passifloraceae – Passion Flower Family

There are over 400 species of passion flowers, mostly from tropical America with two species, *P. incarnata* and *P. lutea*, indigenous to the southern United States. *P. incarnata* is a perennial climber found from Virginia to Florida, west to Texas and Missouri. The fast-growing vines climb with tendrils, and often reach thirty feet in length. They die back to the root when hit by frost. The dull green leaves are four to six inches long, with three to five broad, deep lobes which have serrated margins. The fantastic floral assemblage is one of the most intricate and remarkable of the plant world. Above the ten-part receptacle is a corona with white-purple thread-like filaments. Five stamens with hammer-like anthers surround a three-parted style, topped with reddish stigmas protruding from the flower's center like the antennae of a space ship. The flowers are two to three inches across. The yellowish edible fruits – called maypops – are about the size of a hen's egg and are filled with seeds surrounded by a sweet mucilaginous flesh.

Passion flowers spread from root runners and can be grown from seeds, or cuttings, or by dividing the runners in autumn.

Passion flowers need a place to climb. They often grow along fence rows or climb trees along railroad tracks. A slightly acidic sandy loam with full sun will create a good patch. In areas where temperatures dip below -15° F., passion flowers will not survive the winter.

The above-ground plant parts are harvested when in bloom. The fruits are sweet and edible. They contain some calcium, iron, and phosphorus.

Passion flower is a gentle herbal tranquilizer and antispasmodic. A tea can be used for insomnia caused by worry and overwork, tension headaches, and neuralgia. Passion flower will slightly reduce blood pressure while increasing respiration and depressing motor activity. Extracts of the rhizome were formerly used to treat hemorrhoids, burns, and erysipelas.

The plant contains variable amounts of indole alkaloids including harman, harmine, harmaline, passiflorine, plus flavonoids, sterols, and sugars.

Pennyroyal. *Mentha pulegium* L., *Hedeoma pulegiodes* (L.) Pers.
(men´-tha pul-ee´-ji-um head-ee-oh-ma pul-ee-ji-oi´-dees)
Labiatae – Mint Family

European pennyroyal, *Mentha pulegium*, is a perennial member of the same genus to which peppermint and spearmint belong. It is native to Europe and west Asia, grows to a foot tall, and has rather a sprawling habit. The opposite leaves are smooth or slightly hairy, oval or roundish, about an inch long, with small or no teeth. Tight whorls of small irregular lilac flowers bloom from July to August. It spreads by underground runners. *M. pulegium* var. *gilbraltarica* has fuzzy white leaves. *M. pulegium* has become naturalized in a wide variety of California plant communities.

Hedeoma pulegioides, American pennyroyal, is an annual plant of open woods

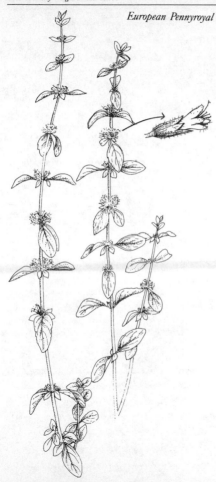

European Pennyroyal

and fields from eastern North America. It grows to fifteen inches in height with leaves three-fourths inch wide and about one inch long, resembling those of *M. pulegium*. The one-fourth inch long bluish-purple flowers appear in summer in whorls around upper leaf axils.

H. pulegioides must be grown from seed sown in the spring or fall. *M. pulegium* is best propagated by dividing root runners in spring or early September and by summer stem cuttings. Space plants eight to twelve inches apart.

Pennyroyal needs fairly rich, sandy loam, with a good supply of moisture and a pH range from 5.5 to 8. Full sun or partial shade are tolerable. European pennyroyal must have room to spread. After the plant flowers, it shoots out root runners from the crown. A pennyroyal lawn needs only occasional mowing. North of Pennsylvania, pennyroyal will need a winter mulch. At the Sabbathday Lake Shaker gardens, we had three 250-foot rows from which we harvested about eighty pounds of dried herb. One winter I decided not to mulch the bed. Even though most of the pennyroyal winterkilled, enough runners survived to more than double the size of the original planting. An acre of either species may produce 1,000 to 1,400 pounds of dried material.

Pennyroyal has carminative, diaphoretic, and emmenagogic properties. It has been used to settle upset stomachs and nervous headaches. In recent years, pennyroyal tea has become popular to promote menstrual flow, relieve cramps, and in some instances to induce abortion. However, sad consequences have resulted from using pennyroyal oil for such purposes. In 1978 a Denver woman died after ingesting a one-ounce dose of pennyroyal oil reportedly to induce abortion—though she apparently wasn't pregnant. A rash of newspaper articles condemning pennyroyal herb followed. Speaking at the third International Herb Symposium held in 1979 at the University of California, Santa Cruz, Dr. Norman Farnsworth of the University of Illinois, Chicago, put the case in proper perspective. You would have to ingest about seventy-five gallons of strong pennyroyal tea (within a short time) to equal the effect of a one-ounce dose of pennyroyal oil. He also noted that almost any plant-derived essential oil in a one-ounce dose could be fatal.

European and American pennyroyal are interchangeable. Pulegone is the chief constituent of their oils. Both can be used as an insect repellant.

Perilla. *Perilla frutescens* (L.) Britt.
(per-il'-la frou'-tes-senz)
Labiatae—Mint Family

Perilla is an erect, branching, tender annual native to parts of Asia and naturalized in North America. It reaches a height of four feet. The leaves are about three inches broad, oval or rounded, up to five inches long, toothed, with hairs especially on the vein. The foliage is ruffled with a metallic lustre. The flowers are white to light lavender, hidden by longer calyces, and borne on a terminal raceme up to six inches long. In autumn, the dried calyces rattle as you walk through a wild patch, earning perilla the name "rattlesnake weed" in the southern United States. It blooms from August to October. *Perilla frutescens* 'Atropurpurea' has dark purple leaves. *P. frutescens* 'Crispa' has strongly wrinkled leaves somewhat more rounded with coarser teeth than the normal species.

Perilla can be sown in the spring. Seeds need light to germinate and should be sprinkled over the soil surface, then gently tamped into the soil. Start seed indoors about six weeks before the last spring frost.

Perilla will grow in a variety of soils. In the wild it grows in dry woods, pastures, and meadows, or along sand and gravel bars near creeks, and in the adjacent moist, rich woodland soil. For best culture the soil should be light and well-drained with a pH of 5.3 to 6.3. It will tolerate full sun or partial shade.

The Japanese consider perilla a culinary delight. The fresh leaves are eaten in salads, and the flower stalks flavor fresh fish. Purple perilla imparts its fragrant piquancy and color to Japanese pickled apricots. As the flowers fade, the inflorescence is fried or used to flavor soups. The salted seeds are eaten as an after-dinner cordial.

The leaves are high in calcium, iron, potassium, riboflavin, and fiber. They are a rich source of vitamins A and C, and contain niacin, phosphorus, thiamin, and

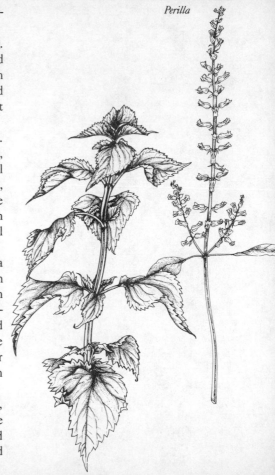

Perilla

protein in measurable amounts. The seeds are high in calcium, niacin, iron, thiamin and proteins.

In Chinese medicine perilla has been used as a carminative, stimulant and anti-nauseant. It has been used to stimulate appetite, to expel phlegm, relieve cold and flu symptoms, and quiet a restless fetus.

Perilla is grown in Japan for its seeds which contain about 40 percent of a fatty, quick-drying oil used as a substitute for linseed oil in manufacturing lacquers, inks, Japanese oil papers, artificial leather, paper umbrellas, and waterproof cloth.

The essential oil of the leaves contains up to 55 percent of monoterepene perillaldehyde. This chemical is easily converted to perillartine which is 200 times sweeter than sugar and used commercially in Japan to sweeten tobacco. Perilla ketones have been implicated as being potentially unhealthy, causing pulmonary disease. Therefore, the herb should be used sparingly.

Pleurisy Root, Butterfly Weed.
Asclepias tuberosa L.
(as-klee′-pi-as tube-er-oh′-sa)

Asclepiadaceae – Milkweed Family

Of the 200 or so species of *Asclepias*, *A. tuberosa* is one of the showiest. Butterfly weed or pleurisy root is, in fact, one of the most glorious flowering roadside weeds of America. It well earns both common names. It is one of the best herbal remedies for pleurisy, and it attracts hordes of butterflies. It is a perennial growing from two to three feet tall native to dry gravelly soils from Maine to Florida, west to Arizona, and north to Minnesota. Unlike other milkweeds, it doesn't produce a milky juice and its leaves are alternate rather than opposite or whorled. The plant is hairy and rough. The lance-shaped to oblong leaves, two to six inches long, are entire, sessile or with short leaf stalks, dark green above and paler beneath. The one-fourth inch hooded and horned orange flowers are borne on showy, erect umbels, appearing in late May in the southern part of its range, lasting through September in the north. Occasionally flowers may be reddish or yellow. The slender furry seed pods are three to four inches long .

Pleurisy root is propagated from root cuttings made in the spring or fall or by seeds sown in late autumn to germinate the following spring. The thick, fleshy, horizontal roots break easily when dug, but if you're careful to excavate as much root and surrounding soil as possible, the plant transplants well. It is always best to purchase wild plants from nurseries specializing in such stock, rather than deplete wild populations. Plants grown from seed may take two to three years to flower.

A dry sandy, well-drained, slightly acid soil is best. Full sun is essential.

Harvest roots in the fall. Older woody roots may have to be split with a small ax.

The young seed pods of this and other milkweeds can be cooked as a vegetable. The Sioux made a crude sugar from its flowers.

Pleurisy root has been used more extensively for medicinal purposes than any other milkweed. Plains Indians ate the raw root for bronchial and pulmonary afflictions. The root was also chewed and put on wounds, or dried and powdered, then blown into wounds. The root has diuretic, tonic, diaphoretic, expectorant, and antispasmodic properties. Doses as small as a tablespoon of chopped root boiled in water may have emetic and laxative effects. This plant is effective as an expectorant and diaphoretic in pleurisy, bronchitis, pneumonia, and other lung inflammations. Flu, asthma, stomach problems, colic, and rheumatic pains have been treated with this plant. A teaspoon of the dried root can be boiled in a cup of water and taken one or two times a day.

A glycoside—asclepiadine—is contained in the root, along with asclepione, a bitter principle, an essential oil and resin.

Rosemary. *Rosmarinus officinalis L.*
(rose-ma-rye′-nus off-ish-i-nail′-iss)
Labiatae—Mint Family

This pine-scented evergreen perennial shrub has been a favorite plant of herb gardeners for centuries. It's native to the western Mediterranean region, especially Spain, Portugal, southern France, Tunisia, and Morocco. It grows from two to six feet tall though heights above four feet are rare. The young branches are hairy. The opposite, leathery, lance-shaped, needle-like leaves are glossy on the upper surface with grayish fuzz beneath. The margins curve downward. The leaves

Rosemary

are ½ to 1½ inches long. The three-eighths-inch long flowers, usually blue, but sometimes pink or white appear in whorls on short racemes arising from upper leaf axils. Rosemary flowers from May to July in warmer climates. Plants in the North may not bloom. There are a number of cultivars including the white flowered 'Alba'; 'Collingwood Ingram,' with bright blue flowers and graceful curving foliage; 'Majorica,' with pink flowers; 'Lockwood de Forest,' a prostrate variety with delicate foliage and vibrant blue flowers; 'Prostratus,' with a creeping habit; and the rigid upright 'Tuscan blue' with rich green foliage and bright blue-violet flowers.

Rosemary is propagated from seeds, stem cuttings, layering, or division of older plants. Seeds are best started in early spring. They will germinate in about three weeks, but resulting seedlings are very slow to develop. Most of the cultivars are best propagated from stem cuttings taken from vigorous spring growth. Plants can be layered at any time during the growing season. Transplant or pot resulting seedlings in autumn. Root divisions are the least-recommended propagation method. Give young plants spacings of two feet.

A light, sandy, chalky soil with good drainage, and a pH of 5 to 8 is good for rosemary culture. Full sun is essential. If over-watered, rosemary may develop root rot. It is a tender perennial, even though I've known it to survive without cover where temperatures reach -5° F. Where temperatures dip into the teens, rosemary should be mulched heavily, or better yet, potted and brought indoors for the winter months. Place in a south-facing window and mist the leaves once or twice a day, especially if you're heating with wood. Rosemary is a good hedge plant or border in California gardens. The prostrate variety makes an excellent cover for banks and slopes or along walls. The plants can be trimmed to encourage bushy growth. Remember to keep the trimmings to dry and use.

Rosemary is harvested when in flower for its essential oil. For home use, harvest leaves as needed.

Rosemary is great with pork, beef, poultry, fish, wild game, veal, peas, carrots, onions, and soups. One potted rosemary plant has served my kitchen for two years. I pinch back sprigs nearly everyday. Rosemary contains vitamin A, vitamin C, phosphorus, potassium, iron, magnesium, zinc, and is high in calcium.

A strong infusion of the leaves makes a good rinse for dark hair.

Rosemary has a multitude of medicinal uses. It is diuretic, diaphoretic, stimulant, astringent, stomachic, carminative, cholagogic, emmenagogic, and antispasmodic. The tea has long been used to relieve headaches and soothe nervous tension. It stimulates digestion, circulation, and bile secretion. It will bring on menstruation and has been reported to be abortive in large doses. A gargle will relieve mouth ulcers and canker sores. Externally, rosemary is used in liniments and ointments for rheumatism, neuralgic pains, bruises, sprains, and as a cosmetic rubefacient.

The oil contains alpha-and beta-pinenes, camphene, limonene, cineol, borenol, and other substances. Rosemary extracts are proven powerful antioxidants or preservatives comparable to BHA and BHT, due to the action of carnosic and labiatic acids. The oil has antifungal and antibacterial properties.

Rue. *Ruta graveolens* L.
(root´-a grave-ee-oh´-lenz)
Rutaceae – Rue Family

Rue is a beautiful, lacy, herbaceous perennial with a woody base. Native to the
Mediterranean, it grows to a height of three
feet. The finely divided fern-like leaves
distinguish the plant, earning it the name
"herb of grace." The leaves are in alternate arrangement on the stems. The
dissected leaf segments are oblong or
spatular shaped, up to one-half inch long,
smooth, glaucous, bluish-green, and dot-
ted with oil glands.

The comb-like inflorescence of
yellow-green flowers appears from late
spring to autumn. The one-half inch
diameter, five-parted corolla surrounds
a green center, appearing on close ex-
amination to be similar to citrus fruit skin.
Citrus fruits are in the rue family. 'Variegata'
has creamy white mottled leaves. 'Jackman
Blue' has a dense compact growth and
blue foliage.

Propagate by stem cuttings or root
division in spring or plant by seed. Seed
germinates readily and self-sows freely.
In southern regions where plants may
become several feet wide, give seedlings
two foot spacings. In the North, space
plants at one-foot intervals.

Rue is not particular about soil conditions. A poor, well-drained soil with a
pH of 5.8 to 8 will suit rue. Full sun is
preferable. Some gardeners must approach
this plant with caution as the juice can
cause a rather unpleasant dermatitis with
irritating burning, reddening, and blistering. The condition looks much like poison
ivy rash.

Gather the herb before it flowers.
Rue's culinary use is limited. The
leaves can be used very sparingly in salads
and have been used in pickles. Rue has
a bitter flavor suggestive of black pepper. Since the time of Greek naturalist,
Dioscorides, (first century A.D.) it has
been known that internal consumption
of rue may be dangerous to pregnant
women.

Medicinally, rue has been used for
its diaphoretic, antispasmodic, emmenagogic, stimulant, and mild sedative
properties. Rue may also be an
anaphrodisiac and an abortificant. Rue
has been used to expel worms, to break
fevers and colds, relieve toothache, and
as an antidote for insect and snake bites.

The plant contains numerous
alkaloids, bergapten – a coumarin – and
rutin (vitamin P). The oil contains methyl-
n-nonyl ketone as its main component,
which is a base for perfume chemicals.
Rue oil relieves spasms in smooth muscles
and is an effective worm expellant. Rutin
decreases capillary permeability and fragil-
ity, and studies with X-rays in mice have
shown it to be protective against
irradiation.

Sage. *Salvia officinalis* L.
(sal-vee´-a off-ish-i-nay´-lis)
Labiatae – Mint Family

The genus *Salvia* contains over 700
species distributed throughout the world.
Common garden sage, *S. officinalis*, a
Mediterranean native, is a shrub growing to 2½ feet high, with white woolly
stems and grayish-green leaves with a texture reminding me of reptile skin. The
oblong, entire or slightly toothed, leaves
are about 1½ to 3 inches long and about
one-half inch wide. The whorls of white,
pinkish, or blue-violet one-half inch long
flowers occur in racemes, blooming in
May to June. *Salvias* have two stamens

with two-celled anthers, connecting to a point at the summit of a filament. On each stamen the anterior anther is not fully developed, forming an appendage bees hit when they enter the flower for nectar. This tips the fully developed anther, rubbing pollen into the hairs on the insect's thorax. Thus pollen is distributed to adjacent flowers. There are a number of cultivars. 'Tricolor' has variegated white leaves with purple margins; 'Purpurea' has purple leaves; 'Albiflora' has white flowers; 'Icterina' possesses beautiful golden yellow leaves; 'Holt's Mammoth' has large robust leaves.

Sage can be propagated by seeds, cuttings, layering, or root divisions of older plants. Seeds germinate within three weeks and should be sown to a depth of one-half inch. Resulting seedlings should be spaced six to twelve inches apart. Plants from seed tend to vary in size and color. One to four pounds of seed will sow an acre. Most of the cultivars should be propagated from stem cuttings taken in the spring. Tips can be layered in September then removed from the parent plant and transplanted the following spring. Fully mature plants should be spaced at two-foot intervals.

Sage will grow in almost any soil but requires good drainage, a fair amount of nitrogen, and full sun. It flourishes on a heavy, moist soil but under such conditions will most likely winterkill in the North. Where temperatures dip below 0° F., sage should be mulched in winter months. A pH between 6.2 and 6.4 is best for sage, though it will grow in a pH range from 5 to 8. First-year plants from seed are slow to mature, producing only a tenth of fully matured plants. An acre has yielded up to 2,000 pounds of dried herb.

Weather conditions may affect the color of the dried leaf in a given season. A wet season may produce leaves of a greenish color, whereas a dry season will give grayer leaves. You should pick leaves carefully by hand just before the plant comes into bloom and later in the summer after the leaves have fully matured. Leaves may blacken if not dried quickly under a steady air flow.

Sage is best known as a flavoring for poultry stuffings, sausages, and commercial ground meats. Fresh or dried leaves enhance lamb or pork dishes. It's good

in cheeses—try a few leaves in a toasted cheese sandwich. Use in soups or by itself for teas. The Dutch used to trade one pound of sage to the Chinese for four pounds of tea.

Sage contains vitamin A, vitamins B_1, and B_2, niacin, vitamin C, potassium, calcium and iron.

Sage has been used as a folk remedy for centuries, serving as a digestive and nerve tonic, a gargle for sore throats and bleeding gums, an antiseptic in vaginal infections, a poultice for insect bites, and a cure for diarrhea. Sage is an astringent, tonic, antiseptic, and antispasmodic. Sage tea will dry up milk flow, stop perspiration about two hours after drinking, and relieve gastritis.

The oil contains alpha- and beta-thujones (also found in wormwoods and yarrow), cineole, borneol, and other components. Like rosemary, sage extracts are strong antioxidents (preservatives). The essential oil suppresses fish odors.

Sage of the Seers. *Saliva divinorum* Epling & Jativa
(sal-vee′-a div-in-or′-um)
Labiatae—Mint Family

Salvia divinorum is known in Spanish as *hojas de la Pastora* or *hojas de Maria Pastora* ("leaves of the shepherdess" or "leaves of Mary the shepherdess"). It was first described by Carl Epling and Carlos D. Jativa of UCLA in 1962 from dried specimens supplied by R. Gordon Wasson. It is not known from the wild—only from well-protected cultivated stands held by Mazatec Indians in Oaxaca, Mexico. It is a tender, fast-growing perennial, three to seven feet high, with oval, light green, acuminate leaves, three to nine inches long with slightly curved tips. The serrated leaf margins have hairs between the teeth's sinuses. Leaf stalks are ⅞ to 1½ inches long. The stems are decumbent (bending toward the ground), square, with thin, wavy wings at the corners. Epling and Jativa originally described the flowers as blue. In his *Narcotic Plants*, William Emboden describes the flowers as white. Craig Dremmon, proprietor of Redwood City Seed Company and a supplier of *S. Divinorum* cuttings, has brought plants into flower and reports them as light lavender. Apparently, the color is variable, but the plant rarely flowers. The slightly hairy seven-eighths-inch long flowers are borne on spectacular panicles eleven to fifteen inches long. The calyx tube is bluish and about one-half to five-eighths inches long. The illusive Aztec psychotomimetic *pipiltzintzintli* may well have been this plant.

S. divinorum is not known to produce viable seeds but is grown from cuttings which readily strike in a moist rooting medium or water. Plants may also be produced by layering the long, sprawling stems.

In its native habitat, it grows in rich, black soil of forest ravines at 5,000-foot elevations. It needs a constant supply of moisture. Leaf mold from deciduous trees is the best growing medium. About 75 percent shade is required. The soil should be slightly acidic. It will stand a freeze of 20° F., dying back to the root when hit by frost. Bring indoors in severe climates. This is an exceedingly rare cultivated plant. A buyer usually has to join a waiting list before securing a plant.

The Mazatecs use *S. divinorum*—the sage of the seers—as a hallucinogen when more potent mushrooms are unavailable. *Curanderas* (medicine men) have special rituals and chants for *S. divinorum* use.

Under the plant's influence, patients state the cause of their illness, the whereabouts of lost items, and the truth behind thefts. Intoxication is characterized by a feeling of weightlessness, euphoria, and dancing colors. Effects last only for a short period of time.

The leaves are harvested in pairs, then crushed in a *metaté* to extract the juice which is then mixed with water and drunk. Fifty to one-hundred fresh leaves can also be nibbled with the incisor teeth. However, as few as three pairs of leaves reportedly induce the desired results. The leaves are extremely bitter. Drinking the juice or eating the leaves often brings on vomiting. I've nibbled my way through twenty leaves–leaving me with an upset stomach, a dry, acrid mouth, and a great respect for Mazatecs who can work their way through a hundred! For me the leaves produced hardly noticeable effects. Craig Dremmond suggests that plants cultivated outside of Oaxaca may not develop the active constituents, and I predict that *Salvia divinorum* will never become a popular subculture euphoric.

Testing in several laboratories has not yet yielded the active constituents.

St. John's Wort *Hypericum perforatum* L.
(hi-per′-i-kum per-for-ay′-tum)
Hypericaceae – St. John's Wort Family

Hypericum is a large genus with about 300 species. *H. perforatum* is a perennial herb growing from one to three feet high, native to Europe and naturalized in waste places and along roadsides in North America. The stems are smooth, erect, and branching toward the top. The oblong, pale green leaves are sessile and about an inch long. The leaves are covered by translucent dots easily seen by holding the leaves up to light; these are the perforations of *H. perforatum*. The star-shaped golden yellow blossoms appear on terminal corymbs from June to August. The flowers are about an inch across and marked, especially along the margins, with minute dark dots and lines.

St. John's wort is best propagated from root divisions made in spring or fall, or by spring cuttings.

It is not particular about soil conditions, growing in any average garden soil. It does like good drainage, a slightly acid situation, and full sun.

The herb is harvested just as the

St. John's Wort

plant comes into bloom. A medicinal oil can be prepared by soaking a handful of the fresh flowers in a cup of olive oil for about three weeks. The yellow flowers will turn the oil a deep blood-red color.

St. John's wort oil has been a popular domestic remedy since ancient times. Externally it is applied to bruises, sprains, burns, skin irritations, or any laceration accompanied by severed nerve tissue. Internally a tea or tincture has been used for lung ailments, bladder infections, depressions, dysentery, diarrhea, and worms. It has been highly esteemed as an antidepressant and sedative. It is resolvent, expectorant, nervine, and astringent. St. John's wort contains phototoxins which may cause photodermatitis in fair-skinned persons who use the herb internally, then become exposed to bright sunlight. Because of this propensity, in 1977, the FDA put this herb on its "unsafe herb list."

St. John's wort contains a glycoside – hypericine – (responsible for the plant's fluorescent red pigment and phototoxicity); the flavonoids quercetin, hypercin, and rutin, an essential oil, pectin and choline.

Salsify

Salsify. *Tragopogon porrifolius L.* and *T. pratensis L.*
(trag-oh-poh´-gon por-i-foh´-li-us; pra-ten´-sis)
Compositae—Aster Family

Although not generally thought of as an herb plant, salsify deserves a place in the herb garden for its colorful flowers and useful culinary root. This genus contains about fifty species native to southern Europe, North Africa, and parts of Asia. Several species occur in North America. *T. porrifolius* and *T. pratensis* are erect biennials with a milky sap, growing from two to four feet high. The smooth, narrow, grass-like leaves are alternate and clasp the stems. Plants flower in the second year, sending up a single flower head—a wheel of yellow (*T. pratensis*) or purple (*T. porrifolius*) ray flowers. Beneath the flower heads, long yellow bracts extend beyond the petals making the flower appear larger. Flower heads may reach four inches in diameter. Blooming begins in June or July of the second year. The seed heads are billowy tufts similar to, but much larger than, those of dandelions. The white fleshy roots, about one foot long, resemble a small parsnip.

Salsify is grown from seed sown in spring as soon as the ground can be worked. Sow to a depth of one-half inch. Thin seedlings to stand at six inch spacings. Seeds germinate in about a week. One ounce will plant a one-hundred-foot row, and produce about sixty pounds of root.

A double-dug bed with a rich, light, moist soil provides a perfect home for a good crop of salsify. It likes full sun and will tolerate soil pH from 5 to 8, preferring a neutral pH. Keep well cultivated and free from weeds. One hundred twenty days of growth are required for harvestable roots.

The roots can be harvested in the fall of the first year and stored in moist sand in a cellar for winter use. A stronger, more oyster-like flavor will develop if plants are left in the ground and allowed to freeze through the winter. Harvest the following spring before the flower stalks begin to develop. Once flower stalks develop, the root becomes woody and the flavor very bitter.

Salsify is also known as vegetable oyster, because if you stretch your imagination a little, the root tastes something like oysters. Many people who have tried wild salsify roots can't understand why anyone would want to eat them. The flavor is too bitter. To be enjoyed, the roots have to be prepared properly. They should be scraped, then soaked in water for about an hour to remove the bitter milky sap. The roots can be eaten like parsnip. Boil until tender, or grate them and shape into small balls. Dip the balls into a batter made from egg whites and flour, then roll them in bread or cracker crumbs and fry—delicious! The young three- to five-inch second-year sprouts can be eaten as an asparagus substitute.

The roots contain a fair amount of vitamin C and potassium, plus measurable amounts of calcium, iron, niacin, thiamin, riboflavin, phosphorus, and protein.

Medicinally, salsify has had limited use as a deobstruent in kidney and bladder ailments, and as a mild laxative.

Santolina. *Santolina chamaecyparissus L.*, *S. virens* Mill.
(san-toe-lie´-na kam-e-sip´-a-ris-us; veye´-renz)
Compositae—Aster Family

There are about eight species in this genus, two of which—*S. virens* and *S.*

*Gray Santolina in
Saso's Astrological
Herb Garden*

chamaecyparissus—are found commonly in American gardens. Both are shrubby, growing to about two feet high and are native to the Mediterranean region. The former, green santolina, has smooth green leaves. The latter, gray santolina or lavender cotton, has downy silver-gray leaves. The alternate, finely cut leaves are about 1¼ inch long with lateral segments one-sixteenth inch long or less. In midsummer, santolinas shoot up solitary flower heads on a stem taller than the rest of the plant, with yellow buttons resembling the heads of tansy, though more rounded. They are about three-fourths of an inch across. Cultivars of lavender cotton include 'Nana,' a dwarf form, and 'Plumosus' with lacy foliage. A santolina or two at the Farm and Garden Project at U.C. Santa Cruz are six feet in breadth. Large santolina plants like these tend to part into divided bunches giving the plant an unkempt appearance. Some gardeners like to keep the plant trimmed back. I think the wavy divided wisps of the uncut plant have a character worth retaining.

Santolina can be started from slow-to-germinate seeds in the early spring but is best propagated from spring cuttings or layering. Mature roots can also be divided before new growth begins in the spring.

Santolina likes a sandy, limey soil with good drainage and full sun. It will tolerate drought. The soil pH should be close to neutral or slightly alkaline. In northern climates, santolina will need a heavy mulch to make it through the winter. In any region with winter snows santolina will die back to the root but will grow again in the spring. In temperate climates, santolina is evergreen. *S. virens* is the hardiest species. It makes a good low hedge.

The leaves and flower heads can be harvested as the plant comes into bloom. Both the leaves and dried flowers can be used as moth repellants. The flowers are useful in dried arrangements.

Santolina was once a popular worm expellant and has been used as a stimulant, for stomach aches, and as an emmenagogue and antispasmodic.

The leaves contain tannin, an alkaloid, resin, and an essential oil containing santolineone.

Sassafras. *Sassafras albidum* (Nutt.) Nees.
(sas′-a-fras al-bye′-dum)
Lauraceae – Laurel Family

Sassafras is a small scraggly shrub or large tree, 80 to 100 feet tall and up to six feet in diameter, native to eastern North America from Maine to Florida, and west to Texas. Two other species occur in the world – *S. tzuma* from central China and *S. randaiense* from Taiwan. On older trees, the deeply furrowed bark is grayish with reddish-brown fissures. Young branches are smooth and light green. The aromatic leaves are entire or three-lobed, alternate, petiolate, oval or mitten-shaped, four to five inches long and two to four inches broad. Half-inch diameter yellow-green flowers bloom in early spring in raceme clusters as the leaves emerge. The half-inch long, oval, dark-blue fruits ripen September to October. Trees must be about ten years old before beginning to flower and fruit. The fall foliage is a brilliant yellow or dull orange, streaked with red.

The wood is coarse-grained, brittle, aromatic, and dull orange. It has been popular for fencing, ox yokes, smaller joints of fishing rods, cooperage, and light boats such as dugout canoes.

Sassafras can be grown from seed or root cuttings. Seeds have a viability of about two years and often take that long to germinate. Soon after they ripen, remove the pulp from the seeds and place them in moist sand for cold stratification for four months at 35 to 42° F. Sow seeds outside in well-prepared seed beds at eight- to twelve-inch spacings, one-half inch below the soil. Don't expect a good germination rate.

However, the roots of sassafras send out runners. Cut young seedlings from the parent plant, then let them sit for a year to develop a good set of roots. Transplant the following year – and give new plants plenty of water. Four- to six-inch offshoots with sprouts can also be removed from the parent tree to increase stock.

Sassafras is often found growing on dry, infertile soils. In the garden, a

Sassafras

moderately rich, sandy, well-drained soil with a pH of 6 to 7 will do. In the North a warm sunny location with winter protection is required. Southern trees become very large and will tolerate partial shade. In the North, plants become moderate-sized shrubs and need full sun.

The bark of the root, trunk bark, leaves, pith of the twigs, flowers, and fruits can be used variously. Harvest the bark of the root in spring before leaves appear or in fall after the leaves have dropped. Harvest the leaves after spring blooming.

The leaves have abundant mucilage and were used by the Choctaws to thicken their pottage. Subsequently, sassafras leaves became a prime ingredient in Cajun gumbo. A sprinkling of crumbled flowers adds color and spicy flavor to spring salads. The young tips of sassafrass—those emerging erect leaves—have a soft delicate texture and a pleasing flavor, hinting at a mild anise taste then shifting to light citrus tones. The emerging leaf tips are great in salads. The root bark is a famous herb tea.

A decoction of the bark was used by the Cherokees to bathe open or infected wounds. The Mohawks used an infusion of the twig pith for eye ailments. Sassafras was one of the first export crops from the New World to European shores. Many early English colonies were in part founded on promises of financial return from speculation on sassafras. The tea of the root bark is considered a stimulant, tonic, diaphoretic, stomachic, and blood purifier. In folk medicine, it has been used to thin blood and for high blood pressure, gout, arthritis, rheumatism, kidney ailments, and skin eruptions.

Sassafras contains an essential oil with safrole (comprising up to 80 percent of the oil weight), alpha-pinene, phellandrenes, asarone, camphor, myristicine, thujone, anethole, eugenol, and other compounds. Sassafras oil has carminative, anodyne, diaphoretic, anti-infective, and lice-destroying properties. In the *Federal Register* of 3 December 1960, the FDA banned safrole from use in human foods, because in laboratory tests with mice, safrole was found to cause liver cancer.[13] In the *Federal Register* of 11 May 1976, the FDA clarified the earlier ruling banning the sale of sassafras bark and leaves from herbal teas, stating that the intended purpose of making sassafras tea was to infuse safrole (a food additive) into water (a food).[14] Since that time, sassafras has been sold in health food stores labeled: "not for food use" or "for external use." In 1978, the then-fledgling, now defunct, Herb Trade Association held a tea party at the Boston Tea Party Ship and Museum. In response to the FDA's sassafras ban, a symbolic toss of sassafras was offered to the famed harbor. Safrole is also found in basil, nutmeg, star anise, cinnamon leaf oil, black pepper, and witch hazel.

Savories. *Satureja hortensis L.*, *Satureja montana L.*
(sat-you-ree´-a hor-ten´-sis; mon-tay´-na)
Labiatae—Mint Family

This genus has about thirty species, including both yerba buena and calamint, which are treated separately in this book. *S. hortensis*, summer savory, and *S. montana*, winter savory are treated here. Summer savory is a hardy annual growing to 1½ feet tall, native to the Mediterranean region. Its leaves are linear to lance-shaped, up to an inch long, entire, with the edges slightly rolled back underneath. The stems have a purple cast. The one-fourth inch long, light lavender to white

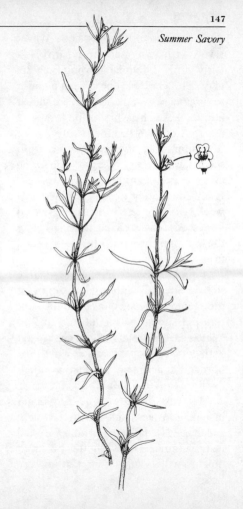

Summer Savory

flowers are borne on sparse whorls. Winter savory, also a Mediterranean native, is a fairly hardy perennial growing from six to twelve inches tall. The leaves are similar to summer savory, though they are shinier and thicker. The white or pink flowers are shorter than summer savory's.

Summer savory is easily grown from seeds sown directly in the garden in spring as soon as the ground can be worked. It self-sows freely. Seeds germinate in a week or so. Winter savory can be started from seeds sown six to eight weeks before the last spring frost but is best propagated from cuttings or layering.

Summer savory likes a moderately rich, sandy soil with a good supply of moisture for the seedlings and full sun. Soil pH should be around 6.5 to 7.5. Winter savory prefers a light, chalky soil with good drainage. It makes a nice low border. An acre may produce as much as three tons of summer savory.

Harvest the flowers as they begin blooming. Winter savory has a woody stem which needs to be removed from the dried leaf. Summer savory should be dried quickly with adequate circulation.

Savory is best known as a flavoring for beans–from lentils to green beans. The fresh or dried leaves are good with cabbage, turnips, brussels sprouts, potato salads, pea soup, and tossed salads. Winter savory has a stronger biting flavor. Both make good pepper substitutes.

The leaves of summer savory are high in vitamin A and contain niacin, iron, calcium, and potassium.

Medicinally, savory is carminative, antispasmodic, and expectorant. The tea is gargled for a sore throat, used for diarrhea, indigestion, and as an aphrodisiac. Fresh leaves rubbed on an insect sting will relieve pain.

The essential oil contains carvacrol, rho-cymene, beta-phellandrene, beta-pinene, limonene, and other monoterpenes. Winter savory oil also contains thymol. The oils are antifungal and antibacterial.

Spice bush. *Lindera benzoin (L.)* Blume (lin-der′-a ben′-zoin)
Lauraceae–Laurel Family

About 100 species in this genus are native to Asia with two from North America.

L. benzoin is an aromatic deciduous shrub, three to eight feet tall, found from Maine to Ontario, south to Florida and Texas. The oblong-to-elongated oval leaves are entire, thin, abruptly pointed at the tips, tapering at the base, and up to five inches long. Tiny yellow flowers appear in axils in early spring before the leaves emerge. One-half inch long, oval, scarlet red, shiny, one-seeded fruits ripen after the brilliant yellow fall foliage has dropped. It is found in moist, rich woods, along banks of streams, and under taller deciduous trees. Spice bush is a close relative of sassafras.

Propagate from seeds, layerings, or cuttings made from green wood. The seeds have a short viability and should be placed in cold stratification at 35 to 42° F. for about four months. Plant in the spring or fall at six- to twelve-inch spacings to a depth of one-half inch. Seeds germinate two to four weeks after planting. Root suckers can be removed and replanted like those of sassafras. Cuttings are best done in a greenhouse and take several months to root.

A soil which is fairly moist the year 'round, yet well-drained, high in humus,

Spice Bush

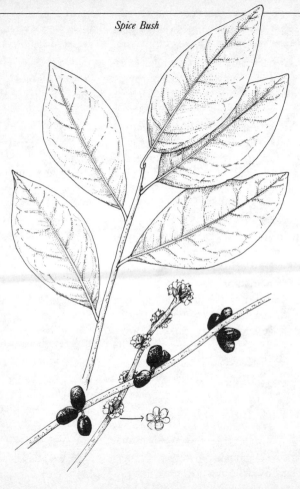

and with a pH of 4.5 to 6.0 is suitable for spice bush. It likes light shade and a warm situation. Expect twelve to twenty-four inches of growth per year.

Harvest and dry the fruits when ripe. Twigs and bark are strongest when harvested in late winter before very early spring flowering. Leaves are ready in midsummer.

The leaves make a good tea. Wild food expert Billy Joe Tatum makes the world's best venison by roasting a haunch with spice bush twigs. The berries can be crushed in a mortar and pestle and used with meats and in soups, salad dressings, and vegetables. During the American Revolution, the berries were used as an allspice substitute.

The bark, leaves, and berries have been used medicinally for their diaphoretic, febrifuge, tonic, and stimulant properties. The berries have been used as a worm expellant, and their oil was once used on rheumatic and neuralgic limbs. The Rappahannocks used a tea of the split twigs to bring on the menses.

The seeds contain an essential oil plus a fatty oil containing capric, lauric, and oleic acids.

Spiderwort. *Tradescantia virginiana L.*
(trad-es-kan′-ti-a vir-gin-ee-ay′-na)
Commelinaceae–Spiderwort Family

There are about twenty species represented in this genus and numerous varieties originating in North and South America. The spiderwort is a close relative of the familiar house plant–the wandering Jew. *T.* × *Andersoniana* is a hybrid with numerous cultivars that is often sold as *T. virginiana*. Spiderwort is a perennial growing to three feet in height with smooth, delicate, grass-like leaves, about a foot long and one inch wide. The flowers are usually blue, though sometimes rose, pink, or white, and are characterized by three petals alternately arranged with three sepals. Flowers are about an inch in diameter and bloom from May to August. Blooms open in early morning and close around noon. *Tradescantia* has six stamens whose filaments are unusual because each stamen has between fifty and ninety hairs. The stamen hairs are elongated chains of between twenty and thirty-five cells so large they can be seen with the naked eye and easily observed under a 20x-powered microscope. A single flower may have between 8,000 and 15,000 stamen hair cells. In certain clones of spiderwort, the normally blue stamen hair cells turn pink when exposed to chemical or radiological mutagens.

Spiderworts can be propagated from seeds, cuttings of offshoots, and spring divisions of the rootstocks. Clones propagated for test use should be increased asexually to maintain genetic homogeneity. Spiderworts hybridize readily, changing their genetic stability.

These are easy plants to grow–so easy, in fact, that the well-known late botanist, Dr. Edgar Anderson, in his *Plants, Man and Life* calls spiderwort "the kind of plant not even a botanist can kill."[15] A light, well-drained, humus-rich soil with a neutral pH is preferable. Spiderworts will tolerate full sun or partial shade.

The spiderwort is edible. The young leaves and stems can be added to salads or boiled for ten minutes as a pot herb. The flower petals make a colorful addition to salads.

This interesting garden perennial has a number of laboratory and educational uses. The beginning botany student may well have used the root tips or pollen grains to study chromosome strucures. Compared with other plants, spiderworts have a relatively low number of large chromosomes. The spiderwort was chosen as a passenger on the first United States biosatellite sent up in the late 1960s to explore the effects of weightlessness on living organisms. As early as 1950, spiderworts were used to indicate the effects of radiation on living organisms. In 1977 this plant was used by the Brookhaven National Laboratory and the Environmental Protection Agency to monitor the effects of air pollutants in eight high-risk areas of the United States. Spiderworts close to petroleum refineries and mixed chemical processing plants have exhibited the greatest increases in mutation rates.[16]

How does the spiderwort's detection system work? A percentage of the normally blue stamen hair cells turn pink when exposed to mutagens. The spiderwort clones used in such testing possess a dominant gene for blue and a recessive gene for pink. Upon exposure to even minute levels of radiation or chemical mutagens, a mutation may occur, causing the loss of the dominant blue gene

Sweet Cicely

which shows up as a pink mutation cell. The pink cells appear eight to eighteen days after exposure to the mutagen. The same kind of somatic (body cell) mutation in humans, from short-term exposure to low levels of radiation, may only be noticeable after several decades.

Techniques for using the spiderwort system were developed at the biological department of the Brookhaven National Laboratory and the Laboratory of Genetics, Kyoto University. In conjunction with Dr. Sadoa Ichikawa, a major *Tradescanticia* researcher, a Japanese high school teacher, Motoyuki Nagata, placed spiderworts near a nuclear power plant in Japan and, over a period of nearly five months, spent about six hours a day, in addition to teaching full-time, recording data on over a half million stamen hairs. He counted about 17,600,000 stamen hair cells and detected 2,778 pink mutation cells from the forty plants. Interpretation of the data by Dr. Ichikawa revealed that somatic mutations occurred only when the reactors were in operation and mostly from the leeward side of the power plants. Spiderworts have also been planted near other Japanese, European, and United States nuclear power plants producing similar results.

Some might ask what spiderworts are doing in an herb book. I have included them because of this biological ability to point to mutagens in our environment. If we heed those warnings, then spiderworts are, in the broadest sense of the term, a preventative medicine.

Sweet Cicely. *Myrrhis odorata (L.)* Scop. (mer´-iss- oh-dor-ay´-ta)
Umbelliferae – Carrot Family

Sweet cicely is a hardy perennial of European origin growing to a height of two to three feet. The leaves are finely divided, fern-like, about one foot long and covered with downy hairs. The leaf segments are coarsely toothed. The stem is hollow and striated. Inconspicuous white flowers are borne on compound umbels in May and June. The shiny, dark brown fruits are like those of chervil, only larger, reaching a length of one inch.

Propagate by planting the seeds as soon as they ripen in late summer, or divide the crowns of roots in the fall. Each piece of root should have a bud or "eye." Give plants one-foot spacings. The seed is viable only a short while.

Sweet cicely makes a good border plant in a moderately rich, well-drained, slightly acid to alkaline soil. Partial shade is required.

The leaves can be harvested as they develop and the seeds when ripe.

The leaves have a mild anise-like flavor and are good for flavoring cabbage, carrots, parsnips, and fruit dishes. The young shoots can be eaten raw or cooked as a spring pot herb. Chop the leaves fine and add them to salads. The boiled roots have an excellent flavor.

The roots have been used as a cough remedy and as a diuretic. The seeds and leaves possess mild expectorant, carminative, stomachic, and diuretic qualities.

The essential oil contains anethole.

Sweet gum. *Liquidambar styraciflua L.* (lik-wid-am′-bar stie-ray′-si-flu-a) Hamamelidaceae – Witch Hazel Family

Four species of deciduous trees in this genus are native to North America and Asia. *L. styraciflua* is a North American native with wide distribution from Connecticut, south to Florida and Central America. Sweet gum attains a height of

Sweet Gum

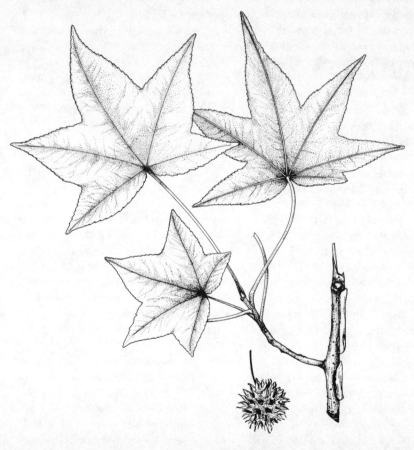

150 feet or more, with a five-foot diameter and a foliage spread of over 100 feet. It grows straight and tall. Young trees are more or less cone-shaped. The bark of twigs often has corky wings an inch or more wide. Old trunks have a light gray bark with deep irregular fissures. The lustrous leaves are almost star-shaped with five to seven lobes and toothed margins. The fruits are globular, up to 1½ inches in diameter and covered with projecting points. The brilliant autumn foliage varies from yellow through red to golden bronze or purple. There are a number of cultivars. The handsome, dark, straight-grained, and close-grained wood has a reddish tint that takes an exceptionally fine polish.

The seed has a short dormancy period. Germination is improved by cold, moist stratification for thirty days. Plant seeds one-half inch deep in well-prepared seed beds in spring. Sometimes seed may take more than a year to germinate. Transplant, six to ten feet apart.

Sweet gum is planted as a street shade tree throughout the United States. It rarely attains a height of more than fifty feet in cultivation. A neutral to slightly acid, rich, moist soil with good drainage is best.

Like oaks, it grows moderately fast, straight and tall under the shade of other trees.

In Central America, the exudate from the bark is collected in hanging buckets, often producing forty to two hundred pounds of gum per tree. Usually a pocket of gum is found in the tree, then slashed and allowed to drip. I once came across a stand of old-growth sweet gums that had been girdled by beavers. Gum was running down the sides, and I spent an hour scraping a few pounds of gum from the damaged bark. The gum or balsam, called American storax, is in liquid as it comes from the tree but hardens when exposed to air.

Antiseptic, expectorant, antimicrobial and anti-inflammatory qualities are attributed to the gum. It has been chewed for sore throats, coughs, colds, and used for diarrhea, dysentery, ring worm, and other skin ailments caused by parasites. The gum is applied to sores and wounds to promote healing. It has been used in hemorrhoid ointments and is an ingredient in compound tincture benzoin. I've chewed the gum on occasion. The taste is fine but the more it's chewed the more resilient it becomes.

The gum contains storesin, styracin, phenylpropyl cinnamate, and tannins.

Syrian Rue. *Peganum harmala L.*
(peg-ay′-num har-may′-la)
Zygophyllaceae – Caltrop Family

Syrian rue is a relatively tender perennial native to southern Russia, the Balkins, North Africa, the central Asian steppes and the Iranian plateau. It grows from one to two feet tall and has a somewhat sprawling habit. The stems are smooth, rather succulent and blue-green. The finely divided, linear, alternate leaves resemble deer antlers. The five-pointed star flowers have creamy white petals streaked with green veins. Flowers are about 1½ inch in diameter. The ovary is spherical, surrounded by eighteen stamens. It blooms from June to September and produces an abundance of seeds that are dark brown, about three-sixteenths inch long and one-eighth inch in diameter. The seeds are the source of the colorfast Turkish red dye used in Persian and Turkish rugs.

Syrian rue grows easily from seed sown in spring, taking about two weeks

Syrian Rue

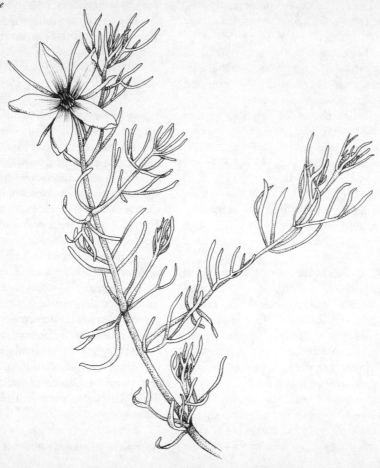

to germinate. The plant self-sows freely.

Soil should be fairly rich, sandy, and well-drained. Full sun is required. The plants die back to the crowns every winter and should be mulched where temperatures dip below 10° F. An alkaline pH between 7.3 and 8 is preferable. In some states, county extension agents frown upon the cultivation of this plant as it may escape and become weedy in pastures. It is reportedly toxic to livestock.

The seeds are used as narcotics and worm expellants in Pakistan and India. In recent years *Perganum* has been noted as a possible source of the Vedic soma. Other uses are as aphrodisiacs, to increase lactation, to bring on the menses, treat genito-urinary disorders and fevers, as a diuretic, and, in large doses, as an abortifacient.

Ingesting the seeds can reportedly cause paralysis and even death. Poisonous doses act as a central nervous system depressant. Smaller doses stimulate the motor tract of the cerebrum. Syrian rue contains the alkaloids harmine, harmaline and harmalol. In minute doses, harmine has been used to treat encephalitis lethargica (sleeping sickness) and Parkinson's disease. The Nazis used it as a narcotic truth serum. Harmine is also the chief constituent of the hallucinogenic jungle vine used by natives of the upper Amazon basin in the genus *Banisteriopsis*.

Tansy. *Tanacetum vulgare* L.
(tan-a-see'-tum vul-gay'-ree)
Compositae—Aster Family

Tansy is a hardy perennial native to Europe and Asia and is naturalized in many parts of North America. It grows to four feet tall and has coarsely divided leaves three to five inches long. The leaves are deeply incised and toothed. The quarter-inch diameter, button-like, yellow flower heads appear from late July to September in flat clusters. Tansy has a creeping rhizome that can spread and take over a garden border if not kept in check. *T. vulgare var. crispum* has more finely divided leaves and luxuriant foliage.

Tansy is grown from seed, or better, from spring or fall root divisions. Any piece of root with a bud will produce a new plant. Seeds can be sown indoors in early spring. Give young plants twelve to eighteen

Tansy

inch spacings. Plants may self-sow.

Tansy is not particular about soil conditions as long as there is good drainage. A moist, rich soil makes for lusher growth. Tansy tolerates a pH range between 5 and 7. An acre may produce 1500 to 2000 pounds of dried leaves, but any grower would be hard-put to sell a ton of tansy leaves.

The plant is harvested and spread or hung to dry when in full bloom.

Tansy is said to be of some utility as a moth or ant repellant, but I've never found it particularly useful in that regard.

Its primary medicinal use is as an intestinal worm expellant. Tansy oil and tea have also been used to bring on the menses, as diaphoretics in fevers, and as a digestive tonic. Tansy has also been suggested as an abortifacient, but any internal use should be discouraged because of potential toxicity even in moderate doses.

The essential oil contains thujone, with varying amounts of borneol and camphor. Tansy also contains tanacetin—a toxic bitter principle.

Tarragon

Tarragon. *Artemisia drancunculus L.*
(are-te-miz′-ee-a dray-kun′-kyou-lus)
Compositae—Aster Family

There are two varieties of tarragon—*A. drancunculus var. sativa*, French tarragon, and *A. drancunculus*, Russian tarragon (formerly known as *A. redowskii*). They are native to southern Europe, Asia, and western North America. The stems are usually shiny and smooth, though sometimes hairy. The linear to lance-shaped leaves of French tarragon are one to three inches long and of a darker color than Russian tarragon. I have rarely seen it flower. It grows to about three feet tall. Russian tarragon stretches to five feet tall, and its leaves may be as long as six inches. It has tiny (one-eighth-inch diameter) greenish-white flowers blooming in loose clusters in June or July. Both varieties spread by creeping rhizomes. Russian tarragon does not have the fine flavor of French tarragon so often appreciated by French chefs.

Tarragon is best propagated by carefully dividing the roots in spring and transplanting one-inch sections of root tips. Tarragon can also be propagated by summer cuttings which take about eight weeks to root. French tarragon, the flavorful clone cherished by herb gardeners, must be propagated asexually. If you buy tarragon seed, you are getting Russian tarragon. Seeds germinate in about twenty days. Give plants one- to two-foot spacings.

A moderately rich, well-drained soil with a pH range from 6.2 to 7.8 is suitable for tarragon. Optimum pH range should fall between 6.2 to 6.5. Plant under full sun. It's a relatively hardy plant if soil drainage is good, but if the roots sit in water, plants will invariably winterkill. Where temperatures dip below 0° F., mulch well after the ground freezes. Tarragon does best in areas where it has a period of winter dormancy.

Like basil, tarragon leaves bruise easily and must be handled with care during the harvest and drying process. Harvest should occur in late June.

Tarragon has one of the finest flavors of any culinary herb. It is good with chicken, fish, salad dressings, salads, and all vegetables – especially asparagus. Use the leaves to season chicken livers and roast duck for an unusual treat.

The leaves contain vitamin A, niacin, phosphorus, potassium, calcium, and iron.

Medicinal uses are very limited. The leaves have been used to stimulate appetite, settle an upset stomach, promote the menses, and as a diuretic. The root has been chewed to cure toothaches.

Tarragon contains an essential oil with up to 70 percent estragole, plus lesser amounts of capillene, ocimene, nerol, thujone, and phellandrine. Tarragon also contains coumarins and the flavonoids – rutin and quercetin.

Thymes. *Thymus vulgaris L.*, *T. pseudolanuginosus* Ronn., *T.* × *citriodorus* (Pers.) Schreb ex Schweiggt. and Korte *T. serpyllum L.*
(time-mus vul-gay′-ris; sue-doe-lan-gwin-oh′-sus; sit-ri-oh′-door-us; ser-i-fil′-lum)
Labiatae – Mint Family

Like the genus *Mentha*, *Thymus* is a taxonomical Pandora's box. There are about 400 species – or 100 species with 400 names. They are creeping, woody-based, evergreen perennials concentrated in the Mediterranean region and western Asia. Leaves are small, entire, and opposite.

Creeping Thyme

Flower heads are usually terminal, compact whorled bunches of tiny flowers. We will deal only with a handful of species.

T. vulgaris, common or English thyme, grows from about six to eighteen inches tall and has linear or elliptical leaves up to five-eighths inches long. The dense whorls of lilac or white flowers are terminal or interrupted on upper branches.

There are several important cultivars including the silver-leafed 'Argentis,' 'Narrowleaf French'–French thyme, 'Broadleaf English'–English thyme, and the golden-foliaged 'Aureus.'

T. × citriodorus, lemon thyme, is a branching perennial with a distinct lemon fragrance. It grows up to one foot high. Flowers are light lilac, and the leaves are oval in shape. The cultivar 'Aureus' has golden yellow leaves; 'Silver Queen' is a silver-leafed cultivar. Trout Lake Farm (see mints) grows lemon thyme commercially.

T. pseudolanuginosus, creeping woolly thyme, is a low-growing (one-half inch tall) perennial, with one-eighth-inch long, woolly, gray leaves that are elliptical. It produces a few tiny, pale pink flowers in the leaf axils. This plant makes a fabulous ground cover.

T. serpyllum, creeping thyme, is perhaps the most ambiguous name of the *thymus* classification. According to *Hortus Third,* it is rarely cultivated in the United States, and most material offered as *T. serpyllum* is probably one of five other species. It is a small-leaved, low-growing perennial, with thin creeping stems which

Creeping Woolly Thyme

form dense mats. The tiny flowers range from white through pink, purple, and red shades.

Thymes are propagated from seeds, cuttings, layering, and root division, although cultivars must be propagated asexually. Give plants six- to twelve-inch spacings. Six pounds of seed will sow an acre of thyme. Root division is the easiest and fastest means of increasing thyme stock. The roots of the low-growing species reach as deep as two feet. Remove them carefully, retaining as much of the original soil material as possible. Give transplants a generous supply of water.

The soil should be light, warm, rather dry, well-drained, and with a pH of 6 to 8 for good thyme culture. Plants may be killed by frost heaving the crowns or burning the foliage in areas where winter temperatures dip below 10° F. Provide plants with a heavy mulch. Clumps tend to become woody and die out in the center. They should be divided every three or four years. One-half to one ton of dried herb can be expected per acre.

Harvest just before it blooms.

Thyme is a well-known culinary herb. Use in fish chowder, poultry stuffings, egg

Variegated Thyme

dishes, meats, cheese and with vegetables such as broccoli, brussels sprouts, asparagus, and onions.

The leaves contain vitamin A, niacin, potassium, phosphorus, calcium, iron, magnesium, and zinc.

Thyme has a wide range of medicinal applications. It has tonic, expectorant, stomachic, carminative, antispasmodic, sedative, and diaphoretic properties. The

tea can be gargled for a sore throat or laryngitis. Headaches, gastritis, diarrhea, bronchitis, and intestinal atony have been treated with the tea. It has also been used as a worm expellant.

The essential oil contains thymol, linalool, carvone, cineole, limonene, and other substances. The leaves contain tannins. Thymol, a powerful antiseptic, is the chief constituent of the oil. The oil has antioxidant, antispasmodic, antibacterial, antifungal, expectorant, and carminative properties. Thymol itself can be highly toxic.

Valerian. *Valeriana officinalis L.*
(val-er-i-ay′-na off-iss-i-nay′-lis)
Valerianaceae – Valerian Family

Valerian is a hardy perennial growing to five feet in height native to Eurasia and naturalized in some parts of North America. The stems are fairly succulent, hollow, and grooved. The deeply divided leaves are larger at the base, becoming progressively smaller on the flower stalks. Seven to ten pairs of oblong or lance-shaped leaf segments characterize the fern-like leaves. The leaves are entire or toothed. The fragrant, tiny, white, pink

Valerian

or lavender flowers are borne in flat umbel-like clusters. Blooms shoot up in late May lasting through August.

Propagate by seeds or spring and fall root divisions. Seeds have a short viability and should be sown when ripe. Plants will self-sow and spread by root runners. They can become weedy. Seeds germinate in about twenty days. Give plants one-foot spacings.

Full sun or partial shade are suitable for valerian. It will grow on a wide range of soils but does best in a moist, rich loam. A soil pH of 6 to 7 is best. Commercial plantings have produced yields of 2,000 pounds per acre.

Harvest the roots in the fall of the second year's growth. Roots three-fourths inch and thicker should be split before drying. Care must be taken to wash off all dirt adhering to roots. Valerian's characteristic odor develops upon drying.

Valerian is one of the best of herbal tranquilizers. The tea and tincture are good antispasmodics, anodynes, carminatives, hypnotics, and nervines. Valerian also possesses worm-expelling qualities. It will help relieve stress, muscle spasms, mental depression and despondency, migraine, insomnia, stomach cramps, fatigue, and nervous conditions in general. The root is a central nervous system depressant, stimulating in fatigue and calming in agitation.

Valerian contains the valepotriates— valtrate and didrovaltrate, tannins, choline, alkaloids, and an essential oil composed mainly of bornyl acetate and isovalerate.

Wild Ginger. *Asarum Canadense L.*
(ass-ar'-um can-a-den'-see)
Aristolochiaceae — Birthwort Family

Wild ginger is a perennial denizen of the Eastern deciduous forest from New Brunswick, to North Carolina, west to Arkansas and Kansas. The three- to seven-inch wide, hairy, heart-shaped leaves have stems up to one foot long. The peculiar reddish-brown, fleshy, urn-shaped flowers have three corolla-like sepals but no petals. Flowers appear in forks between the leaf stems and are often hidden by leaves fallen the previous autumn. Blooming is from April to June. The root is a creeping rhizome.

Propagate by dividing the roots in fall or spring. Root cuttings can be started in a medium suitable for stem cuttings.

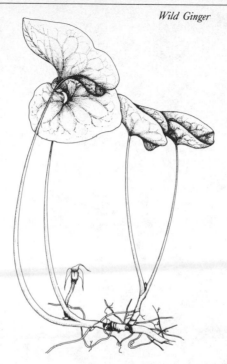

Wild Ginger

Give plants six-inch spacings.

Wild ginger likes a moist, rich soil with lots of humus provided by leaf-mold. A pH range of 4.5 to 6.0 is suitable for *Asarum*. About 75 percent shade should be provided. Plant ginger among goldenseal and ginseng beds.

In the nineteenth century, the root was used as a substitute for true ginger. The fresh roots are fun to nibble while hiking through the forest. Candy the roots as you would calamus or angelica roots.

The Rappahannocks used an infusion of the root for typhoid fever. Mixed with red cedar berries, *Juniperus virginiana*, wild ginger was used to treat asthma. Spikenard *Aralia racemosa* and wild ginger were used as a wash by the Ojibwas for fractured limbs. The Montagnais found the plant to be a general tonic. Sore throats, earache, and stomach cramps were treated with wild ginger by the Meskwakis. Many tribes thought the root made other food palatable and safe to eat. Wild ginger possesses stimulant, carminative, tonic, diuretic, and diaphoretic properties. Stomach ailments, kidney problems, and delayed menstruation were treated with ginger root by early settlers.

Its essential oil contains pinenes, delta-linalool, borneol, terpineol, geraniol, eugenol, methyl eugenol, asarene, and azulene. The oil is antibacterial especially against Gram-positive and pus-forming bacteria.

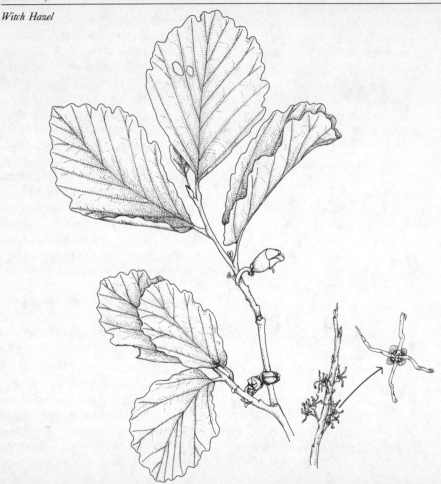

Witch Hazel. *Hamamelis virginiana L.*, *H. vernalis* Sarg.
(ham-am-́e-lis vir-gin-i-ay-́na; ver-nay-́lisl)
Hamamelidaceae –Witch Hazel Family

This genus has about six species of small trees and shrubs native to temperate regions of eastern North America and eastern Asia. *H. virginiana*, common witch hazel, is a shrub growing to fifteen feet tall, native from New England, south to Georgia, and west to Minnesota. The straight-veined scalloped-edged leaves are oval. Branches are long, angled, and curve upward. The bark is light brown to gray and marked by light-colored circular spots and scales. The round slender twigs are covered with rough brown hairs. Crimson and yellow hues of autumn foliage are particularly striking. September through November as the leaves drop, the flowers unfold in clusters or heads tightly hugging the stems. The four, yellow, long, narrow, petals give the flowers a spider-like appearance. Each seed capsule contains two shiny black seeds, with oily, white, edible interiors. When mature, the capsules burst, projecting seeds several feet from the shrub with a pop.

H. vernalis, vernal witch hazel, is native to the Ozark plateau from southern Missouri and Oklahoma, to Louisana and Alabama. Here in the Ozarks, the orange-red blossoms emerge in the last week of December after the last flowers of common witch hazel wither. These two species insure that at least one plant is blooming year 'round in the Ozarks—surviving the bitterness of -5° F. temperatures. In the North, plantings of vernal witch hazel will bloom in early spring.

Witch hazel is not the easiest plant in the world to propagate, but it can be increased by seeds, cuttings, or layering. Ripe untreated seeds can be sown in late fall and may either germinate the following spring or take two years to emerge. Cold stratification at 41° F. for ninety days will help break the seed's dormancy. Sow stratified seeds in spring in a moist, humus-rich soil under shade. Plant seeds at eight- to twelve-inch spacings. Cuttings can be made of green twigs pencil-size or smaller and rooted in moist sand. Roots develop in about 2½ months. Young suckers from an established plant can be layered to increase stock.

Common witch hazel grows naturally on a wide range of soils from poor, rocky, high mountain soils, to rich stream banks with silty loam. Vernal witch hazel prefers a rich moist soil with a pH between 6 and 7. Tolerant of air pollution, this shrub will grow in cities. Full sun or partial shade are acceptable.

The practical uses for witch hazel, as is the case with most American medicinal plants, are products of native Americans' ingenuity. The Potawatomi used witch hazel to relieve sore muscles. The twigs were infused in water, then hot stones were added to create steam. A poultice of the bark was used for eye inflammations. The Iroquois made a beverage tea from the leaves sweetened with maple sugar. Some tribes rubbed a decoction of the bark on the legs of game participants to keep muscles limber.

The leaves and bark are astringent, hemostatic, slightly sedative, tonic, and anodyne. A poultice of the bark will relieve pain and swelling of inflammations. External use of poultices, tinctures, or infusions are useful for bruises and insect bites. I use a homemade tincture of witch hazel on poison ivy. It dries up the discharge and relieves itching. Gather five or six three-foot-long dormant winter branches, scrape off the bark, and add it to twice its weight of vodka. Soak for two weeks, shaking occasionally. Commercial witch hazel products are available at every corner drug store. Products include hemorrhoid suppositories, ointments, lotions, and cloth wipes. These products relieve itching, irritations, and minor pains.

The leaves contain about 10 percent crude protein, phosphorus, calcium, and tannins. The bark contains hamamelitannin, saponins, a wax, a fixed oil, an essential oil, and resin. Steam-distilled witch hazel products are tannin free.

Woodruff. *Galium odoratum* (L.) Scop. (*Asperula odorata L.*)
(gay'-lee-um oh-dor-ay'-tum)
Rubiaceae-Madder Family

There are about thirty species in the genus *Galium. G. odoratum* is an erect or spreading perennial from six to twelve inches high, native to Europe, north Africa, and parts of Asia. Whorls of six to eight lance-shaped leaves, up to 1½ inches long, with rough bristle-tipped margins,

Woodruff

This is an excellent ground cover or edging for shaded areas. It tends to be a rapid spreader in rich, moist soils. To make a poor soil suitable for woodruff culture, fork in a generous supply of leafmold. Soil pH should hover between 6 and 8.3.

Harvest the herb just before flowering. Odorless when fresh, the plant develops a distinctive new-mown hay scent upon drying or wilting.

The dried leaves make a wonderfully fragrant sachet for linen closets. May wine is a refreshing beverage made by soaking the fresh or dried leaves for a couple of hours in a slightly sweet white wine.

Woodruff possesses diaphoretic, diuretic, sedative, antispasmodic, and cholagogic qualities. It has been used primarily as tea to relieve migraines, insomnia, liver infections, jaundice, bladder stones, and nervous tension in children and the elderly. The bruised herb is used as a poultice on fresh wounds and cuts.

Woodruff contains coumarin in a bound glycoside form that is activated by wilting or drying. Asperuloside, montropein, tannin, bitter principles, and a trace of nicotinic acid are found in the

characterize this plant. The white, four-parted, star-shaped corollas bloom on loose, branching, terminal heads from May to June. The flowers are about one-fourth inch long. The fruits have small hooked hairs which catch on the fur of passing animals, thus dispersing the seed. The creeping rhizomes produce lush carpets

in deciduous forests, and favor a beech canopy.

It is best propagated by dividing the creeping rhizomes in spring. Woodruff may also be propagated from cuttings, or seeds planted soon after ripening. Fresh seeds are essential. Space plants at one foot-intervals.

leaves. Asperuloside has anti-inflammatory properties.

Wormwood and Related Artemisias.
Artemisia absinthium L., Southernwood –
A. abrotanum L., Mugwort – *A. vulgaris* L.,
A. Douglasiana Bess., Roman Wormwood –
A. pontica L.
(are-te-miz´-i-a ab-sin´-thi-um; ab-roh-tay´-num;
vul-gay´-ris; dug-las-i-ay´-na; pon´-ti-ca)
Compositae – Aster Family

A. absinthium, common wormwood, is a coarse sprawling perennial native to Europe and naturalized in the northeastern United States. This bitter-tasting herb reaches a four-foot height and has finely divided gray leaves with rounded oblong segments. The nodding, one-eighth inch wide, yellow flowers are difficult to imagine as members of the same family to which sunflowers belong. They bloom in late summer.

 A. abrotanum, southernwood, is a shrubby perennial, usually about three feet tall. The finely divided leaves are smooth and green, with narrow linear leaf segments. The tiny yellowish-white flowers are seldom seen in the herb garden.

Southernwood

A. vulgaris, mugwort, is a six-foot perennial with a creeping rhizome, native to Eurasia. The four inch-long, oval, divided leaves are dark green on the upper surface with tiny whitish hairs underneath. The purple-red, one-eighth inch wide flowers occur in loose panicles in late summer. Its close relative, *A. Douglasiana,* is similar in appearance and native to the western United States.

A. pontica, Roman wormwood, is the most delicate appearing *Artemisia.* It is a short (two-foot) shrubby perennial native to southeastern Europe. The leaves are finely divided and covered with tiny gray hairs. The one-eighth inch wide pale yellow flowers are borne on loose panicles.

These plants are easily propagated by root division with the exception of southernwood which is best propagated from cuttings. Root divisions can be made in the spring or fall. The wormwoods can be grown from seed, but the seed is tiny and difficult to handle. Sow on the soil's surface, as it needs light to germinate. Germination takes place in about three weeks. Give plants eighteen-inch spacings.

Wormwoods will do best in a fairly rich or poor dry soil. Partial shade or full

Yarrow

sun are tolerable. A neutral to slightly alkaline soil is best. Both mugwort and Roman wormwood spread by root runners and must be given room to spread or be kept under control. The leaves of wormwood secrete a bitter principle which inhibits the growth of other plants. Give wormwood at least a three-foot buffer between it and adjacent plants. Once I let an herb garden go wild just to see what would happen. Mints and oregano growing within three feet of the wormwood were about six inches high, where plants outside the perimeter were two feet tall and lush. Wormwoods are winter hardy.

The whole herb is harvested when plants come into bloom.

The leaves of wormwood and southernwood can be placed in drawers to deter moths and beetles. Replenish the supply every six months.

Wormwood and Roman wormwood are used to flavor vermouth. Wormwood was the main ingredient in the now-outlawed alcoholic beverage absinthe. Studies have suggested that absinthe's effects may be similar to marijuana, as they may both interact with the same central nervous system receptors.

Wormwood is used as a bitter tonic to stimulate appetite and aid digestion. It is also used for liver and gall bladder disorders. All of the *Artemisias* mentioned above possess emmenagogic, vermifuge, diuretic, and antiseptic qualities.

A. absinthium contains thujone as the major component of the essential oil along with beta-caryophyllene, pinene, sabinene, phellandrene, and azulenes. Absinthin—a bitter principle—is found in the leaves as well. In large doses, thujone causes convulsions.

Yarrow. *Achillea millefolium L.*
(ak-i-lee′-a mil-e-foh′-li-um)
Compositae—Aster Family

Over sixty species are found in the genus *Achillea*. *A. millefolium* grows throughout temperate and boreal regions of the Northern hemisphere and to some extent in the Southern hemisphere. It is a hardy aromatic perennial growing to three feet tall. The finely divided feathery leaves are about two to eight inches long, becoming progressively smaller toward the top of the plant. The white flower heads are in terminal flat clusters. Each flower head is about one-fourth inch across. The entire cluster is three to four inches in diameter. It blooms from June to September. There are numerous cultivars including the flaming pink 'Rubra' and the light pink 'Rosea.'

Propagate yarrow by seeds or root divisions in spring and fall. Plants should be given eight- to twelve-inch spacings. Clumps should be divided every three to four years to stimulate growth. The tiny seeds can be tamped on the surface of a well-prepared seed bed. They germinate in ten to fourteen days.

Yarrow likes almost any soil but prefers an acidic situation (pH 4.5 to 7). It requires little care, is drought resistant, and should have full sun. Plants become weak and leggy under shade.

Harvest plants as they come into bloom. They dry quickly and easily.

The flowers have stronger medicinal powers than the leaves. Yarrow has been used to stop bleeding and heal wounds by cultures from the ancient Greeks to North American Indians. Wild yarrow grew around the perimeters of the Shaker Herb Gardens at Sabbathday Lake. Whenever herb harvesters cut themselves, we went to the garden's edge, crushed yarrow flowers or leaves in the palm of our hands, washed the wound, then applied the yarrow directly to the cut. Without any additional aid, the bleeding stopped and even deep cuts healed without infection within a few days—often to the amazement of the wounded. It is important to clean the cut before applying yarrow, otherwise the poultice will close the dirt within the wound.

American Indians used yarrow to treat sprains, bruises, swollen tissue, rashes, itching, nose bleeds, fevers, colds, headache, delayed menstruation, and a host of other ailments. Hemostatic, expectorant, analgesic, carminative, diaphoretic, emmenagogic, anti-inflammatory, antipyuretic, antiseptic, and stomachic properties are locked in a tincture of yarrow. I feel it is one of the most useful of home remedies.

Over 120 compounds have been found in yarrow. A complex and variable essential oil contains chamazulene, pinenes, caryophyllene, eugenol, borneol, cineole, camphor and other compounds. Sesquiterpene lactones may be responsible for yarrow's anti-inflammatory qualities. The alkaloid achilleine is an active hemostatic agent. Flavonoids may account for the antispasmodic activity. Yarrow also contains tannins and coumarins.

Yerba buena. *Sateurja Douglasii* (Benth.) Briq.
(sat-you-ree'-a dug-las'-ee-i)
Labiatae—Mint Family

The good herb—yerba buena—was also the original name of the city of San Francisco. Too bad they changed it. This plant is an evergreen perennial with trailing, often rooting, stems up to two feet long. The opposite leaves are oval or rounded, about 1½ inches long and one inch wide, smooth, and scalloped at the edges. Solitary flowers emerge from the leaf axils on one-half to five-eighths inch long pedicels (flower stems) from April to September. Flowers are about three-eighths inch long and white or purple in color. It is native to the shaded coniferous woods of western North America from British Columbia south to Los Angeles County, California. Under the shade of trees it has a more sprawling habit with wider spaced leaves and a less pungent scent than plants grown under full sun. Spanish-speaking peoples give the name yerba buena to spearmint as well.

Yerba buena is easily propagated from stem cuttings and layerings. Offshoots that have become rooted on their own may be cut from the parent plant and transplanted in the spring or fall.

At Taylor's Herb Gardens, a patch of yerba buena receiving full sun during most of the day has a tight compact growth and a strong camphor fragrance. In southern regions with hot summer sun, yerba buena will need shade. In other regions it will take full sun. It is most prolific in a slightly acid, rich, moist, sandy loam. If this plant were indigenous to the Mediterranean region rather than a West Coast American native, it would probably have found its way into European herb gardens, subsequently becoming a favorite plant of American herb gardens.

The leaves can be harvested any time during the growing season. They dry quickly and easily.

The dried or fresh leaves make an excellent tea. Yerba buena was highly esteemed by California Indians as a carminative for colic, a blood purifier, a febrifuge a reliever of arthritic symptoms, and general tonic and panacea. To disguise

the human odor, deer hunters would rub the leaves on their bodies.

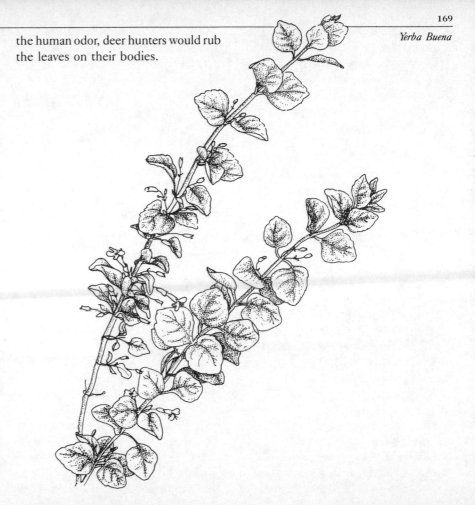

APPENDICES

HERBS LISTED BY COMMON NAME

American ginseng. *See* ginseng
American dittany. *See* dittany
Angelica. *Angelica archangelica, A. atropururea*
Anise. *Pimpinella anisum*
Anise hyssop. *Agastache foeniculum*
    Basils. *Ocimum basilicum*
    Bush. *O. basilicum* 'Minimum'
    Camphor. *O. kilimandscharicum*
    East Indian. *O. gratissimum*
    Holy. *O. sanctum*
    Lemon. *O. basilicum* 'Citriodora'
    Purple. *O. basilicum* 'Purpurascens'
Bearberry. *Arctostaphylos uva-ursi*
Bee balms. *Monarda didyma*
    M. fistulosa
    M. Russeliana
    M. punctata
Bergamot. *See* bee balm
Blue Mountain tea. *See* goldenrod

Borage. *Borago officinalis*
Butterfly weed. *See* pleurisy root.
Calamint. *Satureja arkansana*
Calamus. *Acorus calamus*
Calendula. *Calendula officinalis*
California Mugwort. *See* wormwoods
Camomile
    German. *Matricaria recutita*
    English. *Chamaemelum nobile*
Caraway. *Carum carvi*
Catmint. *Nepeta mussinii*
Catnip. *Nepeta cataria*
Cat thyme. *Teucrium marum*
Cayenne. *Capsicum annuum, C. fructescens*
Chamomile. *See* camomile
Chervil. *Anthriscus cerefolium*
Chicory. *Cichorium intybus, C. endiva*
Chives. *Allium schoenoprasum*
Colt's foot. *Tussilago farfara*

Comfrey. *Symphytum officinale S. uplandicum*

Coriander. *Coriandrum sativum*

Cranesbill. *See* geranium

Dang-qui. *See* angelica *(Angelica sinensis)*

Dill. *Anethum graveolens*

Dittany. *Cunila origanoides*

Dittany of Crete. *See* oreganos

Echinacea. *Echinacea pallida, E. angustifolia, E. purpurea, E. paradoxa var. paradoxa*

Elecampane. *Inula helenium*

Endive. *See* chicory

Fennel. *Foeniculum vulgare*

Foxglove. *Digitalis purpurea*

Garlic. *Allium sativum*

Geranium, wild. *Geranium maculatum*

Ginseng. *Panax quinquefolius*

Goldenrod, sweet. *Solidago odora*

Goldenseal. *Hydrastis canadensis*

Herba mari veri. *See* cat thyme

Herb mastich. *See* cat thyme

Hops. *Humulus lupulus*

Horehound. *Marrubium vulgare*

Horsemint. *See* bee balm

Horseradish. *Armoracia rusticana*

Hungarian camomile. *See* German camomile

Hyssop. *Hysoppus officinalis*

Lady's Mantle. *Alchemilla vulgaris*

Lamb's ear. *Stachys byzantina*

Lavenders

English. *Lavendula angustifolia*

Fern leaf. *L. Multifida*

French. *L. dentata*

Spanish. *L. stoechas*

Sweet. *L. × hybrida*

Lavender cotton. *See* santolina

Lemon balm. *Melissa officinalis*

Lemon verbena. *Aloysia triphylla*

Licorice. *Glycyrrhiza glabra*

Lion's ear. *Leonotis leonurus*

Lion's tail. *See* lion's ear

Lobelia. *Lobelia inflata*

Lovage. *Levisticum officinale*

Maidenhair fern. *Adiantum pedatum*

Mandrake. *See* mayapple

Marjoram. *Origanum majorana*

Mayapple. *Podophyllum peltatum*

Maypop. *See* passion flower

Mints

Apple. *Mentha suaveolens*

Corsican. *Mentha requienii*

Orange. *Mentha × piperita* var. *citrata*

Peppermint. *M. × piperita*

Spearmint. *M. spicata*

Watermint. *M. aquatica*

Mugwort. *See* wormwoods

Nettle. *Urtica dioica*

Oreganos

Dittany of Crete. *Origanum dictamnus*

Oregano, wild marjoram. *O. vulgare*

Pot marjoram. *O. onites*

Winter sweet marjoran. *O. heracleoticum*

Parsley. *Petroselinum crispum*

Passion flower. *Passiflora incarnata*

Pennyroyal

American. *Hedeoma pulegioides*

European. *Mentha pulegium*

Perilla. *Perilla frutescens*

Pleurisy root. *Asclepias tuberosa*

Pot marigold. *See* Calendula

Purple cone flower. *See* echinacea

Oswego tea. *See* bee balm

Roman camomile. *See* English camomile

Roman wormwood. *See* wormwoods

Rosemary. *Rosmarinus officinalis*

Rue. *Ruta graveolens*

Sage. *Salvia officinalis*

Sage of the seers. *Salvia divinorum*

Salsify. *Tragopogon porrifolius, T. pratensis*

Santolina. *Santolma chamaecyparissus, S. virens*

Sassafras. *Sassafras albidum*
Savories
    Summer savory. *Satureja hortensis*
    Winter savory. *S. montana*
Spice bush. *Lindera benzoin*
Spiderwort. *Tradescantia virginiana*
Southernwood. *See* wormwoods
Stone mint. *See* dittany
Sweet cicely. *Myrrhis odorata*
Sweet flag. *See* calamus
Sweet gum. *Liquidambar styraciflua*
Syrian herb mastich. *See* cat thyme
Syrian rue. *Peganum harmala*
Tansy. *Tanacetum vulgare*
Tarragon. *Artemisia drancunculus*
    Russian. *A. drancunculus*
    French. *A. drancunculus* var. *sativa sativa*
Thymes
    Common thyme. *Thymus vulgaris*
    Creeping thyme. *T. serpyllum*
    Creeping woolly thyme. *T. pseudolanuginosis*
    English thyme. *T. vulgaris*
    Lemon thyme. *T. citriodorus*
Uva-ursi. *See* bearberry
Valerian. *Valeriana officinalis*
Wild ginger. *Asarum canadense*

Witch hazel
    Common witch hazel. *Hamamelis virginiana*
    Vernal witch hazel. *H. vernalis*
Woodruff. *Galium odoratum*
Woolly betony. *See* lamb's ears
Wormwood and other artemisias
    California mugwort. *Artemisia Douglasiana*
    Mugwort. *A. vulgaris*
    Southernwood. *A. abrotanum*
    Roman wormwood. *A. pontica*
Wormwood. *A. absinthium*
Yarrow. *Achillea millefolium*
Yerba buena. *Satureja Douglasii*

NOTES

Chapter 1
The Wonderful World of Herbs

1. David Weir, Mark Shapiro, and Terry Jacobs, "The Boomerang Crime," *Mother Jones,* Nov. 1979, p. 43.

Chapter 2
The Common Language of Botany

1. Arthur Cronquist, *The Evolution and Classification of Flowering Plants* (Boston: Houghton Mifflin Company, 1968), p.3

Chapter 3
Designing an Herb Garden

1. William Hepworth Dixon, *New America,* 3rd ed. (Philadelphia: J.B. Lippincott, 1867), pp. 301-54.

2. William Robinson, *The English Flower Garden,* 11th ed. (London: John Murray, 1911), p. 337.

3. The American Herb Association, Rescue, California, publishes a directory to over two hundred public herb gardens in the United States. See resource section.

4. William Cobbett, *The American Gardener* (London: C. Clement, 1821), Ch. 1, para. I.

5. Incorporated as Ch. 4 in John J. Jeavons, Magador Griffin, and Robin Leler, *The Backyard Homestead, Mini-Farm, and Garden Log Book* (Berkeley: Ten Speed Press, 1983).

6. Bring Mitchell and Jesse Wayembergh, *Japanese Gardens: Design and Meaning* (New York: McGraw Hill, 1981), is an excellent reference on the subject.

Chapter 4
Propagating Herbs

1. J. W. v. Goethe, *The Metamorphosis of Plants* (1790; reprint ed. with introduction by Rudolf Steiner, Wyoming, RI The Biodynamic Farming and Gardening Association, Inc., 1974).
2. Glenn Clark, *The Man Who Talks with Flowers: The Life Story of Dr. George Washington Carver* (St. Paul, Minn.: Macalester Park Publishing Co., 1939), pp. 44-45.

Section 2
Meet Your Friendly
Neighborhood Herbs

1. Jeanmarie Morelli, "Angelica," typescript, 1980, p. 12; copy in possession of the author.
2. John Hill, *The Family Herbal* (Bungay Town): C. Brightly and T. Kinnersley, 1812).
3. Jeannette E. Gravstein, *Thomas Nuttall Naturalist-Explorations in America 1808-1841.* Cambridge, Harvard University Press, 1967. p. 37.

4. W. A. Hoffer and H. Osmond. *The Hallucinogens* (New York: Academic Press, 1967), pp. 55-56.
5. Anonymus. *The United Homeopathic Pharmacopeia.* Chicago: Duncan Brothers, 1878. p. 84.
6. Andrew Duncan, *The New Edinburgh Dispensatory*, 2nd ed. (Edinburgh: C. Elliot and T. Kay, 1789), p. 557.
7. Samuel Thomson, *New Guide to Health* (Boston: J. Q. Adams, 1835), p. 80.
8. National Institute of Medical Herbalists, "Press Release: Comfrey as Medicine," Leicestershire, England, 1979.
9. Ronald L. McGregor, "Taxonomy of the Genus Echinacea," *University of Kansas Science Bulletin*, 48 (1968): 113-42.
10. John Uri Lloyd, "A Treatise on Echinacea," *Lloyd Brothers, Pharmacists, Inc., Drug Treatise*, No. 30 (1929), p. 3.
11. Merrit Lyndon Fernald, Alfred Charles Kinsey, and Reed C. Rollins, *Edible Wild Plants of Eastern North America* (New York: Harper and Row, 1958), p. 354.

12. Samuel Thomson, *New Guide to Health*, pp. 38-48.
13. *Federal Register* 25 (1960): 12412.
14. Ibid., 41 (1976): 19207.
15. Edgar Anderson, *Plants, Man and Life* (Berkeley: University of California Press, 1952), p. 21.
16. Protech Products, Inc., "Press Release-Spiderwort: The People's Radiation and Pollution Monitor." Santa Barbara, CA., October 10, 1979.

GLOSSARY

Abortifacient: an agent producing abortion

Analgesic: a substance that relieves pain

Annual: a plant that completes its life cycle in one year or season

Anodyne: a pain reliever

Anthelmintic: an agent that expels intestinal parasites

Anthers: the pollen-bearing portion of the stamen

Antioxidant: a preservative which prevents oxidation

Antiperiodic: an agent which prevents regularly occurring symptoms, as those of malaria

Antipyretic: a fever-reducing or- preventing agent

Antispasmodic: a spasm-relieving agent

Antitussive: a cough-preventing or inhibiting agent

Aphrodisiac: a substance which increases sexual appetite or sensitivity

Astringent: an agent that contracts tissue

Bechic: a cough-soothing agent

Biennial: a plant completing its life cycle in two years

Bract: a leaf-like structure at the base of flower stalks

Calyx: the sepals, located below the corolla and enveloping the flower bud

Cardiotonic: a substance that increases heart tone

Carminative: an agent that relieves flatulence

Cathartic: an agent clearing the bowls; a laxative

Cholagogic: an agent stimulating bile flow from the gallbladder

Concoction: a preparation; a mixture of ingredients

Corolla: a flower's petals collectively

Corymb: flowers arranged in a comb-like cluster

Cultivar: a plant variety produced under cultivation which retains its characteristics when asexually or sexually propagated

Decoction: a preparation made by boiling plant parts (usually root or barks) in water for fifteen to twenty minutes

Demulcent: a soothing agent for irritated membranes, especially mucuous membranes

Deobstruent: an agent removing obstructions

Depurative: a general purifying or cleansing agent; blood purifier

Diaphoretic: an agent producing perspiration

Diuretic: an agent producing or promoting urination

Emetic: an agent which produces vomiting

Emmenagogue: an agent that produces or regulates menstruation

Emollient: an agent that soothes and softens irritated membranes

Entire: in leaves, edges that are not serrated

Expectorant: an agent that helps expel pulmonary secretions

Febrifuge: an agent to reduce or eliminate fever

Galactogogue: an agent promoting lactation

Hemostatic: stops bleeding

Hypnotic: an agent producing sleep

Immunostimulant: an agent stimulating the immune system

Inflorescence: all the flowers growing on a single plant

Infusion: a preparation made by pouring boiling water over herbs in a tightly closed vessel

Nervine: an agent that soothes and quiets the nerves

Palmate: having three or more leaflet divisions originating from the same point

Panicle: an inflorescence consisting of several racemes

Pedicel: a flower stalk

Perennial: a plant that lives more than two years

Petiole: a leaf stalk

Psychotomimetic: the effect of a hallucinogen producing phantasms

Raceme: an elongated simple inflorescence with pedicelled flowers

Resolvent: an agent that eliminates or reduces inflammations

Rubefacient: an externally applied agent which reddens the skin

Scape: a flower stem arising from the ground among radical leaves (leaves emerging from the root)

Sepal: the leaf of a calyx

Sessile: without a leaf stalk

Soporific: an agent that induces sleep

Spadix: an inflorescence with a thickened spike

Spike: an elongated inflorescence with stalkless flowers

Stamen: a flower's male reproduction parts, consisting of anther and filament

Stimulant: an agent which increases activity of a specific organ or general organism

Stipules: a leaf-like appendage arising from the base of a leaf or petiole

Stolon: an underground stem from which new plants arise

Stomachic: an agent which stimulates the stomach's action

Tincture: a diluted alcohol solution extracting a plant's medicinal virtues

Tonic: an agent increasing strength and tone

Umbel: a flat-topped inflorescence from which a number of nearly equal flower stalks radiate from the top of a single axis

Vermifuge: a worm expellant

BIBLIOGRAPHY

Altschul, Siri von Reis. *Drugs and Foods From Little Known Plants.* Cambridge: Harvard University Press, 1973.

Anderson, Edgar. *Plants, Man and Life.* Berkeley: University of California Press, 1952.

Angier, Bradford. *Field Guide to Edible Wild Plants.* Harrisburg, Penn.: Stackpole Books, 1974.

Bailey, L. H. *Manual of Cultivated Plants.* New York: MacMillan, 1924.

Bailey, Liberty Hyde. *How Plants Get Their Names.* 1933; reprint ed., New York: Dover Publications, 1963.

Bailey, Liberty Hyde, and Ethel Zoe. *Hortus Third.* Revision by L. H. Bailey Hortorium Staff. New York: MacMillan, 1976.

Beattie, J. H. *Production of Parsley.* USDA leaflet 136, 1937.

Bianchini, F.; F. Corbetta; and M. Pistoia. *The Kindly Fruits.* London: Cassell, 1977.

Bigelow, Jacob. *American Medical Botany.* 3 vols. Boston: Cummings and Hilliard, 1817-20.

Birdseye, Clarence, and Eleanor G. *Growing Woodland Plants.* 1951; reprint ed., New York: Dover Publications, 1972.

Bring, Mitchell, and Josse Wayemburgh. *Japanese Gardens: Design and Meaning.* New York: McGraw-Hill, 1981.

Brown, O. Phelps. *The Complete Herbalist.* Jersey City: O. Phelps Brown, 1878.

Browne, D. J. *Sylva Americana.* Boston: William Hyde and Co., 1832.

Buist, Robert. *The Family Kitchen Gardener.* New York: C. M. Saxton, 1853.

Chaytor, D. A. "A Taxonomic Study of the Genus *Lavendula.*" *Journal* of the Linnaean Society, Botany 51(1937):170-71.

Cobbett, William. *The American Gardener.* London: C. Clement, 1821.

Crooks, D. M., and A. F. Sievers. *Condiment Plants.* Washington, D. C.: USDA, Bureau of Plant Industry, 1942.

_____.*Medicinal Plants.* Washington, D. C.: USDA, Bureau of Plant Industry, 1941.

Culbreth, David M. R. *Materia Medica and Pharmacology.* Philadelphia and New York: Lea Brothers and Co., 1906.

Cuthbertson, Tom. *Alan Chadwick's Enchanted Garden.* New York: E. P. Dutton, 1978.

Darrah, Helen H. *The Cultivated Basils.* Independence, Mo.: Buckeye Printing Co., 1980.

Densmore, Frances. *How Indians Use Wild Plants for Food, Medicine, and Crafts.* 1928; reprint ed. New York: Dover Publications, 1974.

DeWolf, Gordon P. "The Mints." *Herb Grower* 10 (1956): 46-54.

Dremmond, Craig. *The Basils.* Redwood City, Calif.: Redwood City Seed Co., 1980.

Duke, Jim, "Vegetarian Vitachart." *Quarterly Journal of Crude Drug Research* 15(1977): 45-66.

Duke, James A. *Handbook of Legumes of World Economic Importance.* New York and London: Plenum Press, 1981.

_____."Ecosystematic Data on Medicinal Plants." In C. K. Atal and B. M. Kapur *Cultivation and Utilization of Medicinal Plants,* pp. 13-23. Jammu-Tawi, India: Regional Research Laboratory, Council of Scientific and Industrial Research, 1982.

Duke, James A., and Edward E. Terrell. "Crop Diversification Matrix: Introduction." *Taxon* 23(1974): 759-799.

Duke, James A., and Stephen J. Hurst. "Ecological Amplitudes of Herbs, Spices, and Medicinal Plants." *Lloydia* 38(1975): 404-10.

Duke, J. A., S. J. Hurst, and E. E. Terrell. "Economic Plants and Their Ecological Distribution." *Informacion al Dia Alerta. IICA-Tropicos, Agronomia* 1(1975): 1-32.

Duke, J. A., S. J. Hurst, and J. L Kluve. *Botanicals as Environmental Indicators.* Beltsville, Md.: USDA, n.d.

Dunmire, John R., ed. *New Western Garden Book.* Menlo Park, Calif.: Lane Publishing Co., 1979.

Duncan, Andrew. *The Edinburgh New Dispensatory.* 2nd ed. Edinburgh: C. Elliot and T. Kay, 1789.

Dymock, William, C. J. H. Warden, and David Hooper. *Pharmacographia Indica.* Vol. 1, 1890; Vol. 2, 1891; Vol. 3, 1893. Reprint ed. (3 vols. in 1) Karachi, Pakistan: The Institute of Health and Tibbi Research, 1972.

Eastman, L. M. *Sassafras Trees in Maine.* Augusta: Critical Areas Program, 1976.

Emboden, William. *Narcotic Plants.* New York: MacMillan, 1979.

Emerson, George B. *Trees and Shrubs of Massachusetts.* Boston: Dutton & Wentworth, 1846.

Epling, Carl, and Carlos D. Jativa. "A New Species of *Salvia* From Mexico." *Botanical Museum Leaflets.* Harvard University 20, no. 3(1962): 75-6.

Farnsworth, Norman R. *The Lynn Index: A Bibliography of Phytochemistry.* Vol. 6. Pittsburgh: Norman R. Farnsworth, 1969; Vol. 8. Chicago: Norman R. Fransworth, 1974.

Farnsworth, Norman R., Ralph N. Blomster, Maynard W. Quimby, and John W. Schermerhorn. *The Lynn In-*

dex: A Bibliography of Phytochemistry. Vol. 7. Chicago: Norman R. Farnsworth, 1971.

_____."The Current Status of Sugar Substitutes." *Cosmetic and Perfumery* 88(1973):27-37.

_____."The Present and Future of Pharmacognosy." *American Journal of Pharmaceutical Education* 43(1979):239-43.

Farnsworth, Norman R., and Ralph W. Morris. "Higher Plants–The Sleeping Giants of Drug Development." *American Journal of Pharmacy* 147(1976):46-52.

Fernald, Merritt Lyndon, Alfred Charles Kinsey, and Reed C. Rollins. *Edible Wild Plants of Eastern North America*. New York and Evanston: Harper & Row, 1958.

Flannery, Harriet B., and Robert G. Mower. *Gardening with Herbs*. Ithaca: New York State College of Agricultural Life Sciences, Cornell University, 1979.

Fleet, William Van. *Goldenseal Under Cultivation*. USDA Farmer's Bulletin 613, 1914.

Foley, Daniel J. *Herbs for Use and Delight*. New York: Dover Publications, 1974.

Foster, Gertrude B. *Herbs for Every Garden*. New York: E. P. Dutton, 1966.

Foster, Gertrude B., and Rosemary F. Louden. *Park's Success with Herbs*. Greenwood, S. C.: George W. Park Seed Co., Inc, 1980.

Foster, Steven. "A Taste of Sarsaparilla – Medicinal Uses of Maine Plants." *Maine Audubon Quarterly* (Summer 1978): 14-15.

_____."Calendula." *Well-Being* 45(1979): 48-51.

_____."Garlic Lovers Unite." *Well-Being* 47(1979): 14-18.

_____."Ginseng: Are You Confused?" *Well-Being* 46(1979): 43-50.

_____."Spiderwort–Nature's Geiger Counter." *Well-Being* 50(1979): 39-41.

_____."The Historical Battle over Lobelia." *Well-Being* 56 (1980): 32-34.

_____."The Herb Renaissance." *Vegetarian Times* 54(1982): 54-9.

Gibbs, W. M. *Spices and How to Know Them*. Dunkirk N.Y.: W. M. Gibbs, 1909.

Gilbertie, Sal, and Larry Sheehan. *Herb Gardening at its Best*. New York: Atheneum, 1978.

Gill, John D., and William M. Healy. *Shrubs and Vines for Northeastern Wildlife*. Upper Darby, Penn.: Northeastern Forest Experiment Station, United States Forest Service, USDA, 1973.

Gilmore, Melvin R. *Uses of Plants by the Indians of the Missouri River Region*. Rev. ed., Lincoln and London: University of Nebraska Press, 1977.

de Gingins-Lassaraz, Baron Fred. *Natural History of the Lavenders*. 1826; reprint ed., Boston: The New England Unit of the Herb Society of America, 1976.

Gleason, Henry A., *Illustrated Flora of the Northeastern United States and Adjacent Canada*. 3 vols. New York: New York Botanical Gardens, 1952.

Gleason, Henry A., and Arthur Cronquist. *Manual of Vascular Plants*. New York: D. Van Nostrand Co., 1963.

Goethe, Johann Wolfgang von. *The Metamorphosis of Plants*. 1790; Reprint ed. Introduction by Rudolf Steiner. Wyoming, RI. The Bio-dynamic Farming and Gardening Association, Inc., 1974.

Good, Peter P. *Good's Family Flora*. Vol. 1. New York: J. K. Wellman, 1845.

Grieve, Maude. *A Modern Herbal*. 2 vols. 1931; reprint ed., New York : Dover Publications, 1971.

Grohmann, Gerbert. *The Plant*. 4th ed. rev. London: Rudolf Steiner Press, 1974.

Guenther, Ernest. *The Essential Oils*. 6 vols. 1948; reprint ed. Huntington, N. Y.: Robert E. Krieger Publishing Co., Inc., 1972.

Gunther, E. *Ethnobotany of Western Washington*. Seattle: University of Washington Press, 1973.

Hale, Edwin M. *New Homeopathic Provings*. Detoit: E. A. Lodge, Homeopathic Pharmacy, 1864.

Hartman, Hudson T., and Dale E. Kester. *Plant Propagation: Principles and Practices*. Englewood Cliffs, N. J.: Prentice-Hall, Inc., 1975.

Harrington, Suzanne. *Sassafras*. Santa Cruz, Calif.: Herb Trade Association, 1978.

Hassan, I., "Some Folk Uses of *Peganum harmala* in India and Pakistan." *Economic Botany* 21(1967): 284.

Hedrick, U. P. *Sturtevant's Notes on Edible Plants*. Geneva: New York Agricultural Experiment Station, 1919.

Henckel, Alice, and G. Fred Klugh. *The Cultivation and Handling Goldenseal*. Washington, D. C.: USDA Bureau of Plant Industry Circular No. 6, 1908.

Hensley, David L, Susan Alexander, and C. R. Roberts, eds. *Proceedings of the First National Ginseng Conference*. Frankfort, Ky.: Governor's Council on Agriculture, 1979.

Higbee, E. C., and L. Atherton. *New Crops for the New World: Drug and Medicinal Crops*. New York: MacMillan, 1945.

Hill, Sir John. *The Family Herbal*. Bungay: C. Brightly, 1812.

Hills, Lawrence D. *Comfrey: Fodder, Food, and Remedy*. New York: Universe Books, 1976.

Hitchcock, C. Leo, and Arthur Cronquist. *Flora of the Pacific Northwest*. Seattle and London: University of Washington Press, 1973.

Hocking, George M. "*Echinacea angustifolia* as a Crude Drug." *Quarterly Journal of Crude Drug Research* 5(1965): 679-82.

_____. "*Peganum harmala*." *Quarterly Journal of Crude Drug Research* 6(1966): 913-15.

Hoffer, A., and H. Osmond. *The Hallucinogens*. New York: Academic Press, 1967.

Hu, Shiu-Ying. "The Genus *Panax* (Ginseng) in Chinese Medicine." *Economic Botany* 30(1976): 11-28.

_____. "A Contribution to Our Knowledge of Ginseng" *American Journal of Chinese Medicine* 5(1977): 1-23.

Hunan Province, Revolutionary Health Committee. *A Barefoot Doctor's Manual*. 1974; Reprint ed., Seattle: Cloudburst Press, 1977.

Ichikawa, Sadao. "The Spiderwort Strategy." *Bio-Dynamics* 127 (1978): 35-43.

Jacobsen, M., et. al. "*Echinacea angustifolia*" *Lloydia* 36 (1975): 455-72.

Jeavons, John. *How to Grow More Vegetables*. Berkeley: Ten Speed Press, 1979.

Jeavons, John J., Mogador Griffin, and Robin Leler. *The Backyard Homestead Mini-Farm and Garden Log Book*. Berkeley: Ten Speed Press, 1983.

Johnston, A. "Blackfoot Indian Utilization of the Flora of the Northwest Great Plains." *Economic Botany* 24(1970): 301-24.

Khemani, S. P. "Coriander as a Crop." *The*

Herb Grower 8 (1954): 96-110.

Koepf, Herbert H., Bo D. Pettersson, and Wolfgang Schaumann. *Bio-Dynamic Agriculture*. Spring Valley: Anthroposophic Press, 1976.

Krochmal, Arnold. *The Taming of Lobelia*. Upper Darby, Pa.: Northeast Forest Experiment Station, USDA, n.d.

Lathrop, Norma Jean. *Herbs: How to Select, Grow and Enjoy*. Tucson: Horticultural Publishing Co., 1981.

Lawrence, George H. M. *Taxonomy of Vascular Plants*. New York: MacMillan, 1951.

Leung, Albert Y. *Encyclopedia of Common Natural Ingredients Used in Food, Drugs, and Cosmetics*. New York: John Wiley and Sons 1980.

Lewis, Walter H., and Memory P. F. Elvin-Lewis. *Medical Botany: Plants Affecting Man's Health*. New York: John Wiley and Sons, 1977.

Lloyd, John Uri. "The Cultivation of Hydrastis." *Journal of the American Pharmaceutical Association* 1(1912): 5-12.

—————.*A Treatise on Echinacea*. Drug Treatise 30. Cincinnati: Lloyd Brothers, Pharmacists, 1924.

—————. and Curtis Gates Lloyd. *Drugs and Medicines of North America*. Vol. 1. *Ranunculaceae*. Cincinnati: John Uri Lloyd and Curtis Gates Lloyd, 1884.

—————. *Drugs and Medicines of North America*. Vol. 2, 1887; reprint ed., Cincinnati: *Bulletin of the Lloyd Library*, Reproduction Series No. 9, Vol. 2, Bulletin No. 31, 1931.

Loewenfeld, Claire. *Herb Gardening*. Newton, Mass.: Charles T. Bradford Co., 1965.

McGregor, Ronald L. "The Taxonomy of the Genus *Echinacea*." *University of Kansas Science Bulletin* 68(1968): 113-42.

Meehan, Thomas. *The Native Flowers and Ferns of the United States*. Series 1, Vols. 1-2. Boston: L. Prang and Co., 1878.

Meehan, Thomas. *The Native Flowers and Ferns of the United States*. Series 2, Vols. 1-2. Boston: L. Prang and Co., 1880.

Millspaugh, Charles F. *American Medicinal Plants*. 2 vols. New York and Philadelphia: Boericke and Tafel, 1887.

Ministry of Agriculture, Fisheries, and Food. *Culinary and Medicinal Herbs*. London: Her Majesty's Stationery Office, 1960.

Missouri Department of Conservation, Natural History Section, *Proceeding of the Second National Ginseng Conference*. Jefferson City: Missouri Department of Conservation, 1980.

Moore, Dwight Munson. *Trees of Arkansas*. Little Rock: Arkansas Forestry Commission, 1972.

Moore, Michael. *Los Remedios de la Gente*. Santa Fe: Michael Moore, 1977.

—————.*Medicinal Plants of the Mountain West*. Santa Fe: Museum of New Mexico Press, 1979.

Morelli, Jeanmarie. "Angelica." Unpublished manuscript, 1980.

Moring, Steve. "Echinacea: Natural Remedy for Viral Infections." *Am. Herb Assn*. Newsletter Vol. 2, No. 2 (1983) pp. 5-6.

Morton, Julia F. *Major Medicinal Plants*. Springfield, Ill.: Charles C. Thomas, 1977.

Muenscher, Walter Conrad, and Myron Arthur Rice. *Garden Spice and Wild Pot Herbs*. 1955; reprint ed., Ithaca and London: Comstock Publishing Associates, Cornell University Press, 1978.

Munz, Philip A. *A California Flora and Supplement*. Berkeley: University of

California Press, 1968.

Nutrition Research, Inc. *Nutrition Almanac*. New York: McGraw-Hill, 1973.

Pfeiffer, Ehrenfried. *Bio-Dynamic Farming and Gardening*. New York: Anthroposophic Press, 1938.

Philbrick, Helen, and Richard B. Gregg. *Companion Plants*. Old Greenwich, Conn.: Devin-Adair, 1966.

Richter, Robert. *Pesticides and Pills: For Export Only*. "Part One: Pesticides." Transcript of PBS Television Broadcast, 1981.

Robinson, W. *The English Flower Garden*. London: John Murray, 1883.

Rose, Jeanne. *Herbs and Things*. New York: Grosset and Dunlap, 1972.

Rosengarten, Frederick, Jr. *The Book of Spices*. New York: Pyramid Books, 1973.

Russell, G. A. *Drying Crude Drugs*. Washington, D. C.: USDA Farmer's Bulletin 1231, 1921.

Rowntree, Lester. *Hardy Californians*. 1936; reprint ed., Salt Lake City: Peregrine Smith Books, 1980.

Sargent, Charles Sprague. *Manual of the Trees of North America*. Boston: Houghton Mifflin, 1905.

Schauenberg, Paul, and Ferdinand Paris. *Guide to Medicinal Plants*. New Canaan, Conn.: Keats Publishing, Inc., 1977.

Schenck, Peter A. *The Gardener's Text Book*. New York: A. O. Moore, 1857.

Schermerhorn, John W., and Maynard W. Quimby. *The Lynn Index: A Bibliography of Phytochemistry*. 5 vols. Boston: Massachusetts College of Pharmacy, 1957-62.

Schopmeyer, C. S. *Seeds of Woody Plants in the United States*. Washington, D.C.: United States Forest Service, USDA, 1974.

Schultes, Richard Evans, and Albert Hoffmann. *The Botany and Chemistry of Hallucinogens*. Springfield, Ill.: Charles C. Thomas, 1973.

_____. and Norman R. Farnsworth. "Ethnobotanical, Botanical, and Phytochemical Aspects of Natural Hallucinogens." *Botanical Museum Leaflets*. Harvard University 28(1980): 123-214.

Segelman, Alvin B., et. al. "Sassafras and Herb Teas – Potential Health Hazards." *Journal of the American Medical Association* 236(1976): 477-78.

Sherman, John A. *The Complete Botanical Prescriber*. Corvallis, Ore.: John A. Sherman, 1979.

Sievers, A. F. *Peppermint and Spearmint as Farm Crops*. Washington, D. C.: USDA Farmer's Bulletin 1555, 1929.

Steiner, Rudolf. *Agriculture*. London: Biodynamic Agricultural Association, 1958.

Steyermark, Julian A. *Flora of Missouri*. 5th ed., Ames: Iowa State University Press, 1977.

Stille, Alfred, and John M. Maisch, *The National Dispensatory*. Philadelphia: Henry C. Lea's Son and Co., 1880.

Stockberger, W. W. "Production of Drug Crops in the United States." *USDA Yearbook*. 1917, pp. 169-76.

_____. *Ginseng Culture*. Washington, D.C.: USDA Farmer's Bulletin 1184, 1921.

_____. *Drug Plants under Cultivation*. Washington, D.C.: USDA Farmer's Bulletin 663, 1935.

Swain, Tony, ed. *Plants in the Development of Modern Medicine*. Cambridge: Harvard University Press, 1972.

Tatum, Billy Joe. *Billy Joe Tatum's Wildfoods Cookbook and Field Guide*. New York:

Workman Publishing, 1976.

Taylor, Kathryn S., and Stephen F. Hamblin. *Handbook of Wildflower Cultivation*. New York: Collier Books, 1963.

Thatcher, John. *The American New Dispensatory*. 2nd rev. ed. Boston: Thomas B. Wait and Co., and C. Williams, 1813.

The United States Homeopathic Pharmacopeia. Chicago: Duncan Brothers, 1878.

Thomson, Samuel. *New Guide to Health*. Boston: J. Q. Adams, 1835.

Thomson, William A. R. *Medicines From the Earth*. New York: McGraw-Hill, 1978.

Thorton, Robert John. *A Family Herbal*. London: B. & B. Crosby and Co., 1814.

Tierra, Michael. *The Way of Herbs*. Santa Cruz, Calif.: Unity Press, 1980.

True, Rodney H. "Cultivation of Drug Plants in the United States." *USDA Yearbook*, 1903, pp. 337-46.

_____."Progress in Drug Plant Cultivation." *USDA Yearbook*, 1905, pp. 533-40.

Tucker, Arthur O. "Botanical Aspects of Oregano Reconsidered." *The Herbalist* 40(1974): 11-13.

Tyler, Varro E., Lynn R. Brady, and James E. Robbers. *Pharmacognosy*. 7th rev. ed. Philadelphia: Lea & Febiger, 1976.

Underbrink, A. G., L. A. Schairer, and A. H. Sparrow. "*Tradescantia* Stamen Hairs: A Radiobiological Test System Applicable to Chemical Mutagens." A. Hollaender, ed. *Chemical Mutagens: Principles and Methods for Their Detection*. New York and London: Plenum Press, 1973.

USDA. *Mint Oil*. Foreign Agricultural Circular, 1981.

USDA. *Essential Oils*. Foreign Agricultural Circular, 1982.

Vestal, Paul A., and Richard Evans Schultes. *The Economic Botany of the Kiowa Indians*. Cambridge: Botanical Museum, Harvard University, 1939.

Vogel, Virgil. *American Indian Medicine*. Norman: University of Oklahoma Press, 1970.

Wacker, A., and W. Hilbig. "Virus Inhibition by *Echinacea purpurea*." *Planta Medica* 33(1978): 89-102.

Wasson, Gordon R. "A New Psychotropic Drug from the Mint Family." *Botanical Museum Leaflets*, Harvard University 20(1962): 77-84.

Webster, Helen Noyes. *Herbs: How to Grow Them and How to Use Them*. Boston: Charles T. Bradford Co., 1939.

Weiner, Michael A. *Earth Medicines—Earth Foods*. New York: Collier Books, 1972.

_____.*Weiner's Herbal*. New York: Stein and Day, 1980.

Weir, David; Mark Schapiro; and Terry Jacobs. "The Boomerang Crime." *Mother Jones* 4(1979): 40-48.

Weir, David, and Mark Schapiro. *Circle of Poison*. San Francisco: Institute for Food and Development Policy, 1981.

Whallon, Dorothy C. "Oregano—Botanical and Culinary." *Herb Grower Magazine* 4(1974-75): 94-96.

White, Alan. *Herbs of Ecuador*, Quito: ZIKR Publications, 1976.

Wood, George B., and Franklin Bache. *The United States Dispensatory*. 8th rev. ed. Philadelphia: Grigg, Elliot and Co., 1849.

Youngken, Heber W. *Pharmaceutical Botany* 2nd rev. ed. Philadelphia: P. Blakiston's Son and Co., 1918.

RESOURCES

Herb Seeds and Plants

ABC Nursery
Route 1, Box 313c
Lecoma, MO 65540
Catalog: $.25

Abundant Life Seed Foundation
Box 772
Port Townsend, WA 98368
Catalog: $1

Caprilands Herb Farm
534 Silver Street
Coventry, CT 06238

Carroll Gardens
Box 310
444 E. Main Street
Westminster, MD 21157

Casa Yerba
Star Route 2, Box 21
Days Creek, OR 97429
Catalog: $.50

Gilberties Greenhouses
Sylvan Avenue
Westport, CT 06880
Catalog: $1

J. L. Hudson Seedsman
Box 1058
Redwood City, CA 94060
Catalog: $1

Johnny's Selected Seeds
Albion, ME 04910

Kieft Bloemzaden
Box 1000
1695 ZG Blokker, Holland

Le Jardin du Gourmet
West Danville, VT 05873
Catalog: $.25

Lamb Nurseries
101 E. Sharp Avenue
Spokane, WA 99202

Logees Greenhouses
55 North Street
Danielson, CT 06239
Catalog: $2

Meadowbrook Herb Garden
Wyoming, RI 02898
Catalog: $.50

Nichols Garden Nursery
1190 N. Pacific Highway
Albany, OR 97321
Catalog: $1

George W. Park Seed Co., Inc.
Cokesbury Road
Greenwood, SC 29647

Redwood City Seed Co.
Box 364
Redwood City, CA 94064

Otto Richter & Sons Ltd.
Goodwood, Ontario, Canada L0C 1A0

Saso's Gardens
14625 Fruitvale Avenue
Saratoga, CA 95070
(no mail order)

Taylor's Herb Gardens, Inc.
1535 Lone Oak Road
Vista, CA 92083
Catalog: $1

Well Sweep Herb Farm
317 Mt. Bethel Road
Port Murray, NJ 07865
Catalog: $.50

Special Plants

The Buddies Nursery
Box 14
Birdsboro, PA 19508
spicebush

Bigelow Nurseries
Box 728
Northboro, MA 01532
bearberry, sweetgum

Bountiful Garden
5798 Ridgewood Road
Willits, CA 95490
Catalog: $1
organic herb seeds

Charles Fiore Nurseries, Inc.
Box 67
Prairie View, IL 60069
spicebush, witch hazel

Christom Farms Nursery
1746 Highway 73
Cambridge, WI 53523
witch hazel

Dutch Mountain Nursery
Augusta, MI 49012
spicebush

Eisler Nurseries
Box 70
Butler, PA 16001
spicebush, witch hazel

Fox Hill Farm
Box 7/ 444 W. Michigan Avenue
Parma, MI 49269
basils and other plants

Horticultural Enterprises
Box 340082
Dallas, TX 75234
Pepper seeds

Hsu's Ginseng Enterprises, Inc.
Route 3, Box 221D
Wausau, WI 54401

Magee Root Co.
Eolia, MO 63344

Nature's Cathedral
2250 14th Avenue
Marion, IA 52301
(ginseng, goldenseal)

Prairie plants

Prairie Associates
6328 Piping Rock Road
Madison, WI 53711

Prairie Nursery
Box 365
Westfield, WI 53964

Prairie Restoration, Inc.
Box 327
Princeton, MN 55371

Prairie Ridge Nursery
RR 2
9738 Overland Road
Mt. Horeb, WI 53572

Redwood City Seeds
Box 364
Redwood City, CA 94064
Salvia divinorum

Smokey Mountin Ginseng and Goldenseal Gardens
Box 86
Asheville, NC 28802

Native Plants and Wildflowers

Beersheba Wildflower Gardens
Stone Door Road
Beersheba Springs, TN 37305

Clyde Robin Seed Co., Inc.
Box 2855
Castro Valley, CA 94546
California natives
Catalog: $2

Gardens of the Blue Ridge
E. P. Robbins
Box 10
Pineola, NC 28662
Catalog: $2

Griffeys Nursery
Route 3, Box 28
Marshall, NC 28753

Izard Ozark Natives
P.O. Box 454
Mountain View, AR 72560
Catalog: self-addressed, stamped envelope. Supplies *E. paradoxa* seed

Little Valley Farm
RR 1, Box 287
Richland Center, WI 53581

Panfield Nurseries, Inc.
322 Southdown Road
Huntington, NY 11743

Siskiyou Rare Plant Nursery
2825 Cummings Road
Medford, OR 97501
Catalog: $1.50

Soil Conservation Society of America
7515 Northeast Ankeny Road
Ankeny, IA 50024
Excellent booklet, "Sources of Native Seeds and Plants," $2

Walters Garden, Inc.
Box 137
Zeeland, MI 49464
wholesale perennials

Tools

Franz Keim
4783 Wernstein/Inn
Austria
Manufacturer of blueberry rakes—looking for American distributor

A. M. Leonard, Inc.
6665 Spikes Road
Piqua, OH 45356

Mellingers
2310 W. South Range
North Lima, OH 44452

Walter Nicke
Box 6676
Hudson, NY 12534

Smith & Hawken Tool Co., Ltd.
25 Corte Madera
Mill Valley, CA 94941

Woodcraft Supply Corp.
313 Montvale Avenue
Woburn, MA 01801
drawknife

Bio-dynamic and/or French Intensive Educational Programs

Camphill Village
Box 155
Kimberton, PA 19442

Camp Joy
131 Camp Joy Road
Boulder Creek, CA 95006

Ecology Action
2225 El Camino Real
Palo Alto, CA 94306

Emerson College
Forest Row
Sussex, England, RH18-5JX
Two-year and four-week courses

Farallones Institute Rural Center
15290 Coleman Valley Road
Occidental, CA 95465

Farm and Garden Project
c/o Campus Facilities
U.C. Santa Cruz
Santa Cruz, CA 95064
One-year apprentice program

Gasconade Farm, Inc.
Paydown Road
Vienna, MO 65582

Saratoga Community Garden
Box 756
Saratoga, CA 95070
Year-round apprenticeships

Herb Organizations

American Herb Association
Box 353
Rescue, CA 95672
The AHA sells a directory of American Herb
Gardens for $5

Herb Research Foundation
P.O. Box 2602
Longmont, CO 80501

Ozark Bendicial Plant Project
New Life Farm, Inc.
HCR, Box 3
Brixey, MO 65618

Sources of High-Quality Herbs or Preparations

Pipsissewa Potions
Box 777
Blacksburg, VA 24060

Trout Lake Herb Farm
Route 1, Box 355
Trout Lake, WA 98650

Herb-Pharm
Box 116
Williams, OR 97544
Catalog: $1

United Society of Shakers
Herb Department
Poland Spring, ME 04274

INDEX